PRAISE FOR *HIRING FOR DIVERSITY*

"With a steady pulse on this rapidly changing landscape, Arthur and Susanna have crafted a singular guide to creating inclusive hiring practices that not only meet but exceed the heightened standards of the modern era."

—Jennifer Brown, author, *Inclusion: Diversity, the New Workplace & the Will to Change* and *How to Be an Inclusive Leader*

"This book is a must read for any leader, no matter what title you hold. It will give you the actionable plan you need to build a more diverse team."

—Mita Mallick, Head of Inclusion, Equity and Impact, Carta

"*Hiring for Diversity* delivers thoughtful, operationally sound, measurable, scalable, and time-tested methods for hiring and supporting diverse teams."

—Judith Williams, Chief Diversity and Inclusion Officer, SAP

"*Hiring for Diversity* provides a clear, tested, and integrated approach to hiring and retaining talent across all spectrums of diversity, breaking the work down into measurable and actionable steps. This is required reading for any leader serious about improving diversity in their organization."

—Beth Anton Grous, Chief People Officer, Tripadvisor

"If you hope to lead this moment and build diversity into your organization, Hiring for Diversity is a must read. This book dismantles all the misconceptions and barriers to creating real change, regardless of your role or title."

—Keith Ferrazzi, author of Never Eat Alone, Who's Got Your Back and Leading Without Authority

"*Hiring for Diversity* will convert your organization's good intentions into measurable impact by giving actionable strategies for hiring and advancing diverse talent."

—Rocki Howard, Chief Diversity Officer,
SmartRecruiters

"A must-read for leaders who are ready to take action on growing diversity in their organizations. *Hiring for Diversity* gives you a holistic strategy coupled with tangible resources to make progress in diversity hiring."

—Margot Slattery, Global Chief Diversity &
Inclusion Officer, Sodexo

"*Hiring for Diversity* gives leaders actionable direction for growing diversity within their organization. It is an important read for talent, learning, and business leaders."

—Elliott Masie, Creator of e-Learning,
CEO of the MASIE Center

"If you are looking for specific, actionable, and practical advice to attract and engage diverse teams, *Hiring for Diversity* will hit the mark. The book dives deep into various dimensions of diversity, with numerous examples. It doesn't stop at hiring—also covering topics of engagement, retention, and culture—or at diversity—addressing equity and inclusion too."

—Kathi Enderes, PhD, Vice President,
Research, Josh Bersin Academy

"*Hiring for Diversity* provides a roadmap for employers who are serious about diversity, equity, and inclusion (DEI). Its Equal Hiring Index is an innovative game changer for Corporate America and a new way to look at recruiting diverse talent, retaining them, and investing in their success."

—Ingrid M. Duran CEO and Founder,
D&P Creative Strategies

HIRING FOR DIVERSITY

HIRING FOR DIVERSITY

The Guide to Building an Inclusive and Equitable Organization

ARTHUR WOODS

SUSANNA THARAKAN

WILEY

Published by John Wiley & Sons, Inc., Hoboken, New Jersey.
Published simultaneously in Canada.

For general information on our other products and services or for technical support, please
contact our Customer Care Department within the United States at (800) 762-2974, outside
the United States at (317) 572-3993 or fax (317) 572-4002.

Wiley publishes in a variety of print and electronic formats and by print-on-demand. Some
material included with standard print versions of this book may not be included in e-books or in
print-on-demand. If this book refers to media such as a CD or DVD that is not included in the
version you purchased, you may download this material at http://booksupport.wiley.com. For
more information about Wiley products, visit www.wiley.com.

Library of Congress Cataloging-in-Publication Data

Names: Woods, Arthur (Entrepreneur), author. | Tharakan, Susanna, author. |
    John Wiley & Sons, publisher.
Title: Hiring for diversity : the guide to building an inclusive and
    equitable organization / Arthur Woods, Susanna Tharakan.
Description: Hoboken, New Jersey: Wiley, [2021] | Includes index.
Identifiers: LCCN 2021018921 (print) | LCCN 2021018922 (ebook) | ISBN
    9781119800903 (cloth) | ISBN 9781119800927 (adobe pdf) | ISBN
    9781119800910 (epub)
Subjects: LCSH: Diversity in the workplace. | Employee selection.
Classification: LCC HF5549.5.M5 W647 2021 (print) | LCC HF5549.5.M5
    (ebook) | DDC 658.3/1108—dc23
LC record available at https://lccn.loc.gov/2021018921
LC ebook record available at https://lccn.loc.gov/2021018922

Cover Design: Wiley
Cover Image: ©Irina Karpinchik/Getty Images

SKY10027805   062521

CONTENTS

A Note on Accessibility and Available Resources

We are committed to ensuring everything we recommend and write about is reflected in our own work and the delivery of this book itself. We've partnered with our publisher, Wiley, to ensure this book is accessible to people of all abilities through the specific measures detailed below. We have also taken steps to make the resources mentioned in the book available to anyone committed to advancing this work. To that end, we've created an open-source library of resources and assessments available to everyone through our platform, Mathison. Please read below to learn about our accessibility measures and access to open-sourced resources.

Accessibility for This Book

Hiring for Diversity is available in e-book and hardcover, and will be available in audiobook. We offer the following accessibility options:

Text-to-Speech (TTS). This book's text has been converted to audio format by way of a computer-generated voice. Please contact your eReader device or software manufacturer's customer support service for the best solution (e.g. Google Play Support; Amazon Kindle: kindle-accessibility@amazon.com; Apple iPhone and iPad: accessibility@apple.com).

Book Share. This book is available through Bookshare. If you cannot read traditional print books because of a visual impairment, physical disability, or severe learning disability, Bookshare can provide high-quality text-to-speech voices, Daisy, Braille, and large print.

Access Text Network. Our publisher, Wiley, is a participating member of the AccessText Network (ATN). The ATN provides a common interface for Disabled Student Service offices and providers to request, track, and receive electronic files for college textbooks on behalf of students with print-related disabilities. Please visit www.accesstext.org for more information.

OPEN-SOURCED RESOURCES FROM THIS BOOK

We mention a number of resources and tables throughout the book. To make these available to everyone, to ensure you have access to the latest version, and to be eco-friendly, we've centralized everything in an open-sourced resource library here: http://Mathison.io/Book.

Finally, we have created a complimentary assessment called our Equal Hiring Index® to help leaders of any organization size assess the current state of their hiring process, to identify where they can reduce bias, increase accessibility, and reach new diverse communities. You can find this free assessment at: http://Mathison.io/Index.

FOREWORD

Diversity and inclusion may seem like recent buzzwords in the business world. In fact, these concepts trace their origins in corporate and military organizations as far back as the 1940s, when President Harry Truman desegregated the U.S. military. Meanwhile, in the last 20 years, we have watched business owners, shareholders, employees, consumers, and policy makers all increasingly agree that diversity and inclusion are important investments—for almost every company imaginable.

This is for good reason: The talent pool available to founders and leaders is becoming more diverse than ever. Women now outnumber men among U.S. college graduates, and representation among people of color continues similarly to expand. Ten years ago, it would have been difficult to find a technology start-up that mentioned diversity or inclusion in its IPO filing, and very few Fortune 500 public tech companies discussed the topic with their shareholders.

During those ten years, I've spent my career as a leader in the DEI (Diversity, Equity, Inclusion) space. Two poignant observations stick out.

First, the key to successfully building inclusive workplaces and high-functioning diverse teams is to think more like a businessperson and less like a diversity person. What do I mean by that? In all aspects of business, we are constantly looking for data from which we can glean any meaningful insight. Diversity is no different. When your business has the right data systems in place, it is easier to operationalize the processes that result in more diverse hiring. It also becomes much simpler to build and cultivate the culture that you *want* for your company.

Second, when we talk about diversity and inclusion, we are talking about the largest attempt in modern history to fix outdated standards and practices in the field of human resources.

The reason for this is simple. Building diverse workforces and inclusive workplaces is not a new function of human resources. Instead, it is simply a rethinking of the precepts built into some of HR's oldest functions. Indeed, a more recent trend across Fortune 500 and other high-performing companies is to see the head of HR or head of people role also incorporate the title "Head of Diversity."

This can make the solution seem easier than it is. Like many experienced heads of DEI, I am often asked to "rebuild" HR. A common analogy in this situation is "changing the wheels while the car is still in motion," but it's actually even scarier than that. As every executive and founder knows, human resources is a critical operation to the health of a business and not to be messed with capriciously. (Sensitivity to this risk may be another reason HR organizations and practices have remained unchanged for so long.) A wholesale rethinking of HR is not just a significant investment for your business; it's also scary.

The good news is it's doable, and the map has already been made. In more than 20 years designing, building, and overseeing human resources operations, my advice for all leaders is to see how attention to data and a passion for process can yield powerful, scalable results. As entrepreneur Ben Horowitz has written, a great head of HR "must be a masterful process designer." Process design is the key to success. While many business functions require constant innovation, HR in this era simply requires this one significant yet transformational change in process: hiring and supporting diverse teams, implemented via time-tested methods of thoughtful, operationally sound, measurable, and scalable process.

What follows in this book is exactly that. Arthur and Susanna, with their team at Mathison, have trudged the start-up trenches familiar to many of us to build the insights and tools we need as the next generation of founders, executives, and HR professionals to grow diversity in our organizations.

In DEI, many of the challenges we warn founders and executives about have names like "unconscious" bias, meaning some part of the problem we are setting out to solve may require software that eliminates our human fallibility. Other challenges, however—the ones founders face in an era of increased awareness like hiring diverse teams—are just good old-fashioned HR implemented in a new way. What follows in these pages are practical recommendations for founders, executives, and HR professionals and the broader team to implement exactly those systems for their organizations.

As a passionate believer in the power of good HR policy and operations to help companies succeed, it is clear to me that one day, what we call diversity and inclusion won't need a name. We'll just call it HR. I believe this because I believe human resources, people operations, or any name we choose to call it will retain the same core function: helping businesses and employees build a healthy, safe, and mutually thriving relationship. I believe this because 200 years of U.S. history show us that when workers are thriving—no matter what their model of unionization, autonomy, or equity—the standard of employee-employer relationship changes our broader culture, too.

Which is to say, if you'd like to see the future of the United States, to quote a trite phrase of middle management everywhere: You'll need to talk to HR. If you are interested in building the future of our workforce, however, I'd like to personally invite you into the pages that follow. I am certain it's a brighter future, and I'm continually inspired by everyone who aims to make it that way. I can't wait to see you there.

Judith Williams
Chief Diversity and Inclusion Officer, SAP

PREFACE

One of the greatest joys of my career has been to bear witness to the accelerating evolution of diversity, equity, inclusion, and belonging as a maturing industry. It began years ago, with mere whispers about diversity circulating within the corporate vocabulary, mainly focusing on gathering data about representation, and how workforce demographics might be retooled to more accurately reflect the diversity of the talent pool and the marketplace. Then the conversation shifted toward inclusion, or how existing talent—particularly those who are underrepresented and who hold marginalized identities—feel on a day-to-day basis, and what level of trust they hold toward the organization. Next, equity and belonging entered the conversation, raising the critical but as-yet-unasked questions of systemic support and psychological safety as they relate to identity and expression. And still our field continues to expand and broaden, with explorations of what justice might look like, on the heels of a year like 2020, where the call for change crested, and the hard questions became our North Star.

Let me begin by saying that the time for all of these things— diversity, inclusion, equity, and belonging, and yes, justice—is now. The call for accountability and empathy at work has always existed, but it is undoubtedly louder than ever before. I believe each and every one of us can think of a recent event, movement, personal anecdote, or news story that throws into stark relief the need for systemic change. But I also believe many of us have been confused about how we can better support that change.

As a diversity and inclusion consultant with over fifteen years' experience in the field, I have witnessed the vast majority of leaders delegate their responsibility around DEI work. They've outsourced the accountability, and the labor, to people of color, women, and other marginalized groups within their organizations, who they believe can (and should) carry the water because of how they identify, even though there is often less structural power among these identities—and sometimes the smallest numbers—to throw behind efforts. This is particularly dangerous at our current moment in time, because leaders are facing a mounting call to step up or fall behind, and stepping up means challenging this thinking. When those with power and influence shirk accountability or delegate responsibility, or remain inactive, or silent, organizations risk destroying hard-won trust that fuels collaboration, teamwork, innovation, and most important, retention. And leaders cease to grow and evolve; what many don't realize in opting out is that they are also endangering their own futures; the sidestepping around this topic, because of discomfort, lack of competency, or defensiveness can ultimately result in irrelevance.

I say this not to scare or castigate anyone, but rather to set the stage for and demonstrate the pressing need for this book, *Hiring for Diversity: The Guide to Building an Inclusive and Equitable Organization*. With a steady pulse on this rapidly changing landscape, Arthur Woods and Susanna Tharakan have crafted a singular guide to creating inclusive hiring practices that not only meet but exceed the heightened standards of the modern era. If you're reading this book, then your eyes are open to the far-reaching and pervasive nature of DEI challenges, and awareness is always the first step. All that we have been shown in recent years at work and in the world has awakened a vast new cohort of people to the critical issues that many of us in underestimated and underrepresented communities have been laboring against for decades. Some of us may be showing up to "class" late, but what matters is that we're here now, in the room, and rolling up our sleeves.

That awareness and participation is key, because when we surface our biases and arrive at a deeper understanding of the damage they can inflict, we then have choices. We can remain inactive, silent, or apathetic, or we can move forward and embrace the role we each can play in creating cultures of belonging where everyone is empowered to thrive.

As budding agents of change and innovative risk takers choose the latter option (as I hope you do), I see them undergo a metamorphosis of sorts, a liberating journey characterized by radical honesty, joyful storytelling, and generative collaboration. But the process—like so many things worth doing—is also tempered by significant discomfort, challenge, and obstacles. The future will require a greater focus on equity and intersectionality, which can entail loaded conversations with sobering acknowledgments of power imbalances. As you travel this demanding yet gratifying road, I urge you to lean into that discomfort. I like to say that leadership is not truly leadership unless it's uncomfortable. It's a signal that growth is occurring. If you aren't pushing yourself to do more, and pushing others around you to improve, chances are you aren't doing enough. You would expect no less in so many other arenas of your life; the discipline, practice, and "stretch" needed to build new, healthier habits applies very much here, and when we care enough to follow through, despite the "growing pains," we see the results over time. One of the biggest shifts to explore is closing the gap between our intent and our impact. A positive or favorable self-perception—our desire always to "be right"—is much less important than developing a deeper understanding of our place in a given system, how we got there, and our ability to effect change from who we are and where we sit.

As leaders—wherever we sit in a given system—this is well within the possible, for all of us. Progress will happen if we dedicate and prioritize our development and hold ourselves accountable while extending grace and space to ourselves to show up and learn imperfectly. Resilience and agility are key; we must learn how to fail forward, and to have grace for ourselves and others as we do so. We are all poised to be beacons for this conversation, and for progress, and as we share the work more completely, however imperfectly, the burden for change can begin to be more equitably shared—and lightened—by many more heads, hearts, and hands.

The truth is, creating lasting and sustainable cultures of belonging is a task far bigger than any one executive, or any one department, or any one initiative. With that daunting reality in mind, leaders often ask me, "Where do we begin?" This book will provide many answers to that, and more.

Hiring for Diversity will ask you to do three things. They may be difficult, but I guarantee they will also be three of the most transformative steps you can take as a forward-thinking leader. First, you will be asked to leverage what you know to do what needs to be done, however uncomfortable that may be. Second, you will be asked to embrace what you don't know, because this is how you narrow the gap toward systemic change. Often, this is achieved by first admitting there's a lot you don't know and accepting that reality. Finally—and this is the most critical step—you will need to choose to be a leader. You will need to step into your power willingly, enthusiastically even, without all (or even many) of the answers, and actively take intentional and brave steps that inspire and support those who want to follow you. They're waiting, and they care.

If you are ready to make a difference for those people, turn the page, and let Arthur and Susanna lead the way.

Jennifer Brown
Founder and CEO, Jennifer
Brown Consulting, author of *Inclusion* and
How to Be an Inclusive Leader

CHAPTER 1

Setting the Stage: Going from Intent to Impact

You came to this book for a reason. Something compelled you. You might have been moved by a story in the news, a conversation with your team, or your own personal experiences.

When you think about diversity, you might first feel frustrated that not enough is being done. You might feel the pressure to drive results. You might be confused as to how. You might even feel guilt or shame.

When you look at your own organization, you might see where diversity is lacking, where representation is low and you haven't made enough progress. Like many people, you might be angry. You might be focused on the state of the world and the fear of what might happen if you now get this wrong.

But you might also be inspired by the *possibility* of getting this right.

Whether driven by fear or possibility, you, like many leaders, are likely feeling a burning desire to grow diversity in your organization. You have intent.

And because you picked up this book, you presumably have some degree of power: the power to choose, to reframe, to accept, or to influence. This book is designed to help you use whatever power you have to make a difference—not just in your own life or organization, but in the lives of people who deserve more opportunities than life has handed them.

Diversity is personal, perhaps more so than any other topic or decision we make during the workday. It reflects our values and our viewpoints, and it can trigger a surprising array of emotions. Advancing diversity isn't just about facilitating organizational change. It's about reaching the hearts and minds of our people. And it can't happen without leadership.

But leaders alone can't advance this mission. Despite what anyone tells you, there are few experts in this work, if any. There are few leaders with decades of experience in diversity hiring, and there isn't a single organization that has mastered it across the board. Today, this work requires collective learning, invention, and action. We are all writing the playbook that will guide diversity hiring in the years to come, and to do it well, we need everyone to contribute.

The path ahead is filled with extraordinary potential. If you travel it with dedication and persistence, it will lead to a better, more equitable world. Whether you are leading a company, managing a team, working in HR or recruiting, or simply aspiring to make things better, we wrote this book for you. Regardless of the role you hold, or your experience with diversity, your contribution matters, and you have the potential to make a difference. We hope this book gives you inspiration, direction, and support in this work. We hope this book reminds you what is possible and, most importantly, that you are not alone.

WHY THE TIME IS NOW

It took a series of unthinkable events, in a stunningly brief period, to force us all to reckon with injustices we'd been conditioned to tolerate.

We witnessed the murder of George Floyd and its aftermath, the agony of oppression erupting in massive, anguished protests. We watched the rise of Black Lives Matter, a global movement giving voice to people unwilling to remain disposable. We saw the COVID-19 pandemic force marginalized communities into even greater hardship and disparity. If our eyes were closed before, they have now been pried open. We are no longer willing—or able—to ignore the inequality and racism that surrounds us.

In a handful of months, the world discovered an urgent desire for change, and no facet of life has gone unaffected, especially the workplace and the makeup of our workforce. Most management teams and boards for the first time looked around and noticed the lack of diversity in the room. And employees across organizations demanded response and action from their employers.

Leaders were left asking, "Will things ever go back to the way they once were?" But the world as we know it has forever changed. Our new world calls us to move forward in innovative ways and to solve problems we've ignored for far too long.

So what changed? We've always had the intent to do better, to be better. And for the last decade, we have signaled how little diversity, equity, and inclusion is present in the workforce today, but that has yet to translate to real changes in our systems. There has been little impact from our efforts. We are now at a critical juncture. We can no longer tolerate our own lack of progress.

Our personal frustration is a direct indication of our desire for personal engagement. We can no longer say this isn't our responsibility, that this is someone else's problem. Each of us—from chief executives down to entry-level employees—has a sphere of influence in advancing diversity on our teams and our organizations. We each have the opportunity to build awareness of the need for diversity because of the systemic inequities across our hiring process. We have the chance to model new behavior for inclusive hiring in our own work personally, and we can play a role in influencing changes to the way our teams and organizations operate.

We also have more transparency around the lack of representation than ever before. Black individuals make up 13 percent of the U.S. population, yet only in four of the nation's 37 largest employers do they occupy 10 percent or more of the executive and management roles, according to Bloomberg. Hispanics make up 18.5 percent of the U.S. population, yet in only four of those companies do they occupy 15 percent or more of executive and management roles. Meanwhile, white people make up 60 percent of the U.S. population, and all 37 of the largest employers have at least 50 percent white representation at the executive and management levels.

To advance diversity in the workforce, we have often looked to changes we can influence in public policy. In June of 2020, the U.S.

Supreme Court made history by declaring that the 1964 Civil Rights Act protected gay, lesbian, and transgender individuals from discrimination based on sex. For the first time in American history, employers were prevented from firing employees because of who they loved or how they identified. Although this was a victory, it shed light on the cruel reality that the LGBTQ+ community had always faced. It took 56 years for them to be granted the protection under law that their heterosexual and cisgender coworkers had all along.

Slowly but surely, progressive lawmakers are pursuing legislation to grant individuals access to the most basic protections in the workforce. But we can't wait for changes in the law alone to ensure equity for everyone at work. We all need to focus on what *we* can change, and that starts within our own organizations.

WHAT NEEDS TO CHANGE

If we want to increase diversity in our organizations in a sustainable way, we have to abandon old ways of thinking and shift our approach entirely. This begins with stepping back to recognize why most organizations have struggled so immensely to grow their diversity. Most employers have lacked unity or alignment around the issue. They have approached the work with a short-term mindset that has limited the focus to isolated parts of their organizations. They have lacked a sense of shared responsibility in diversity hiring, which has left the work resting on the shoulders of far too few. These challenges combined have collectively stifled the march of diversity and prevented organizations from truly transforming. Here is what we believe must change:

To improve diversity we have to start with inclusion.

If we are serious about increasing representation in our organizations, we have to begin with a unified and inclusive definition of diversity. Many leaders look at diversity through a narrow lens, focusing solely on attributes they believe they can see. But there are visible and invisible aspects of diversity. To accomplish our mission, we can't paint diversity in broad strokes and leave people out. We need to ensure our definition of diversity encompasses all the underrepresented communities we hope to hire.

Next, to grow diversity among our teams, we have to constantly ensure our organizations themselves are places where people feel empowered and included. It's easy to think that driving diversity mainly depends on hiring, but this equality depends on investing in our existing teams and building cultures within our organizations where people feel embraced, supported, and have room to advance. As the civil rights activist Deray McKesson says, "Diversity is bodies. Inclusion is culture." In other words, diversity is the act of identifying and hiring the right people. Inclusion is about creating a space where those people feel welcome. They are two different concepts, but neither one is sustainable without the other.

We need to reframe diversity hiring as a long-term, strategic priority.

Many leaders see diversity hiring as an urgent but short-term effort, a terrible oversight that has often led efforts to feel more like one-off posturing rather than longterm sustainable change. But if we really see growing diversity in our organizations as a strategic priority, we must acknowledge that change often comes slowly. Just as we would never say that growing revenue is a near-term priority that depends solely on one department, we must never approach diversity hiring as a sprint, or a single team's "project." We need to pursue the work in a systematic way that persists regardless of short-term wins or losses. To do it right, we need to reframe diversity hiring as a permanent strategic imperative, an ongoing journey.

We have to inspire collective ownership of diversity hiring across our teams.

In most organizations, people see growing diversity as someone else's job. Most employers don't galvanize their full organization around the shared diversity vision in a way that inspires everyone to feel a sense of responsibility. Instead, diversity hiring typically falls on the shoulders of HR and recruiting teams. But if the rest of your team isn't aware of the need, they might not refer underrepresented candidates or consciously address their personal bias when participating in the hiring process. By mobilizing everyone in your organization around diversity hiring, articulating shared goals, and aligning incentives to meet those goals, you unlock the capabilities and involvement of your full team. This helps the work become a collective effort and, most important, one that is ingrained in your organization's culture and values.

COMING TOGETHER TO WRITE THIS BOOK

We came together to write this book for a multitude of reasons. We were inspired by the thousands of remarkable job seekers from underrepresented communities we've gotten to engage in our daily work. We felt our understanding of the challenges these communities face in the hiring process could help empower employers struggling to make a change. We've been able to intimately partner with many employers on this journey through our company, Mathison, which provides software that sources candidates from diverse backgrounds and reduces bias in the hiring process. We've gotten to hear employers' stories, see their common gaps in the hiring process, and observe which diversity hiring tactics and strategies have made the greatest impact. Finally, we felt a sense of urgency, looking at all that has happened in the world through the lens of our own lived experiences, which have always informed our approach to this work.

From Arthur

I grew up in an evangelical community in rural northern California, and I was taught in church that being gay was a sin. When I came out as gay halfway through college, I was completely lost and uncertain about the effect my identity would have on my career. I was blessed with a mother who was the greatest cheerleader a son could wish for, but as the first in my family to graduate from college, I was often without the professional guidance and mentorship that many of my peers took for granted. Unsure of how to navigate my future, I decided to hide my identity in my earliest job interviews, afraid it would hurt my chances of getting hired. Walking into my first job in a corporate office setting, I overheard colleagues using homophobic and derogatory slurs, and I felt utterly crippled. I realized at that moment I was not safe there. I could not be myself. I had to hide. As this sunk in more, I became convinced for much of my early career that my professional identity and personal identity could not be one and the same. I felt an undeniable sense of shame, anxiety, and frustration.

All this changed, however, when I applied to a mission-driven technology company that embraced diversity and made me feel included at every stage of the hiring process. I was placed on a team that included people from across generations, races, and sexual identities. My new manager was openly gay and proudly out at work. He introduced himself by showing me a picture of his husband and family. It was clear to me that this was a place where I could belong. Within weeks of starting the new job, I came out to my colleagues and was immediately embraced. A weight had been lifted from my shoulders as my professional world invited in the person I was at my core. I felt the most authentic sense of alignment between myself and my work, and I immediately realized a newfound energy to build, to go above and beyond, and to make a difference. By feeling a sense of belonging at work, I was confident and unstoppable.

I imagined how many others in the workforce shared my early experience of not being embraced for who they are, not feeling as if they belonged. I began to feel a deep calling to focus my work and life to advancing diversity and inclusion at work. Over the last decade I've had the chance to work with hundreds of leaders on the journey to grow diversity in their organizations. This has given me the opportunity to launch a number of organizations at the intersection of advocacy and technology. I became so enthralled in the work that I shifted my focus to technology that would help employers scale all of their diversity hiring efforts, which is what led me to co-found Mathison (Mathison.io). Witnessing how hard but necessary the work is at this moment, when it is top-of-mind for so many leaders, I felt compelled to work with Susanna to translate the insights from our collective work into a digestible resource for leaders who want to make progress in diversity hiring.

In this very moment, each of us as leaders has the capacity to create extraordinary change. Just as an inclusive boss did for me years ago, we have the opportunity to empower people who feel underrepresented by giving them a seat at the table. We have a chance to instill a sense of belonging by celebrating people for who they really are. If we can catalyze this change within our organizations, it will propel the change we want to see in society.

From Susan

Who I am starts long before I was even an idea—it starts with my parents and my grandparents. It starts with the country they all left behind over 25 years ago to pursue a better life. Although I grew up in a culturally diverse suburb of New Jersey, American norms were instilled upon me. I quickly learned that you eat PB&J sandwiches for lunch, that straight hair is prettier than curly hair, and that you spend Sundays at church. Like most first-generation immigrants, all I wanted was to find a way to fit in—to connect with my peers and have a sense of belonging. That's why I did everything I could to hide my Indian roots and lean heavily into my family's Christian background. That piece of my identity helped me feel like there truly was a place for me here.

Unfortunately, but not unusually for women of color, I didn't have mentors to tell me what I needed to do to get into a good college or write a resume that would land me an interview or how to handle my finances. I didn't have parents or relatives who understood how to navigate white America as a brown woman, struggling to balance two cultures. I didn't see anyone who looked like me in the TV shows that I watched, so my everyday struggles were never addressed or validated. Navigating my personal and professional life without any guidance was difficult, to say the least. That was, until college.

In college, I found friends, professors, and mentors who were people of color. I took a class called "Experiences for Individuals with Disabilities" that helped me see life through the eyes of my professor, a Latino man with paraplegia. I learned more about how managing multiple identities paved the way for even greater challenges and how important it was to understand intersectionality because of the way it shapes our experiences. The opportunity to see, hear, and live with people from all walks of life showed me just how crucial it is for everyone to be exposed to diversity. Being part of that diversity was comforting for me, but more important, it created an inclusive environment where everyone could share themselves without fear. I learned a lot about the experiences of other people of color, women, individuals with disabilities, immigrants attending university on student visas, and others. All of these people had to overcome so many obstacles to achieve their professional goals. Seeing this left me worried for other women like me who weren't as lucky to stumble upon the kind of people and support I'd encountered.

I'm grateful for where I am today. But one question has remained. What can I do to help others avoid the alienation and uncertainty that I felt growing up? How can I help those trying to navigate their professional lives? To me, the answer was a career in HR. I decided that I needed to have a seat at that table where I could influence organizational leaders. I needed to be part of the decisions that affected all employees.

Today, I'm in the unique position of knowing how it feels to be an outsider, but also what it takes to feel included. The research on the value of diversity and inclusion speaks for itself. If we want to stay ahead of the curve and fruitfully grow our organizations, we need diverse underrepresented talent. It can feel like a daunting task, but organizational leaders have the opportunity to champion initiatives that will make a difference. I hope this book will inspire you to take on the challenge without feeling overwhelmed by it.

What We Are Striving For

For this work to make a difference, we need to determine what success looks like. We should be striving to do more than posturing to change the look of our organizations. Our goal should be fundamentally shifting culture, reimagining the equity of our systems, and being intentional about the way we make people feel. How we gauge success directly ties to the way we think about diversity, equity, inclusion, and belonging:

Diversity: We are striving for a workforce that equally represents society at all levels.

We are seeking to build diverse representation throughout our organizations. This encompasses how we source from all communities, how we acknowledge that diversity is more than what you can see, how we ensure that people advance in our hiring process to get the job, and how we support and promote people when they become our coworkers. Diversity that is limited to junior positions or particular departments is not true diversity at all.

Equity: We want to eliminate barriers and ensure opportunities for everyone.

Creating equity within our organizations means ensuring impartiality and fairness for all communities we hope to hire and advance. This means addressing historical inequity and oppression that has existed in our systems to date. It means developing structure and consistency across the hiring process, building policies that ensure accessibility for all groups, and taking ongoing steps to intentionally address bias in decision-making.

Inclusion: We are striving for everyone to feel invited, understood, and heard.

Instilling inclusion means consciously taking steps to ensure that people of all communities feel invited to participate in and engage with your organization. It means making sure that people feel understood, and that their voices are heard. This experience starts in the hiring process but continues long after employees are integrated into your organization.

Belonging: We want everyone to feel valued and embraced.

This is what we are ultimately striving for in our diversity efforts—that people are celebrated for who they are and feel like they can bring their full selves to work. Belonging gets to the heart of people feeling psychological safety and emotional connection to their work. Belonging inspires a sense of empowerment and commitment. There is no stronger litmus test for the impact of your work than helping people feel like they belong.

How to Mobilize Change Using This Book

Wherever you find yourself in this work, remember that you are striving for progress and not perfection—and that every step is progress. Too often, we make the mistake of waiting to act until the path is clear and the goal easily attainable. Or we wait for problems to reveal themselves rather than actively rooting out problems. We need to be less afraid of taking the wrong actions and more afraid of inaction.

It's important to note that every team and organization is different, and there is not a single, universal way to successfully approach this work. Rather than provide proscriptive recommendations, we aim to help you assess where your team and organization are today and then serve up options for the ways you can advance this work. Each chapter of this book explores in detail a different part of the hiring process where you have the opportunity to make change.

The book begins with uncovering your diversity needs and setting your goals in Chapter 2. In Chapter 3, we profile 12 underrepresented job-seeker communities. From there, we shift gears to tactics for building an inclusive brand (Chapter 4), writing inclusive job descriptions (Chapter 5), diversity sourcing (Chapter 6), minimizing selection bias (Chapter 7), inclusive interviewing (Chapter 8), ensuring equitable job offers (Chapter 9), and strategies for retaining and advancing underrepresented job seekers (Chapter 10). We conclude the book in Chapter 11 with insights on how you can mobilize this work across your organization by engaging other leaders, hiring managers, HR, and your broader team in diversity hiring.

Each chapter includes an assessment. Rather than share policy and have everyone ask, "Does this belong to me?" these assessments prompt you to expand your perspective and question assumptions about what you can advance and what job belongs to whom. Usually, when someone is affected by a policy, they should have a say in it—and a little shift in perspective can bring that principle into focus. The assessment accounts for a simple truth: despite how much you already know, you might find there is still more to discover.

To ease the transition from intent to impact, we end each chapter with one thing you can do to get started: a single action you can take now regardless of your current situation. It's our hope that taking these steps will mean measurable progress in your diversity goals.

As you take this journey, remember that uncomfortable discussions can inspire changes in perspective. Educating yourself, the way you're doing now, is its own kind of progress. Be willing to go further. Lean into the discomfort the way you have in other areas of business, and you will reap the shared rewards of purposeful risk-taking.

Thank you for your leadership in advancing this work. If you've decided to continue, you've already started.

REFERENCES

Green, Jeff, et al. "New Data Expose Precisely How White and Male Some U.S. Companies Are." *Bloomberg*. March 22, 2021. https://www.bloomberg.com/graphics/diversity-equality-in-american-business/.

"Women in Contemporary Comics." Powered by Whitman College Blog Network. October 24, 2018. http://blogs.whitman.edu/biznidjam/2018/10/24/diversity-is-bodies-inclusion-is-culture/.

CHAPTER 2

Building Your Diversity Hiring Vision, Goals, and Reporting

If you look at organizations that have made the greatest strides in their diversity hiring, you find that they all have certain things in common: they set clear goals, measured their results, and reported their progress.

This may sound obvious, but you'd be surprised how many smart, well-meaning organizations think they can skip these steps. And when they do, it rarely goes well.

In 2016, the New York Times Company published its first public diversity report. The report showed that in 2015, women made up 45 percent of the company and 40 percent of leadership. However, people of color represented just 27 percent of the company and 17 percent of leadership. For an organization that had long prided itself on holding those in power to high standards of diversity, equality, and justice, the report was an embarrassment. The Times' own public editor, Liz Spayd, wrote a scathing column headlined, "Preaching the Gospel of Diversity, but Not Following It."

"When you ask managers about the issue individually, everyone genuinely seems to care," she wrote. "Collectively, however, not much changes." Other publications were even less forgiving in their coverage.

The Times had made a bold move in sharing its representation data publicly, even knowing it would reflect badly on the company. Now, the Times needed a plan to do something about it. Stacey Olive, the Times' then VP of Talent Acquisition, and her team knew this was a critical moment for the organization and that all eyes were upon them.

Olive's team had been searching for a strategy for diversity hiring but needed a powerful goal they could use to galvanize the organization around the work. They knew that setting arbitrary diversity quotas could be hard to enforce, and it was difficult to know where to even start. Instead, she and her team decided to set process goals and center their diversity efforts around "four pillars" of operating. Every job at the Times would be expected to adhere to these pillars to ensure equity and representation in the process:

1. All jobs must be posted publicly.

2. All candidates must apply (even if the team knows them).

3. No offer can be made unless there is a diversity of candidates in the process.

4. No offer can be made without a representative interview panel.

After successfully testing the model on her own team, Olive got the green light from leadership to implement it across the organization. That meant making sure that everyone at the Times not only understood the principles but embraced them. Olive and her team knew that if the people in charge of hiring didn't take ownership over the mission, it was unlikely to succeed. They took careful steps to ensure every leader fully understood the model and had everything they needed to execute it.

But they also understood that principles and directives don't mean much without some means of enforcement, so they established a rule that any exception to the model required executive approval. They also built a reporting structure to verify the process was taking place and built a new system for capturing exceptions to see where any patterns arose. Now, when leaders received exception requests, they were more likely to ask for reasons and less likely to grant the request.

Olive and the team witnessed a culture shift around this work and a visible change in the way team members were operating. It became clear that they were starting to care about getting it right.

The results were encouraging. In the first year, the team achieved 90 percent diversity in the candidate pipelines and interview panels and saw their diversity numbers rise in every department. By 2017, women represented 50 percent of the company and 46 percent of leadership, up 5 percent and 6 percent, respectively. People of color rose to 28 percent at the company and 20 percent in leadership (up 1 percent and 3 percent, respectively). The four pillars had become embedded in the hiring process for every role and in the daily vernacular of every team member. For Olive, what started as a unique approach to diversity goal-setting resulted in a more diverse New York Times.

DEI remains a work in progress at the Times, but this peek behind the scenes demonstrates how setting clear goals and guidelines and taking the time to encourage stakeholder adoption can lead to change. There's also something to be said for the motivational effects of exposing yourself to public scrutiny.

Your organization may not have the resources or the profile of the Times, but leaders at most levels of any organization are already accustomed to setting goals. They just need to apply those skills and mindset to their diversity hiring efforts. Doing so requires finding the right balance and answering some important questions: What goals are ambitious yet achievable? How can we apply quantifiable measures to this more human space? What additional stakeholders will support these goals?

WHY DIVERSITY GOAL-SETTING, STRATEGY, AND REPORTING MATTERS

If we think of diversity hiring as building a house, then reporting data and setting goals are the foundation. But too many organizations try to build their house without first laying that foundation, which is one reason DEI efforts so frequently fail. In fact, according to a 2021 study by Josh Bersin, founder of talent management consultancy Bersin & Associates, 76 percent of companies have no diversity or inclusion goals at all.

As with most aspects of business, you can't manage what you can't measure. If you are serious about diversifying your organization, you need to apply the same rigor to those efforts as you do to other strategic priorities. That means assessing the situation, setting clear and realistic goals, sharing those goals across your organization, and then measuring your progress against those goals.

And you need to be willing to share your findings with employees, customers, shareholders, applicants—anyone who has a vested interest in your organization. If the people most responsible for diversifying your organization don't have a firm understanding of your current situation, they are not truly empowered to do the job. And sharing data publicly is a critical aspect of accountability; even embarrassing news builds trust among stakeholders and signals that you are serious about making a change.

Unfortunately, too many organizations resist sharing their DEI data publicly. They fear being called out by critics or competitors, or losing applicants who don't want to work for a homogenous organization. That fear is why only 59 out of 931 of America's largest corporations—a mere 6.3 percent—had reported their diversity data as of January 2021, according to nonprofit research company JUST Capital.

At a time when so many employers have publicly stated their commitment to diversity, the public—which includes your potential employees—is expecting to see real results. They are more likely to be patient with an employer that is honest about its challenges and sets out a clear goal for doing better. This is where your organization's mindset can make a difference. Bersin's 2021 study showed that roughly 40 percent of companies were operating their DEI programs from a risk-management perspective, suggesting they were more focused on compliance and risk mitigation than the actual benefits of diversification. But if you're going to "talk the talk" about diversity, you need to be prepared to walk the walk. And that means being clear about where you are *and* where you hope to end up.

Translating those goals into action is its own challenge. Knowing where you want to end up is different from knowing how you'll get there. With so many approaches and tactics, it's a common mistake to assume there is a viable "one size fits all" approach. Leaders will often copy the diversity goals and tactics used by other organizations without thoughtfully considering what's best and most natural for their own group. Because every organization has its own unique culture and challenges, what works well for one may not work for another. This is why it's important to do some soul-searching to find the most authentic approach for you.

Don't make the common mistake of compartmentalizing your DEI efforts. Instead, approach your diversity goals the way you would any other goal at your organization. Find the North Star that will galvanize your organization and devise a plan to get there. It's rarely a quick or easy journey, but hopefully this chapter will help you find the right path.

Assessing Where You Are in Your DEI Goal-Setting, Strategy, and Reporting

Human nature is a funny thing. When presented with a set of rules and guidelines from someone in a position of authority, we tend to react with skepticism and a dash of ego. Even if those rules are in our best interest and we agree with the ultimate objective, we still can't help but bristle a bit. "Who are you to tell me what to do?"

But those same rules and guidelines, arrived at by mutual effort, can be something we embrace with great enthusiasm. It's why Winston Churchill called democracy "the worst form of government except for all those other forms that have been tried." If we're going to follow the rules, we would like to have a hand in making them. Really, it's only fair.

The same is true for diversity and inclusion policies. When setting goals, we need the broader team to buy in wholeheartedly, so we need to give people a sense of shared ownership. Simply put, if you want your team to embrace your diversity goals, they need to be part of building them.

We'll discuss later in this chapter how to engage your entire organization in this process. But as you start to think about setting goals and finding the right strategy and tactics, here are some questions that will help you see where you need to focus.

- Have you asked your organization and team what they want to see change with diversity? Where do their passions lie in this work? And what will they commit to contributing to the process?

- Have you determined your vision and goals for your diversity efforts?

- Do your diversity goals naturally align with the culture and process of goal-setting that already exists in your organization?

- Do you know the current representation of your team or full organization?

- Do you have a system to track your ongoing progress in diversity hiring?

- Do you have any capabilities to track the diversity in your applicant pool?

- Do you have a process to report your diversity progress and results?

- Do you share your diversity progress internally with your team or externally to the public? Or both?

For additional resources to assess your diversity hiring efforts visit: http://Mathison.io/Index.

Whether you are part of leadership, the talent team or neither, these are the high-priority questions you need to address to gain support from upper management. If you're a leader by nature and not (yet) by title, you have every right to ask these questions; use them as the bridge to partner with leadership ambassadors and to find your way to get involved and demonstrate value in the process. You can use these questions to assess current levels of impact and where your shared intent can be applied to create better results.

Uncover Where Your Organization Is Passionate and Ready for Change

To get your team engaged with setting diversity goals, start by asking them about their vision for diversity at your organization, where their energy lies, what they believe needs to change, and what they can commit to contributing as partners in the process (this will be key for activating the work later on). This can be done by hosting a casual conversation in your next team meeting, facilitating a more formal focus group, or circulating an anonymous survey.

Sarah Nahm, co-founder of applicant-tracking system Lever, found that the most effective way to advance the team's diversity goals was to source creative input and ideas from her team. "Some of our earliest diversity and inclusion tactics came straight from our team," she said. "One team member walked through our hiring process and found that we may be deterring candidates from applying based on rigid skills or experience requirements. As a result we started experimenting with displacing job descriptions with 'impact descriptions,' where we removed skills and experience requirements and instead highlighted the impact the candidate would make in the role. This gave candidates the ability to speak uniquely to how they would make that impact and proved to be highly effective for us. This would not have come to life without the input of the team."

This collective input and involvement from your team is critical to ensuring you have a holistic, inclusive approach that hasn't left out any underrepresented groups or critical steps of your process.

Assess Your Current Diversity Representation

Before you can set your diversity goals, it's important to understand what diversity looks like at your organization. If you don't yet have this data, you can capture it through an anonymous survey. We recommend including diversity questions alongside any other engagement or culture surveys you might be doing so they are naturally included. The survey should be voluntary and anonymous, and it should use that treats your employees with dignity, respect, and fairness.

As you are sharing the survey with your team, you can emphasize that the diversity questions are included to better understand the current representation of the team and more accurately set goals for improvement. It's helpful to remind the team that results will remain anonymous and not be used for any purpose other than DEI initiatives.

When writing your survey—or, for that matter, any time you talk about diversity—it's important to use inclusive terms. When asking about specific disabilities, use affirmative terms such as *visually impaired, neurodiverse individuals,* or *people who use a wheelchair,* instead of negative terms such as *blind, autistic,* or *wheelchair-bound.* This is known as person-first language: terminology that puts the human being before the disability or condition. It emphasizes the value and worth of the individual by recognizing each as a person instead of a condition. When asking about gender, the default demographic options have long been *male* and *female,* but today, the biological implications of those terms are increasingly considered exclusionary. Instead, use *women* or *men,* which is more inclusive of transgender people. You should also provide additional response options like *nonbinary* or *gender nonconforming.* This will give you a more holistic view of your organization and where you stand in terms of gender diversity. It also sends a signal to candidates that the organization knows how to adapt to changing times and wants to be an inclusive workplace for all. For a fuller discussion of these terms, see Chapter 3.

To get the fullest possible picture of your organization, be sure to go beyond the usual questions about gender, disability, veteran status, and race. First-generation immigrants, refugees, formerly incarcerated individuals, and LGBTQ+ are among the communities that continue to face discrimination in the workforce. Including them in your survey will empower individuals from these communities to participate and feel included. It's important to remember that some people may not identify with a particular group or may not be comfortable responding, so offering individuals the opportunity not to respond or to select "other" is key.

Example diversity survey

Survey questions	Response options
What is your gender identity?	Man Woman Nonbinary Gender nonconforming I prefer not to respond Other (please specify)
Which of the following best describes your sexual orientation?	Heterosexual or Straight Queer Asexual I prefer not to respond Other (please specify)
What is your racial or ethnic identification? (select all that apply)	American Indian or Alaska Native Native Hawaiian or Other Pacific Islander Asian Black or African American Hispanic or Latino White or Caucasian Two or more races Other (please specify) Prefer not to respond
Here we loosely define disability as having been diagnosed with one or more of the following: sensory impairment (e.g., vision or hearing), mobility impairment, learning impairment (e.g., ADHD, dyslexia), mental health disorder, or other impairment.	I am a person with disability Other (please specify) Prefer not to respond

(continued)

Survey questions	Response options
Please check one of the answers: If applicable, please indicate your veteran status:	I am not a Veteran Disabled Veteran Special Disabled Veteran Armed Forces Services Medal Veteran Other (please specify) Prefer not to respond
Are you a parent?	Yes No Prefer not to respond
What is your age?	<18 18–25 26–33 34–41 42–49 50-59 60-69 70+ Prefer not to respond
What is the highest level of education you have completed?	High school diploma 1–3 years of college, no degree obtained Bachelor's degree Some graduate school Graduate degree PhD Prefer not to respond
Do you identify with any of the following communities?	Refugee or immigrant First generation Formerly incarcerated community Neurodiverse community Older, experienced worker community Other (Please specify)

Uncover Where Your Real Diversity Needs Exist and What Is Possible

As you are drawing insights from your existing diversity representation data, try to look beyond organization-level insights to gain a more detailed understanding of your diversity profile. Matt Sigelman, CEO of job market analytics company Burning Glass Technologies, has observed that many employers get fixated on organization-wide averages that don't always give a useful picture of where the needs exist. "Employers need to focus on specific contours of diversity that enable them to gauge representation by function, level, and region," he says. "If Amazon only looked at its company-wide diversity average, they wouldn't realize that the representation in its distribution centers is far greater than in its corporate functions. In some high-tech roles, the representation of Black and Hispanic talent is less than one-twentieth of Amazon's company-wide average." Sigelman says that this detailed analysis needs to extend to levels of seniority as well. "A lot of organizations have great representation at the entry level, but the more senior the position, the less diverse they become,".

To set realistic targets for diversity, you also need to understand what representation looks like in your market, industry, and location. This better helps you determine the diversity of the total candidate pool you are trying to recruit from. For example, if an organization is trying to set representation goals for data scientists in its Chicago office, it's important to first consider the diversity of the total market of the city's data scientists, which may be low to begin with. You can use U.S. Census data or private, real-time job market data to get an understanding of these baselines.

Ultimately, understanding your existing diversity profile by function, level, and location will give you a clearer picture of where you need to focus your energy. Considering the diversity of the market and talent pool you're recruiting from will give you a realistic sense of what is possible. The two insights combined will help you form focused and realistic goals.

Identify Where You Have Gaps and Opportunities in Your Hiring Process

To better capture representation data in your hiring pipeline, consider adding self-identification questions to your job applications. This will allow you to gauge the diversity of your pipeline and pinpoint where underrepresented applicants drop off—or if you're even attracting them in the first place. You can use this information to provide extra support to candidates from underrepresented communities and to augment your efforts to source and recruit candidates from communities you're not currently reaching. Then, by collecting the same data from new hires at the 30-, 60-, and 90-day mark, you can measure your attrition rates among underrepresented candidates. If they are leaving at higher rates than the rates of your team overall, you may need to work on your inclusion efforts (see Chapter 10).

When setting your goals for increasing diversity representation, don't overlook goals for improving the accessibility and equity of your hiring practices. Your DEI success depends not only on defining a strong outcome but on the process itself. As you consider the current state of your hiring process, reflect on the areas where you might have the biggest gaps or the least structure. Where can you remove bias, increase accessibility, and shift policies and practices to help you meet your overall objectives? And, of course, take into account where your organization has the most energy and least resistance for change. Here are some areas to consider:

- How you can increase awareness of underrepresented and marginalized communities overall

- How you can build a more inclusive and inviting brand

- Where you can expand your diversity sourcing

- How you can write more inclusive job descriptions

- Where you can minimize candidate selection bias

- How you can develop more fair and structured interviews

- How you can ensure more equitable job offers

- Ways you can better retain and advance uderrepresented team members

- Ways you can mobilize the rest of your organization in diversity hiring

We'll be spending the next nine chapters of the book exploring these areas, each in great detail, to help you understand where you are and where you can take action. We recommend tailoring your goals as you uncover more here.

Set Your Diversity Goals

Setting your diversity goals can feel like an insurmountable task. You might be wondering, *Where do I start? What does success look like?* It is important to approach this process in a way that is natural and realistic for your organization. What works for you might not work for someone else. Luckily, you aren't the first to pursue this path. Many great organizations have taken distinct approaches to setting their diversity goals. Below, we've divided common diversity goals into three types with a few examples of each. Which one makes the most sense for your organization?

Goal Type	Detail	Examples
Representation goals	Measurably increase diversity representation of a specific group	• Airbnb: Increase underrepresented groups in its U.S. workforce from 12% to 20% by the end of 2025. • Goldman Sachs: Increase the number of women vice presidents to 40% by 2025. • Coca-Cola Co.: Have its workforce mirror U.S. Census data for race (known as "population parity") by 2030.

(continued)

Goal Type	Detail	Examples
Process or activity goals	Change a process or complete a step or action in the operations of the organization to reduce bias or increase access.	• General Motors: Create an inclusion advisory board chaired by the Chairman and CEO. • Snagajob: Rewrite all job postings to remove exclusionary language and bias.
Organizational achievement goals	Achieve a new diversity status or recognition, or change the overall state of equity at the organization.	• T-Mobile: Become a member of the Billion Dollar Roundtable (BDR) by 2025. (The Billion Dollar Roundtable association recognizes businesses that spend at least $1 billion a year with minority- and women-owned suppliers.) • Salesforce: Achieve pay equity across all job functions and levels by the end of 2015.

Here are the tactical steps we recommend taking when crafting your diversity goals:

1. **Translate everything you've learned into diversity targets that address your gaps.**

   Consider the feedback from your team, your existing representation data, and the state of your hiring process to determine where your greatest needs exist. Review these needs to set specific goals that will address each of the gaps you've found. Many employers simply just set goals for increasing diversity representation but it's important that your goals are well-rounded. For example, if you see a need to increase representation in a department while also addressing bias in part of your hiring process, be sure your goals account for the target increase and needed process changes.

2. **Ensure that your diversity goals naturally align with your culture and mission.**

It's key that your diversity goals feel like a natural fit for your organization. They need to resonate with your team and fit into the culture of goal-setting that already exists. If your diversity goals don't feel clear and inspiring for your colleagues or don't resemble what you are already doing, they could fail to take flight. "We can't treat diversity goals as mutually exclusive with our culture, mission, and vision," says Barry Marshall, CEO of consultancy P5 and a human resources lecturer at King's College in New York.

3. **Set goals that reflect an inclusive definition and focus on diversity.**

Many leaders hold a narrow view of diversity that greatly limits how they define success in their goal-setting. Be sure your goals account for an inclusive definition of diversity that encompasses the broad range of underrepresented communities you hope to hire. Focused short-term goals may be ideal, especially when looking to increase representation of a particular group, but don't let that cause you to deliberately exclude other underrepresented groups from your long-term goal-setting.

4. **Make sure your diversity goals are specific and realistic.**

A common challenge for many leaders is to oversimplify their diversity goals or make them so broad that they become immeasurable. Be sure to structure your goals so they are specific, measurable, and attainable. In some organizations, there is a tendency to intentionally set low targets that can easily be hit. Others make goals exorbitantly high or impossible to achieve. Your goals should be realistic, or you risk convincing your team and yourself that any meaningful change isn't possible. For example, if women make up less than 10 percent of your organization, a goal to increase representation to 40 percent in under a year is probably not realistic.

5. **Give yourself a deadline and account for the actual time this will take.**

Set a timeframe for achieving your diversity goals so they don't feel open-ended. Make sure this timeframe isn't overly ambitious. Many leaders fail to acknowledge the time needed for diversity efforts to have a noticeable effect. On the other hand, don't allow deadlines to become moving targets. If you don't achieve your goals by a reasonable deadline, accept that your methods may not be working and you might need to take steps to change them. Rome wasn't built in a day, but it did eventually get done.

Map Strategies and Tactics for Achieving Your Goals

Now comes the exciting part of bringing your diversity goals to life. After you've included your team in the goal-setting process, ensure your tactics for achieving those goals are equally empowering and actually work for your team.

Aligning your diversity goals to the right tactics is key for your impact and the morale of your team. Adam Ward, partner at recruiting firm Growth by Design Talent (GBD) and a former head of recruiting at Pinterest, says organizations should be wary of the damage that failed diversity tactics can cause within the workforce. "It can create stress, slow down your diversity efforts, and deflate employee morale if they feel their efforts have failed," he says.

Here are three things to consider when approaching your tactics and strategies for translating your diversity goals to reality:

1. **Start internally before going external.**

The classic mistake that many employers make is to assume they can only increase diversity through external recruiting efforts without first looking to their own internal teams. This is especially problematic as diversity tends to decrease as you look to more senior roles in most organizations. Your most immediate opportunity with any role you're hiring for is to first see if there are people already in your organization from underrepresented groups that you can promote.

Many employers miss the step of communicating open roles they are trying to fill to their existing team. Take steps to proactively communicate all new opportunities internally to allow people to raise their hands and apply, just as you would external candidates. Be sure your process accounts for internal candidates from underrepresented groups in the same way you do external candidates. For example, if you set a rule mandating specific diversity representation in the hiring process, be sure you are equally accounting for your internal candidate slate as well.

2. **Develop a role-specific diversity strategy and avoid a one-size-fits-all approach.**

In 2003, frustrated and embarrassed by the lack of non-white representation among the league's coaches, the NFL created the Rooney Rule. Named for former Pittsburgh Steelers owner Dan Rooney, the rule stipulates that teams must interview at least one non-white candidate for every available coach position. In 2020, the rule was amended to require that teams interview "minorities and/or female applicants" for all executive positions. Since its inception, the Rooney Rule has been adopted by a wide range of organizations looking to diversify.

While the rule has proven effective for many groups, its widespread adoption has also laid bare its shortcomings. "In leadership hiring, the Rooney Rule might be a great approach," says Ward, "but it might not be as effective if you are hiring 20 accountants for finance." The Rooney Rule was designed for one specific role in a specific industry. That doesn't mean other groups can't adopt it. It just means they have to do so thoughtfully and take the time to make changes that suit their particular role and situation.

The truth is, there is no silver bullet when it comes to diversity hiring tactics. To best succeed, try to develop a game plan tailored to each kind of role in your organization. This strategy should account for who you can advance internally and what your options are for external hiring. Try to resist the urge to force a universal diversity hiring tactic on all of your roles.

By the way, it's worth noting that, despite all its popularity, the Rooney Rule has proven largely ineffective in the NFL. As of 2021, there were still only three Black head coaches—the same number as there were when the rule was passed.

3. **Experiment, learn, iterate, and build a playbook for your tactics.**

One thing that every leader deeply engaged in diversity hiring tactics will tell you is that this work is hard and it's never perfect out of the gate. Diversity hiring requires shifting systems, changing many people's perspectives, and also addressing historic inequities that have existed in society since the beginning of time. It requires constant iteration and experimentation. Some strategies will fail; some tactics will prove to be misguided. What is important is the fact that you are trying and constantly learning.

If one strategy doesn't work, try something else. If your team members get demoralized, remind them what's at stake. Think of every step that doesn't go according to plan as another key learning to file away. We recommend developing an internal playbook for diversity hiring at your organization to capture at every step which tactics work or don't work with each role you are hiring for. This will enable your team to collectively build institutional knowledge and every insight you glean will be shared by everyone.

Make Your Progress and Results Transparent

It can be frightening to throw back the curtain on your diversity efforts. But transparency is an essential part of building trust and galvanizing others around your goals. If you want to transform diversity from an activity into a movement in your organization, it comes down to building transparency around your efforts.

1. **Be brave and start building awareness, even if it feels early.**

    It can be hard to imagine an upside to letting the world know that your DEI numbers are less than desired. But there's ample evidence to show it's the right thing to do. In 2013, despite having low representation numbers, Pinterest shared its first public diversity report as a way of holding itself accountable, and it immediately drove the company to take meaningful action. Seven years later, the public accountability and recruiting efforts had paid off. In its 2020 annual report, Pinterest stated that it had exceeded all three of its external hiring goals, increasing hiring rates of full-time women engineers to 27 percent, underrepresented minority engineers to 9 percent, and underrepresented employees across the company to 14 percent.

2. **Get started on a reporting routine, even if it's informal.**

    While many organizations have made a point of publishing full diversity reports, we know this requires capacity and resources that not every organization has. You can opt for alternative, light-lift, and low-cost ways to share your efforts. Many organizations use their own blogs. In 2020, Uncommon Schools, a nonprofit education organization, published a letter on its website to share updates on its DEI commitments as well as actionable changes it had planned for the new school year. The blogging platform Medium used its own site to share its diversity report in a brief article—something any organization could emulate at practically no cost.

3. **Consider accessibility and what your community will understand.**

    When deciding how to release your diversity progress, remember that less is more. Not many people will care to wade through a dense 50-page report in search of your relevant numbers. In its 2019 report, eBay published a colorful 20-page slide deck that distilled information using engaging visuals and descriptive captions. That same year, Target went an even simpler route with a four-page report consisting of graphics showing its diversity data and how the company measured against comparable companies in the industry.

4. **Make this a conversation with your team and community.**

Your diversity reporting shouldn't feel like you're unveiling results to your team and broader community in a one-way direction. Rather, this is your opportunity to build a shared conversation around your goals and progress to date so it's clear to everyone how you will take next steps together. Streaming service Netflix made its diversity reporting a team effort. In the spirit of its own platform, it released a mini-documentary featuring members of its inclusion team, CEO Ted Sarandos, and testimonials from employees. Like Netflix, you can use diversity reporting as a chance to engage your team and empower them to play a role in telling your story. This will be much more profound and personal.

FIRST STEP TOWARD IMPACT

The most powerful way you can start your diversity goal-setting efforts is to initiate a conversation with your team. Of any step in this process, this is the one that will require the broadest range of orchestrated inputs from across your organization. The more representative the perspective you have feeding into your work, the clearer and more focused your results will be.

Rather than do this alone or make guesses as to where the need exists, schedule some time with your team to ask them:

- Where do you see the greatest need to increase representation in your organization?

- Where do you believe, tactically, you have the greatest opportunity to first implement this work?

- What role are you committing to playing to help us get there?

This sets you up to make your diversity goals a shared pursuit across your organization.

REFERENCES

Barbour, Heather. "25+ Examples of Awesome Diversity Goals." *Ongig* (blog). July 8, 2020. https://blog.ongig.com/diversity-and-inclusion/diversity-goals/.

Bersin, Josh. "Elevating Equity: The Real Story of Diversity and Inclusion." Accessed March 25, 2021. https://ss-usa.s3.amazonaws.com/c/308463326/media/7667603358a67626883312490210463/202102%20-%20DEI%20Report_Final_V2.pdf.

"Black Employee Representation Goals: Mirroring the Markets We Serve." Coca-Cola Company. Accessed March 17, 2021. https://www.coca-colacompany.com/shared-future/diversity-and-inclusion/racial-equity/internal-action/black-representation.

"Civil Rights Groups Sign Groundbreaking Diversity Agreement with T-Mobile US." National Urban League. March 16, 2021. https://nul.org/news/civil-rights-groups-sign-groundbreaking-diversity-agreement-t-mobile-us.

Dennis, Jo. "What We're Learning as We Build a More Inclusive Company." *Pinterest Newsroom.* January 16, 2020. https://newsroom.pinterest.com/en/post/diversity-report-2020.

Dickey, Megan Rose. "Airbnb Sets New Diversity Goals." *TechCrunch.* December 15, 2020. https://techcrunch.com/2020/12/15/airbnb-sets-new-diversity-goals/.

Granderson, LZ. "Column: NFL's Rooney Rule Still Ineffective and Needs Enforcement." *Los Angeles Times.* January 6, 2021. https://www.latimes.com/sports/story/2021-01-06/nfl-black-coaches-rooney-rule-enforcement.

Hackett, Robert. "Goldman Sachs CEO's Diversity Advice: 'Set Very Specific, Aspirational Goals.'" *Fortune.* September 30, 2020. https://fortune.com/2020/09/30/goldman-sachs-ceo-david-solomon-diversity-mpw-summit/.

"Inclusion Takes Root at Netflix: Our First Report." Netflix. January 13, 2021. https://about.netflix.com/en/news/netflix-inclusion-report-2021.

"Letter to Our Community." Uncommon Schools. December 17, 2020. https://uncommonschools.org/letter-to-community/.

Munoz, Raquel. "Medium: Diversity and Inclusion 2017 Edition." *Medium* (blog). December 18, 2017. https://blog.medium.com/medium-diversity-and-inclusion-a90062f8e39d.

"Our 2019 Diversity and Inclusion Report." eBay. Accessed March 26, 2021. https://static.ebayinc.com/assets/Uploads/Documents/eBay-DI-2019-Report.pdf.

Seiter, Courtney. "An Incomplete Guide to Inclusive Language for Start-ups and Tech." *Buffer* (blog). June 6, 2018. https://buffer.com/resources/inclusive-language-tech/.

Spayd, Liz. "Preaching the Gospel of Diversity, but Not Following It." *New York Times*. December 17, 2016. https://www.nytimes.com/2016/12/17/public-editor/new-york-times-diversity-liz-spayd-public-editor.html.

"Target 2019 Workforce Diversity." Target. Accessed March 26, 2021. https://corporate.target.com/_media/TargetCorp/csr/pdf/Target-Workforce-Diversity-Report_FY2019.pdf.

"2020 Salesforce Equal Pay Update." Salesforce News. September 18, 2020. https://www.salesforce.com/news/stories/2020-salesforce-equal-pay-update/.

Vaghul, Kavya. "A Small Fraction of Corporations Share Diversity Data, but Disclosure Is Rapidly on the Rise." *JUST Capital*. January 19, 2021. https://justcapital.com/news/a-small-fraction-of-corporations-share-diversity-data-but-disclosure-is-rapidly-on-the-rise/.

Wayland, Michael. "GM CEO Mary Barra: 'It's my responsibility' to Ensure Company Changes Following Death of George Floyd." *CNBC*. June 9, 2020. https://www.cnbc.com/2020/06/09/gm-ceo-its-my-responsibility-to-drive-change-after-floyds-death.html.

CHAPTER 3

Understanding Underrepresented Job Seekers

If we want to increase diversity in our organizations, we first have to be intentional about how we define diversity itself.

How we see people—and how we approach them—is rooted in the way we talk about them. The language we use matters, and when we paint *diversity* itself in broad strokes, we miss the important distinctions and challenges of each community we are trying to hire. According to the *Harvard Business Review*, many leaders misuse the term "diverse" as a shorthand for underrepresented populations. "But lumping a wide range of people into the category of 'diverse' erases the racial, gender, and disability characteristics leaders want to value," it says.

Going deeper than the broad strokes that have often painted diversity comes down to developing a deeper understanding of the different communities that are underrepresented in our workforce. Rather than lump these communities together and generalize, we have the chance as leaders to educate ourselves on each underrepresented group, the challenges they face, and how we can better hire and support each.

To paint the picture of the cross-section of underrepresented communities from which we can hire, we have profiled 12 groups in this chapter. Our work here is not to imply that this is an exhaustive list of all underrepresented job seekers, but rather a starting point. We chose groups that we found faced marginalization or a lack of representation in the workforce, or where there was little awareness of their challenges or needs in the workforce. We believe it's important to build awareness of underrepresented communities as an ongoing and collective process. The needs of each community will continue to evolve, and we should never treat these insights as static.

We have emphasized what we believe is most important to know about each community, including the most inclusive terminology and how we as leaders can better hire and support each one. The communities we explore, in no particular order, are:

- Working parents
- Older and experienced workers
- Refugees and immigrants
- LGBTQ+ community
- People with disabilities
- Veterans
- Formerly incarcerated individuals
- Black community
- Hispanic and Latinx community
- Indigenous and Native American community
- Women
- Asian American and Pacific Islander community

We encourage you to consider this information in the context of your organization's unique diversity priorities. The nature of your product, service, or geography might lead you to focus on some communities over others, or shift your focus to groups other than those we've profiled. As you familiarize yourself with different underrepresented groups, this list will naturally expand.

You may find that you are already aware of and advocating for some communities while finding that others are less familiar to you. We encourage you to keep an open mind and resist the urge to assume or generalize. As you read through each section, consider the following questions:

- What do I already know or believe to be true about this community?

- Am I aware of the challenges this community faces?

- Is this a community I have considered when thinking about diversity representation?

- What are the unique challenges this community faces in the hiring process?

- What can my organization do to better hire and support this community?

- What are my sources for data on the needs of this community?

- How can I engage this community to be a direct voice in innovations and solutions that will guide my hiring practices?

- How can I be a better advocate for this community?

For additional resources to assess your diversity hiring efforts visit: http://Mathison.io/Index.

Of course, no community of people exists in isolation. Members of one community will inevitably overlap with others. There are Black members of the LGBTQ+ community, Asian veterans with disabilities, and, of course, women members of every community. This *intersectionality* is an important concept to grasp, because every individual has their own experience of oppression and discrimination. While we begin with a framing of community by community, know that by the end of the journey, we're going to address the nuances of intersectional aspects of identity.

As we increase our awareness of each underrepresented group, it's important to avoid generalizing at all costs, even with the language we use when referencing each community. Bella De Soriano, who leads conscious language research at Healthline Media, observes that there is no universal approach or best-practice inclusive language for a given underrepresented group. "It's important to respect a person's autonomy to use the language they choose to describe themselves, their communities, or their experiences, even if it goes against language recommendations. Letting people define themselves even if it's contradictory to language 'best practice,' including person first versus identity first language, is a key part of respecting who they are," she says.

For now, we'd encourage you to go into each of these community sections the way you would enter any conversation as a leader: aware that the other person or group you're about to encounter has something to teach you—something you likely don't fully understand yet. An open mind and a curious spirit will go a long way in empowering each group.

WORKING PARENTS

"The workplace has only become more challenging for working parents in recent years—many must wear multiple hats and have manyfold responsibilities, from working to teaching and doing all the housekeeping."

—Jenny Galluzzo,
co-founder of the Second Shift, a network of
professional women who work on a project basis

Working parents probably aren't the first people who come to mind when you think about diversity. After all, working parents make up a significant portion of the workforce. In more than half of U.S. families, both parents work. In 2019, 33.4 million families, or two-fifths of all families, included children under age 18, and 91 percent of those families had at least one employed parent.

But consider that there are many different ways to be a parent, or a co-parent or stepparent. There are same-sex parents, single parents, and parents of special-needs children. There are surrogate mothers and those who become parents through surrogacy. Parenting may be an elemental human activity, but it is also one of constant evolution.

While parents do enjoy some systemic advantages and targeted benefits in our society, they also face some distinct challenges—especially those who don't fit the traditional mold. Many of these challenges were exacerbated by the COVID-19 pandemic, when parents suddenly had to accommodate remote learning with the simultaneous loss of childcare options.

"Parenting is not a monolith," says Mita Mallick, Head of Inclusion, Equity, and Impact at software company Carta. "We have to be inclusive of all forms of parenting and move beyond the stereotype of the traditional nuclear family. This includes single parent households, two dads caring for their children, and in many cases, grandparents helping to raise the next generation."

While working parents can often be falsely perceived as being less committed or effective because of obligations at home, in reality their ability to balance responsibilities is what makes them effective. This makes it all the more critical that employers offer flexible work environments that embrace working parents.

Today, 58 percent of working parents believe more flexible working arrangements would have a positive impact on their work experience, and 27 percent of working parents with children under 18 have real concerns about managing work and children's needs while working at home. Although flex work has become more popular since the shift to increased remote work that occurred in 2020, we need to explore what the next set of initiatives looks like, whether that's additional sick leave or more paid time off.

Terms to use	Terms to avoid
Working Parents	*Where possible, reference*
Parental Policies	*"Parental" to be gender inclusive*

Challenges Affecting Working Parents

- **Caregiving responsibilities.** A large percentage of working parents are also caring for a parent with a disability or other family member with special needs. According to the Pew Research Center, 47 percent of working parents are also supporting aging parents.

- **Self-inflicted pressure.** Nobody can balance work and family perfectly. The burden of trying to do so creates unrealistic self-expectations.

- **Lack of flexible scheduling.** Juggling family needs with work demands is challenging and even harder when working from home, where the line between work and home is blurred. Many potential employees going through the application process may feel the need to hide the fact that they have children in order to be considered for the job.

- **Gender perceptions.** The same actions are perceived differently depending on whether they are taken by a man or a woman. For example, a man is generally applauded for taking time off to attend a child's dance recital, whereas a woman would be criticized for a lack of commitment to her job.

Single working parents face additional pressures with the absence of a partner to take on half the load. Often, single working mothers face the general misconception that if a working mom is single, she must be struggling. We should also acknowledge the differences in perceptions as it relates to working mothers and working fathers.

It's worth acknowledging that although single people don't face the same biases as those mentioned in this section, single people without children often face their own challenges. The best practice is to adjust work structures to accommodate working families without putting additional pressure on employees who don't have children. There is always an opportunity to make the workplace more equitable for one group without taking away support for another.

Top biases and challenges

- Working parents are thought to be less effective and less committed. Employees who are not parents often judge their parent colleagues when family needs conflict with work hours.
- Working parents place enormous pressure on themselves to balance work, caretaking, and home life.
- Working parents are often mistakenly thought to be unable to travel or have regular obligations outside of work.
- Some professionals believe it is a faux pas if a working parent's child appears in a video or conference call.

Ways to Hire and Empower Working Parents

Research strongly suggests there are many benefits to having parents in the workplace. However, the lack of accommodations and programs to support working parents leaves many with no choice but to prioritize childcare responsibilities over work. By understanding the challenges and adopting the measures listed below, we can pave a way to empower and better support this community.

1. **Be flexible.** Provide virtual interviews. Be flexible with your hours of availability and scheduling.

2. **Fight for better benefits.** Assess current policies and how they support families. Offering PTO, childcare benefits, flexible work schedules, and other family-friendly options opens the field considerably for working parents.

3. **Be accommodating; use a "candidate-first" mindset.** Offer support, empathy, and compassion. When a candidate's child suddenly appears in a video conference or an interview, for example, be understanding. Make sure your actions reflect your intent to be accepting toward working parents.

4. **Offer mental health support.** Offer counseling services to help your working parent employees.

5. **Have an open dialogue with teams.** Set expectations and daily goals and encourage employees to be honest about their capacities.

First Step in Supporting Working Parents

Our first step really has two parts. The two questions you can use to start empowering working parents are:

- How can I be more flexible and supportive for working parents on my team?

- How can I encourage my organization to develop more consistent policies to support working parents longer-term?

Make flexibility a core part of your approach, and consider how policy could shift if you built it around parents' daily work.

OLDER AND EXPERIENCED WORKERS

"We are on the edge of a huge change in how people live their lives. While previous generations retired early, individuals in their 50s and 60s, older workers, want to find meaning and fulfillment, and they want to contribute."

—Ginny Brzezinski,
co-author of *Comeback Careers*

In your focus on diversity efforts, age may have taken a backseat to your other priorities. That's not unusual, because most leaders fixate on more commonly discussed factors such as race and gender. However, older and experienced workers are one of the fastest-growing populations in the workforce. By 2024, they will make up nearly a quarter of all American workers, and by 2026, the number of workers over 55 years of age will reach 42.1 million, up nearly 7 million since 2016 (U.S. Senate, 2017).

Older workers bring unique contributions to the workplace, but most employers have been slow to recognize their value. While 83 percent of business leaders say multigenerational workforces are key to the growth and success of their companies, 92 percent of companies do not include age as a part of their DEI strategies, according to a 2016 PwC report, and 53 percent do not include age in diversity and inclusion policies. If you haven't addressed this, you're not alone. But also, let's get to it.

There are many advantages to hiring older workers. Heather Tinsley-Fix, Senior Adviser for Financial Resilience at AARP, says, "Our research repeatedly shows that older workers are eager to grow and learn new skills, particularly if their employer provides opportunities to do so. After the [COVID-19] pandemic hit and so many people had to adjust overnight to working remotely, many employers found that there were no age-related patterns to who adapted well and who didn't."

When referencing the community, which is defined as individuals over the age of 50, it is best to use the terms *Older and Experienced Workers*, *Older Workers*, or *Mid- or Late-Career Workers*:

Terms to use	Terms to avoid
Older Workers	Retirees
Older and Experienced Workers	Seniors/Senior Citizens
Mid- or Late-Career Workers	Aging Workers
	Old Workers

Challenges Affecting Older Workers

Older and experienced workers face many challenges in the workforce. While age discrimination remains by far the biggest age-related challenge, increased caregiving needs, job insecurity, and lack of access to training may also keep many older workers from thriving in their chosen career. Here are some of the major challenges facing older workers in the workplace today:

- **Age discrimination.** According to AARP, 61 percent of workers have either seen or experienced age discrimination in the workplace, and 76 percent see age discrimination as a hurdle to finding a new job. Age bias is so prevalent, in fact, that many of us are desensitized to it. Comments such as "I'm having a senior moment" conjure up images of older workers as addled or forgetful but are largely thought of as harmless.

- **Lack of training.** A common issue facing older workers is a lack of access to training opportunities and a shortage of guidance on what skills to acquire in order to remain competitive.

- **Financial insecurity.** One-third of older workers are not financially prepared to retire and therefore must work longer than originally anticipated.

- **Slow rebound.** "When older workers are unemployed, or there is a shock and they lose their jobs or they are down-sized, it takes them about twice as long to get back into the workforce as it does younger workers," says Tinsley-Fix from AARP. "And almost always when they get back into the work-force, it is at a diminished income level."

- **Caregiving needs at home.** Caregiving responsibilities for a spouse or family member can conflict with work schedules, especially if employers cannot offer flexible scheduling.

Top biases and challenges

- Misconception that older workers won't be able to learn or use technology
- Belief that older workers will not be willing to take a more junior or lower-paying job to make a career shift, learn new skills, or continue working
- Belief that older workers will require extra training and/or training methods
- Belief that older workers will be less committed or will have lower retention

---

Ways to Hire and Empower Older Workers

Given the clear benefits of hiring older workers, the challenges the community faces, and the low priority most organizations continue to place on recruiting them, there is a huge opportunity for forward-thinking organizations to make an impact by hiring and supporting older workers. Here are some key ways you can serve this community:

1. **Revise your definition of diversity to include older and experienced workers.** Create a more inclusive definition of diversity by accounting for them in your diversity agenda and reporting. Including age in your metrics not only helps ensure they are hired in equitable numbers, but it also communicates to the world that your organization is committed

to doing so. Given the staggeringly low number of organizations that include older workers in their diversity metrics, this is a chance for your organization to become an advocate in this space.

2. **Take steps to address age bias in your hiring process.** Because age bias is so prevalent in hiring, take time to educate your team about the risks involved. Also consider using tools that can redact age and graduation years from candidate profiles so you can focus on older workers' qualifications. When composing job descriptions, watch out for words like "energetic" or "dynamic" or "digital native." These can serve as subtle signals that older applicants are not welcome.

3. **Offer flexible scheduling options.** Work-life balance is even more important for older workers, who may need time off for caregiving duties. According to the U.S. Senate Committee on Aging, even though 80 percent of employers say they are supportive of older workers, only 39 percent offer flexible scheduling options.

4. **Relax your requirements and consider transferable skills.** Don't disqualify potential candidates because they don't satisfy all your requirements. Older workers have learned and adapted through the years and are open to being trained if you give them the chance.

5. **Create mentorship relationships.** Older, experienced workers have a wealth of experience behind them and have much to offer. Being given the opportunity to mentor a younger, less experienced worker can be empowering for both the mentor and the mentee. In a 2018 AARP study, about two-thirds of the 1,000 employees surveyed had experienced mentorship, either as a mentee (53 percent) or as a mentor (55 percent), and found it a positive component of an age-diverse workforce.

6. **Promote training opportunities for older workers to brush up on new skills.** According to a study by the Center on Aging and Work at Boston College, more than 80 percent

of workers ages 45 to 64 believe the opportunity to learn something new is an essential element of their ideal job, and more than 70 percent claim that on-the-job training is, too. Certain industries have recognized this need and have taken the lead, including the scientific, financial, insurance, and healthcare sectors.

First Step in Supporting Older Workers

A single question you can start with in your pursuit to empower older and experienced workers is: **How do I address my own potential age bias when I am recruiting?**

One suggestion is to take two employee profiles—one newly graduated and one older worker—and consider how you view their performance and expertise through the lens of their age. If you notice any imbalance or unfairness, make a mental note to proactively think of this the next time you view a candidate profile.

REFUGEES AND IMMIGRANTS

"There are about two million immigrants and refugees currently in the U.S. who have college degrees but are unemployed or working far below their skill level, according to research from our partners at the Migration Policy Institute. We believe that starting over in the U.S. shouldn't mean starting at the bottom."

—Jina Krause-Vilmar,
President and CEO of Upwardly Global

Although politicians and the media often portray immigrants and refugees as a threat to the American workforce, they are in fact a large and vital part of the U.S. economy. They bring a wide variety of rich cultural perspectives to the workplace and help support key industries and often take jobs for which they are vastly overqualified simply for the chance to work in this country.

"Immigrants are the future of the U.S.," says Gitanjali Rawat, Program Director of Upwardly Global. "They're innovators and very resilient." Yet both immigrants and refugees face a host of challenges across the spectrum, from restrictive policies to language barriers and cultural divisions.

According to the Census Bureau, immigrants make up about 17 percent of the U.S. workforce. And compared to the general population, a greater proportion of immigrants are working. For example, among male immigrants, 77.8 percent are working, compared to 67.5 percent of men born in the U.S.

In 2018, a Fiscal Policy Initiative study found that 73 percent of employers reported that their refugee employees had a higher retention rate than their American-born workers. Nearly one-third, however, do not have authorization to work legally. Hiring teams often use the lack of work authorization as a barrier to even having a conversation with a potential candidate. Consider the benefits of offering visa sponsorship when you are likely to have significantly fewer costs in turnover.

A 2010 Social Influence study found that the term "illegal alien" evokes greater prejudice against Mexican immigrants because the term is associated with "increased perceptions of threat." When referring to this community, stick to using the terms "refugee" or "immigrant." When we use alternative terms like "aliens" or "illegals," we are inherently criminalizing them as wrong. People are not illegal.

Terms to use	Terms to avoid
Refugees	*Illegal immigrants*
Immigrants	*Illegal worker*
Undocumented immigrants	*Migrant*
	Illegals
	Aliens
	Anchor baby

Challenges Affecting Refugees and Immigrants

Refugees and immigrants must overcome a multitude of obstacles to find work in a foreign land. They face the obvious challenges of navigating an unfamiliar country with very few, if any, connections to help them.

- **Difficulties getting work.** Many immigrants take low-paying jobs far below their educational or experience level because employers prefer domestic credentials or because certifications and licenses from overseas don't transfer. The next time you hop into an Uber driven by an immigrant, ask them about their story. You might be surprised how many of them used to be doctors, lawyers, or teachers in their home country.

- **Accessing services and resources.** Undocumented immigrants may hesitate to seek essential services, such as medical or legal assistance, for fear of being deported. Even when they do seek such services, the language barrier can create misunderstandings and misdiagnoses. This language barrier also prevents individuals from attempting to form stronger connections to expand their professional network.

- **Transportation limitations.** Getting a driver's license can be difficult for immigrants and refugees. If they have trouble speaking English, they may need an interpreter for the driving test, and they must also pass a written exam. Often only one member of the family will get a license, making it difficult to commute to work or engage in spontaneous business travel.

- **Access to childcare.** The world is a scary place and it's hard to know whom to trust. Immigrants and refugees who do not have extended family nearby face great challenges in finding quality child care.

- **Housing.** As housing costs soar, immigrants with low-paying jobs and poor English skills may struggle more than most. As a result, large families often live together in overcrowded situations. Language barriers, furthermore, make it difficult for tenants to get a fair resolution to housing problems.

Top biases and challenges

- **Language barrier.** For non-English-speaking immigrants and refugees, it can be challenging to perform simple tasks like shopping and meeting people, much less applying for jobs or filling out financial forms.
- **False perception.** The inability to speak English fluently can give someone the appearance of being unintelligent or uneducated, regardless of their education or fluency in other languages. Remember, someone speaking with an accent is smart enough to learn more than one language and brave enough to work using their second language.
- **Cultural differences.** Resumes and LinkedIn profiles may be written in a different format without much awareness of how to optimize them for recruiters.
- **Prejudice and racism.** Immigrants and refugees often struggle in the face of ignorance, indifference, and a lack of understanding.

Ways to Hire and Empower Refugees and Immigrants

1. **Prepare now.** Develop a firm immigration policy so you're not making decisions on a case-by-case basis. Under what circumstances will you sponsor visas? Will you pay for travel and relocation expenses? What support will you extend to an applicant's family? Preparing these policies now will make for an easier hiring process.

2. **Recognize cultural differences.** Not speaking English or a lack of familiarity with American customs are not signs that someone is uneducated or rude. In some cultures, eye contact is considered disrespectful. In others, it is impolite to talk about money. Each person has a unique cultural background and is capable of making an individual contribution. Think in terms of cultural *add*, not cultural fit.

3. **Consider mentorship of refugees.** Providing mentorships is a great way to support refugees who may not be able to network. For example, in 2020, the Tent Partnership for Refugees, a nonprofit organization that promotes the hiring

of refugees, partnered with the Human Rights Campaign to mentor LGBTQ+ refugees throughout the United States.

4. **Consider employment-based Green Card sponsorship.** Offering Green Card sponsorship is a great way to accommodate foreign employees who want to become permanent residents.

5. **Other integration services.** Employers can offer English language classes during off-hours or lunchtimes, mentorship opportunities with bilingual senior employees, and citizenship training to help immigrant and refugee employees better acclimate to U.S. society.

6. **Partner with recruitment agencies.** There are numerous refugee-focused recruitment agencies in the U.S. and abroad. For example, the Tent Partnership for Refugees provides a variety of services for employers that are open to hiring or otherwise supporting refugees.

First Step in Supporting Refugees and Immigrants

Granting opportunities to immigrants and refugees can be challenging if you don't understand their credentials and experience. If your hiring managers are uncertain about how a foreign applicant's skills measure up, an independent skill translation company such as Enic-NARIC USA can help by comparing foreign qualifications with U.S. standards.

LGBTQ+ COMMUNITY

"With every generation, more and more people identify as LGBTQ. And even those who don't identify as LGBTQ are increasingly determined to work at an organization that has a culture where LGBTQ+ folks can belong. Businesses see this. They don't want to be left behind or lose the competitive edge of inclusion. That's why more and more of them are doing what it takes to build cultures of belonging."

—Erin Uritus,
CEO, Out & Equal Workplace Advocates

You might have noticed the changing and demographically expanding aspects of the LGBTQ+ community. Within the community, new discussions arise every day and new vocabulary reflects new understanding. Emerging conversations are rooted in culture, medical science, history, and policy. And yet, despite the nature of these discussions—which are being met with unprecedented national acceptance—queerness is not new.

There's a juxtaposition of old and new, of emerging justice and longstanding imbalances, that presents unique challenges for the community. The culture is empowering people to identify and celebrate themselves in new ways, but the mechanics of the hiring process and adapting to people's unique needs are historically slow to change.

Despite large scale support from LGBTQ+ allies, the number of organizations that practice inclusion and create policy changes is significantly fewer than those that brand themselves as allies. According to McKinsey, about 5 percent of women and 3.9 percent of men in the United States identified as LGBTQ+ as of 2020. These statistics are not inclusive of nonbinary people, because most surveys do not measure them, and that's a barrier they face when seeking representation and inclusion.

Despite great legal strides being made for the community in recent years, 25 percent of LGBTQ+ Americans have experienced discrimination based on sexual orientation or gender identity, and a 2020 research study by FCB and Out Leadership shows that only 57 percent of people are out at work. As leaders, it is our responsibility to ensure that we build a more inclusive culture for all employees. This is challenging with a demographic that is still making strides to unite and include different parts of its own population.

According to Catalyst, 40 percent of the LGTBQ+ community work in industries more prone to economic insecurity, such as the service industry and healthcare. This employment uncertainty is distressing and made worse by the fact that many states and employers have been slow to adopt inclusivity of the community in the workplace. However, there's been progress on the legal front for workers in the LGBTQ+ community, with the landmark Supreme Court LGBT ruling in June 2020. This case ruled that the 1964 Civil Rights Act protects gay, lesbian, and transgender individuals from workplace discrimination and will help improve economic conditions for members of the community moving forward.

Terms to use	Terms to avoid
LGBTQ+ people	*Homosexual*
Queer person	*The term "queer" may not resonate with every*
Gay	*member of the community, and for some it is offensive. It has a history of being used as a slur, but has*
Lesbian	*sive. It has a history of being used as a slur, but has*
Transgender	*been reclaimed by younger generations.*

Challenges Impacting LGBTQ+ Individuals

As with many of the identities we highlight, intersectionality adds complexity to the challenges that LGBTQ+ individuals face during the job search and beyond. According to a Human Rights Campaign report, Black transgender women face the highest levels of lethal violence in the LGBTQ+ community. Data from NPR and Harvard also shows that 32 percent of LGBTQ+ people of color say they've experienced discrimination because of their identity when applying for jobs, which is two times more than their white counterparts.

Equally unsettling are the statistics surrounding workplace discrimination of LGBTQ+ workers. According to the FCB and Out Leadership study, 47 percent of LGBTQ+ employees have experienced microaggressions at work, which causes at least 70 percent of these employees to cover up certain behaviors at the office. Additionally, about one out of five LGBTQ+ Americans report not being paid equally or promoted at the same rate as their cisgender, heterosexual peers.

Violence against members of the LGBTQ+ community is also extremely prevalent. Almost one-fifth of hate crimes committed in 2015 was due to sexual orientation, according to FBI Hate Crime Statistics. Overall, these are some more universal challenges that the community faces.

Top biases and challenges

- Fear of bringing their authentic self to work for fear of discriminatory behavior or being seen as "unprofessional."
- Thirty-one percent of LGBTQ+ workers say they have felt unhappy or depressed at work.
- One in five LGBTQ+ workers report having been told or had coworkers imply that they should dress in a more feminine or more masculine manner.

Ways to Hire and Empower LGBTQ+ Individuals

1. **Develop more targeted recruiting efforts.** Partner with LGBTQ+ organizations, post on LGBTQ+ specific job sites (Tjobbank, Outpronet, Pink-Jobs), and attend professional recruiting events.

2. **Develop more inclusive policies.** Talk with employees of various genders, sexualities, and gender expressions about what would make them feel more included:

   - Create an inclusive dress code that avoids enforcing gender stereotypes.

   - Scrub internal communication/imagery that assumes heterosexual relationships as the norm.

   - Make it easier to report discrimination and harassment.

   - Clarify what will and will not be tolerated as "office banter."

   - Add a space for preferred pronouns in email signatures and job applications.

   - Educate yourself on typical challenges the community faces such as bringing spouses to work events or discussing family-related challenges that impact their work life with a supervisor.

3. **Diversify your board.** Increasing representation among members who hold power will give you more insight into the needs of this community and how to take action.

4. **Culture of communication.** Focus efforts on creating a culture where employees can feel comfortable speaking up about discrimination or harassment in the workplace. This likely includes visual representation both in branding materials and the actual power structure of your organization.

5. **Business resource groups (BRG).** Also known as ERGs or affinity groups, these can help create a space of safety and comfort to discuss obstacles the community faces in their day-to-day lives at work. It's important to make sure the BRG has executive sponsorship with a direct line to voice their concerns or ideas to management.

6. **Public support.** Publicly support the LGBTQ+ community by participating in PRIDE events and supporting LGBTQ+ charities/causes.

7. **Advocacy.** Advocate for and act as an ally to members of the community through your day-to-day interactions. According to a 2015 U.S. Transgender Survey, 80 percent of the transgender population who were employed that year experienced harassment or mistreatment on the job or took steps to avoid it. Public advocacy will help end such treatment.

8. **Benefits.** Ensure that existing policies and benefits are inclusive of the LGBTQ+ community and that domestic or same-sex partners are covered by health insurance. Leave policies, particularly parental leave policies, should be revised to be more inclusive.

9. **Identify where you stand.** The Corporate Equality Index is the national benchmarking tool on corporate policies and practices pertinent to lesbian, gay, bisexual, transgender, and queer employees. Remember that each subgroup within the community has unique needs that are unlikely to be met by any one policy.

First Step in Supporting LGBTQ+ Individuals

There are many accessible ways to signal your support and commitment to the LGBTQ+ community within your organization. To begin this work, you may want to ask yourself the following: Is my organization's stance on LGBTQ+ rights public and consistent with our current policies? If you don't have policies because you've not communicated a stance, what's the best way to onboard the organization to develop the stance that will inspire policy?

PEOPLE WITH DISABILITIES

"You do not have to be an expert on all things disability in order to get started. Imperfect action is better than no action. Just get started, and let's co-create a culture of inclusion and belonging together."

—Tiffany Yu,
CEO and Founder, Diversability

Tiffany's suggestion is a powerful one, and of course, one we've tried to apply throughout this book. For all groups, we advocate finding an imperfect starting point and advancing from there. In regard to hiring people with disabilities, you'll certainly encounter policy and perspectives that are unique to this community, but understand that self-education is vital to the process, and know that you can always ground yourself in the basics to give you clarity on the specifics as you progress.

The term "disability" itself is one that is subject to many questions on the part of people trying to better understand the community. Disability is a purposefully vague term that reflects the vast diversity within the community of disabled people. The CDC defines a disability as "any condition of the body or mind (impairment) that makes it more difficult for the person with the condition to do certain activities (activity limitation) and interact with the world around them (participation restrictions)." It's important to remember that not all disabilities are visible. Generally, disabilities are categorized by physical and mental limitations, though many diagnoses overlap both categories. Disabilities encompass a person's sensory impairment, mobility impairment, learning impairment, mental health disorders, or any other impairment.

As of 2018, 61 million adults in the United States—approximately 26 percent of the adult population—were living with a disability. But due to stigmas and social norms, many people with disabilities (PWD) do not identify as part of this community. People with disabilities, both physical and mental, are frequently isolated by mainstream concepts of normalcy and acceptable skills. One of the most prevalent examples of othering occurs in the labor market.

Unfortunately, this group has some of the highest and most disproportionate unemployment in the country. For instance, 69 percent of people with a disability ages 16 to 64 were not employed in 2019, versus 25 percent for people *without* a disability, according to data from the U.S. Bureau of Labor Statistics. That lack of employment is partly why one in three persons with a disability between the ages of 18 and 44 lacks access to consistent and regular healthcare.

Notably, there is a marked intersection between race and diagnosed disabilities in the United States. Data from the National Disability Institute shows that Black Americans have the highest likelihood of having a disability (14 percent), followed by white, non-Hispanic Americans (11 percent). Within the Latinx community, 8 percent of people have a disability.

Terms to use*	Terms to avoid
People with disabilities **Person with _____**	*Handicapped, Handicap, Handi-capable, Special needs, Special, Gifted, Differently abled, Crippled, Defective, Invalid*

*Using person-first and ability-centric language is preferred (e.g., "person who uses a wheelchair" instead of "wheelchair-bound").

Acceptable terminology is constantly evolving and can depend on individual preference. That said, while the term "disabled" used to be frowned upon, it is now one of the more preferred terms within the community of people with disabilities. "Disabled" should not be perceived as a bad word or a negative; it's more straightforward and inclusive than terms that can seem patronizing, like "special" or "differently abled."

Challenges Affecting People with Disabilities

- **Pay inequity.** According to the U.S. Census Bureau, the median salary of individuals with disabilities in 2017 was $41,332, whereas the median salary of individuals without disabilities was $47,279.

- **Poverty.** Poverty has been shown to cause disabilities, but it can also be a result of having a disability. The poverty rate for those with disabilities is 27 percent, compared to 12 percent for people without disabilities.

- **Discrimination.** Once people with disabilities are given the opportunity to work, many often face significant discrimination within their organization: 33.4 percent of discrimination charges filed to the EEOC in 2019 were about disability discrimination.

- **Financial insecurity.** People with disabilities are more likely to be "unbanked", meaning they do not have a checking or savings account. Without a formal financial footprint, it can be particularly difficult to reach financial security, even while employed full time. Almost half of households with disabilities (48 percent) are unbanked.

Top biases and challenges

- Using language that describes the community in a derogatory or negative way (e.g., crazy, psycho, blind) is prevalent in our culture. Many advocates are building awareness around exclusive language through discussions of what neurodiversity is and how it's representative of our population.

(continued)

- Prejudice, discrimination, and the fear of workers being a physical or financial burden on the organization.
- AI like HireVue that attempts to predict a candidate's employability based on gestures, poses, lean, tone, and cadence put those with physical disabilities at a disadvantage.
- Negative attitudes toward hiring people with disabilities usually come from those who have not had previous experiences with them.

Ways to Hire and Empower People with Disabilities

1. **Policies.** Implement or refine your organization's anti-ableism, anti-harassment, and antidiscrimination policies.

2. **Accommodations.** Understand your workers' needs and provide the necessary accommodations (e.g., more time on a project, proper equipment, etc.).

3. **Training.** Provide training to build awareness in the workplace—not all disabilities are visible or talked about.

4. **Accessibility.** Prioritize access for all by ensuring inclusive design through your website, public materials, and digital tools.

5. **Self-identification questions.** During your recruitment and interview processes, you may offer opportunities to potential employees to self-identify as a disabled person. These questionnaires can empower people with disabilities while signaling your organization's commitment to establishing a more inclusive workplace.

6. **Flexible work options.** The COVID-19 pandemic has proven that work can continue even when we are all engaging through screens. Offering remote work options and flexible schedules will benefit all employees.

7. **Amplify, don't tokenize.** Invite current employees with disabilities to share their journeys and success. It's important to engage community members without placing responsibility on them to "fix" the glaring issues in an organization.

First Step in Supporting People with Disabilities

Because disabilities are far-reaching and broadly defined, it can feel overwhelming when trying to address your organization's accessibility. One place to start may be to ask yourself if you as an employer are familiar with your organization's accessibility statement, and how you make accommodations for your employees with disabilities. Once you've become more familiar with your policies, you'll be able to readily shift them to become more inclusive of your entire workforce.

Veterans

"When I was coming out of active duty, the one thing I didn't have was the ability to translate those skills, and to be able to figure out exactly what I could do. We learned the same things, but with different terms. I was lost."

—Tim Cochrane,
U.S. Marine, SVP of American Corporate Partners

As of 2019, 18.8 million Americans were classified as veterans by the Bureau of Labor Statistics. This group of individuals holds a vaunted position in American society, revered for their service and admired for their sacrifice. But that admiration often fails to translate to the workplace. Military personnel can be high-performing individuals with a wide variety of skills, an acute sense of discipline, and well-honed leadership abilities. Nevertheless, a high incidence of mental and physical disabilities, paired with the misconception among employers that military experience doesn't translate to civilian work, prevent them from fully engaging in the workforce. As of 2019, veterans in the U.S. had a 5.4 percent unemployment rate, as opposed to a 3.5 percent rate for the general population.

The data indicates a deep intersectionality of challenges facing America's veterans. Between 2000 and 2019, almost 20 percent of those who served in the military were women. Of the entire veteran population, about one-fourth have a diagnosed service-related disability. Black veterans have a 5.9 percent unemployment rate, as opposed to 3.1 percent for white veterans. While all veterans face similar biases, the added identities put these veterans at an even greater disadvantage. We cannot adequately hire and support veterans without understanding the other communities they also belong to. A few stats from the Bureau of Labor Statistics to keep in mind:

- **Forty-one percent** of veterans who served on active duty in the U.S. Armed Forces since September 2001 have a service-connected disability.

- Of the **284,000** veterans who were unemployed in 2019, 56 percent were between the ages of 25 and 54.

Terms to use	Terms to avoid
Veteran	*Ex-military*
	Avoid nicknames: jarhead, flyboy, squid, grunt, pog

Challenges Affecting the Veteran Community

- **Appearing unqualified.** Veterans are not always adequately prepared to find a civilian job because their language and skills have been acquired specifically for military service. Additionally, employers may falsely believe these skills won't transfer to a civilian role.

- **Associated stigmas.** Employers are often wary of hiring veterans due to concerns over mental health or long gaps in employment.

- **Lack of on-the-job training.** When veterans reenter civilian life, they tend to be older than the average entry-level worker, and their lack of familiarity with the workplace can be mistaken for incompetence. For many veterans, this proves to be a barrier to employment.

- **Lack of connections and resources.** Eighty-five percent of people get their jobs via network connections, according to a 2016 survey conducted by the Adler Group. Military roles are often siloed and may not provide many civilian networking opportunities.

Top biases and challenges

- Veterans are not always adequately prepared to explain their transferable skills to find a civilian job.
- Veterans' profiles are often misunderstood by hiring teams who don't know how to relate military experience to civilian duties.
- Veterans often face stereotypes and misconceptions that all veterans have PTSD and mental illness that will impact their ability to do their job and connect to coworkers.

Ways to Hire and Empower Veterans

1. **Understand success.** Rather than focus narrowly on a handful of surface qualifications, rethink job descriptions to understand what attributes might really contribute to success (e.g., an infantry squad leader could make a great customer success manager).

2. **Check your biases.** Confront your preconceived notions about veterans. This will allow you to remain objective and focus on the candidate.

3. **Be understanding.** Veterans typically don't have previous private-sector work experience or access to resources to learn how to properly interview and navigate the hiring process.

4. **Be an advocate.** Push back on hiring managers who don't express interest in hiring veterans due to bias or a lack of understanding around transferable skills.

5. **Mentorship.** Encourage mentorship within your organization or through the American Corporate Partners' (ACP) free Mentoring Program. These opportunities will help veterans get assimilated into the civilian workforce.

6. **Demonstrate appreciation.** Show that you appreciate and understand veterans beyond just offering a "thank you for

your service." Educate employees so they have some degree of military literacy. Develop policies and benefits structured to support your veteran employees and their families.

7. **Value tangible skills.** Don't dismiss candidates because they don't have direct experience in certain areas. They likely have used similar skills, only in a different capacity.

First Step in Supporting the Veteran Community

Educate yourself so you have some degree of military literacy. Veterans will have less difficulty connecting if their colleagues have done their homework on the basics. The U.S. Department of Veteran's Affairs has a great employers toolkit we share on our book resource page. Use tools like Careeronestop or ONETonline to learn about military occupation codes and specialties used in the military. This will clear up any confusion when reviewing resumes and give you a broader understanding of military skills that can be applied to your workplace.

FORMERLY INCARCERATED INDIVIDUALS

"There's not this absolute morality, bad people and good people. We're talking about people who probably made a mistake when they were a kid . . . and if they had a white father who could afford a lawyer, they probably would've not been in trouble."

—Richard Bronson,
CEO of 70 Million Jobs

When talking about diversity, we often refer to systemic imbalances that lead to inequity. Nowhere are those systemic imbalances more prevalent than in the lives of formerly incarcerated individuals. People from underrepresented groups are disproportionately arrested and imprisoned for any number of crimes. And once inside the system, the lethal combination of stigma and poverty can make it hard to climb out, much less to start a promising career.

The United States criminal legal system currently incarcerates 2.3 million people, including those in jails, prisons, juvenile facilities, state psychiatric hospitals, and immigration detention centers. Six hundred thousand people enter prisons each year, and over 10 million go through the jail system. This is a significant statistic, as it shows the majority of incarcerated individuals are held in short-term facilities that are not meant to be sustainable housing.

One in four people who have been incarcerated will be incarcerated again in their lifetime due to the cycles of mental illness, substance abuse, and poverty or unemployment that are associated with imprisonment.

Many employers avoid hiring or even accepting applications from individuals with past criminal histories. And while there is a growing movement today to encourage more employers to consider justice-impacted individuals, finding and sustaining gainful employment remains a uniquely taxing challenge for this community. Although background checks are in place to ensure the safety of an organization's employees, they can often unfairly and inaccurately disqualify people who have been formerly incarcerated.

There is substantial evidence to show that these individuals are not more prone to recidivism, largely because they now have stable and secure employment. It's common for at least one in four formerly incarcerated individuals to be facing unemployment, according to the Prison Policy Initiative. Because poverty, a direct result of unemployment, is the highest predictor of whether an individual will reenter the prison system, it is vital we work with this community.

Language can be especially harmful to formerly incarcerated individuals seeking employment upon reentry. Without using modifiers and adjectives, labeling this community with some of the more common terms is dehumanizing and unproductive. Below are some examples of preferred language versus what to avoid. The Fortune Society, a nonprofit organization dedicated to seeing justice-impacted people thrive upon release, also offers a comprehensive guide to language called *Words Matter*.

Terms to use	Terms to avoid
Formerly incarcerated individual	Ex-convict
Returning citizen	Ex-criminal
Justice-impacted person	Ex-prisoner
	Ex-inmate
	Ex-felon
	Ex-offender

Challenges Impacting Formerly Incarcerated Individuals

Being part of the justice-impacted community is already challenging, but the nature of the American correctional system also proves to be an intersectional nightmare for people who identify within multiple underrepresented groups.

- **Race.** Due largely to systemic racism in the U.S., 1 in 3 Black men and 1 in 6 Latino men will be incarcerated in their lifetime as opposed to the 1 in 17 white men.

- **Gender.** Most prison programs are specifically dedicated to men, despite a staggering 834 percent increase in women in the criminal justice system over the last 20 years.

- **Mental health vulnerability.** Thirty-seven percent of people who have been incarcerated have a diagnosis of mental illness.

- **Education.** The school-to-prison pipeline refers to punitive discipline practices that many school-aged people experience. This leads to juvenile delinquency and truancy, which then leads to a cycle of incarceration, unemployment, and poverty.

Top biases and challenges

- Misconception that formerly incarcerated people are dangerous
- Misconception that formerly incarcerated people do not want to work, are lazy, or lack discipline
- Misconception that formerly incarcerated people already have lower-level, manual labor, and customer-service employment options and don't need to be considered

Ways to Hire and Empower Formerly Incarcerated Individuals

To support the people within the formerly incarcerated community, we have to commit to changing the narrative around hiring people with criminal records. There are many ways in which your organization can provide gainful employment opportunities and positively affect this community in particular.

1. **Support with transportation.** Finding roles that can be performed remotely or at a location easily accessed by public transportation will significantly lower the barriers to maintaining employment for reentrants. In a 2006 study by the Urban Institute's Justice Policy Center, one-third of reentrants named transportation to and from work as their biggest barrier to sustained success.

2. **Professional development and continuing education opportunities.** Offering professional development training and continuing education partnerships to employees will help not just formerly incarcerated employees, but everyone in an organization. Investing in your employees' futures demonstrates a commitment to their well-being and professional growth, which can lead justice-impacted individuals to find more success in the future.

3. **Transferable skills in place of education minimums.** While this measure is helpful to all underserved communities, removing barriers in our job descriptions such as required years of experience and level of education can open many doors for formerly incarcerated individuals, since there is such a strong connection between poor access to education and incarceration.

4. **Ban the Box and background check adjustments.** Ban the Box is a movement that encourages employers to make their hiring policies more welcoming to justice-impacted people, specifically by eliminating the box—standard on many job applications—that asks whether the applicant has ever been convicted of a crime. By agreeing to do so, you are signaling to applicants (and your own organization) that you see

candidates as people first. It's important to note that Ban the Box and background check adjustments don't require businesses to get rid of these measures all together. They simply ask them to let a more diverse set of applicants participate in the hiring process before identifying their conviction history.

5. **Partner organizations (WPA, Osborne, REfoundry).** Many nonprofit organizations have partnerships and programs that act as an intermediary between formerly incarcerated individuals and businesses. Organizations like Women's Prison Association (WPA) and Osborne Association, for example, help the formerly incarcerated community in New York City and its surrounding areas. These organizations have programs to help justice-impacted persons learn soft skills and work release programs that can lead to long-term employment opportunities. Refoundry is an LA-based start-up that cultivates entrepreneurship in reentrants to help them achieve stability and meaningful career trajectories.

First Step in Supporting Formerly Incarcerated Individuals

A single question you can start with in your efforts to support formerly incarcerated individuals is: Am I advocating for formerly incarcerated individuals by banning the box at my organization? Resources like Prison Policy Initiative and the partner organizations mentioned above are excellent resources to learn more about this underrepresented community.

BLACK COMMUNITY

"Advancing racial representation in your organization depends on rebuilding trust—step one is really starting from an authentic place about what you truly believe, and step two is internally examining the ways you are actually perpetuating systemic racism within your workplace. Only then can you start to rebuild that trust."

—Valerie Williams,
Managing Partner at Converge Firma

When it comes to understanding the mindset of the Black community today, there is perhaps no more vital concept than "rebuilding trust," as Williams puts it. For centuries, the Black community, a remarkably diverse and heterogeneous community in itself, has endured the false promises of government, politicians, corporations, and yes, employers. Talk of inclusion and equity in the workplace for Black people is hardly new. On the contrary, these conversations have taken place so many times, over so many years, that many Black job seekers regard them with justifiable skepticism.

It's vital for employers to appreciate this history when dealing with members of the Black community. As good as your intentions may be, they mean little without concrete action. Do not make promises you don't intend to keep, and do not fail to keep the promises you make.

Black individuals make up roughly 12.5 percent of the labor force in the United States and regardless of education, they hold a disproportionately large percentage of low-level, underpaying positions, according to a 2021 report by McKinsey. This data quantifies one aspect of the systemic racism that Black Americans face in the workplace.

More than half of the Black workforce lives in the South, and 60 percent live in only 10 states, meaning employers in other regions may need to look harder or work more creatively to attract Black candidates.

Given the fraught political climate today, organizations that say they are dedicated to equity and racial justice must do their part to amplify Black voices and provide more equal opportunities. Supporting (ERGs) or affinity groups for Blacks is no longer an option, but a necessity and requirement for the development of workplace belonging. It is time for organizations in every industry, of every size, to look inward and actively seek more creative and inclusive solutions.

Regarding compensation, we mentioned earlier that Black Americans disproportionately hold more underpaying positions. On top of that, Black men are paid 13 percent less than white men, and

Black women are paid 39 percent less than white men and 21 percent less than white women. In 2018, 6.5 percent of Black people were unemployed, the second highest rate among all races, according to data from the U.S. Bureau of Labor Statistics. Our fellow Black colleagues deserve better, and it's up to you to be an ally and advocate by first asking your organization to conduct annual pay equity audits.

Terms to use	Terms to avoid
Black man or woman	*Historically derogatory words*
Person of color	*If you're questioning whether a word can be*
Person of African descent	*used, the answer is probably no.*

One thing to note with regard to language is the diversity within the Black community itself. For decades, "African American" was used as a blanket term for Black Americans. It's important to consider, though, whom this term excludes. For example, "African American" does not apply to Caribbean Americans, to Black Americans with unknown ethnic ancestry, or to those who don't feel comfortable claiming a specific geographic identity. It is always best to ask individuals how they prefer to be identified and use language accordingly.

Challenges Affecting the Black Community

Top biases and challenges

- **Microaggressions.** Passive-aggressive comments or backhanded compliments about intelligence, ability to speak English ("articulate" is not an appropriate compliment for a Black adult), or the way they carry themselves.
- **Pressure to "fit in."** The pressure to create "facades of conformity," suppressing personal values, views, and attributes to fit in with organizational ones (e.g, "whitewashing" resumes by deleting ethnic-sounding names or companies).

- **Reliance on Black employees for education.** They are often tapped as the voice or main resource for diversity training and informal conversations, putting all the emotional labor on them.
- **Lack of representation.** Being the only Black person on a team can place undue pressure by taking on the responsibility of representing Black people everywhere. It also means you don't see yourself in leadership positions, which makes it difficult to believe that climbing the ladder is achievable.

Ways to Hire and Empower Black Employees

The emotional sacrifice required of Black employees is unparalleled among underrepresented groups in the U.S. For example, even when violent crimes against Black Americans make national news, Black employees are often expected to show up to work as usual without sharing their experiences or expressing their opinions.

As the United States becomes more steeped in racial justice initiatives, many organizations are publicly and internally committing to DEI work. To do this, many leaders put the onus of the movement on the Black employees, hoping to inspire change with their support. This can be a huge mistake, since the very group negatively affected by injustice should not be expected to upend the systems that allow for the injustice to thrive. For some perspective, Black employees have only 3.2 percent of senior-level and executive roles, despite making up 12.5 percent of the labor force.

1. **Evaluate your hiring processes from start to finish.** Where are you recruiting from? Are you partnering with any organizations that can help expose you to more Black talent? Do your recruiters have tools in place to reduce their own personal racial biases? Do you have people of color on your interview panels? Without giving your Black employees more work, seek honest feedback from individuals of color to identify areas in the process that could be improved to be more inclusive.

2. **Target your recruiting.** Develop a more targeted recruitment strategy by forming partnerships with diversity-focused organizations, HBCUs, multicultural professional associations, and student groups (see chapter 6 on Diversity Sourcing).

3. **Consider the core competency of your organization.** Ask your team members where they see inequity or injustice in your industry or space. Challenge them to submit ideas for how your organization could make a difference.

4. **Make space without singling people out.** Many leaders' first inclination is to increase engagement by Black and brown employees. Help ensure Black and brown employees aren't feeling the burden of becoming your DEI "consultants" or facilitators on top of their normal activities.

5. **Build sharing into your culture.** Communicate your priorities to your people and be authentic. Leaders can begin to gather feedback from their Black employees and further circulate information on meaningful ways to speak about race.

6. **Elevate through mentorship.** Consider developing a formal or informal mentorship program to support diversity. Create affinity-based leadership development programs, with one dedicated to Black and brown employees. Also, consider establishing ongoing educational programs and events that build awareness and advocacy among your team members.

7. **Provide budgetary resources.** Invest in affinity groups and provide funds for Black employees to become members in associations and networking groups in the community. Then, plan to set aside resources and time for Black employees to lead programs that will improve awareness throughout your organization.

First Step in Supporting the Black Community

It can be challenging to know where to start on a journey to workplace equity. Inviting Black employees to share their experiences through

ERGs or affinity groups can allow them to process how the world outside of work influences their world inside. Continuous feedback and safe spaces for honest dialogue are great first steps. Show them that you care about them as people more than you care about making sure others know you're "woke."

HISPANIC AND LATINX COMMUNITY

"There's an incredible amount of diversity within the Hispanic community. It's one of our biggest strengths, and something I believe can benefit not just Hispanics, but the entire global economy. We're resourceful, resilient, resolute, and we're ready to tackle any challenge that's put in front of us. Diversity is a business imperative. Hispanics are the future imperative. The sooner we all embrace that fact, and the more we all see that diversity is a strength, the better our collective community and society will be."

—Raquel Támez,
Chief Inclusion and Engagement Officer,
Charles River Associates

The Hispanic community is the second fastest growing demographic in the United States. It makes up nearly 19 percent of the workforce today and, by 2030, will make up 21 percent of the U.S. population. In fact, according to SHRM research, one of every two new workers joining the workforce will identify as Hispanic by 2025.

It is clear that as we continue pushing for diversity and inclusion in our organizations, we need to consider the magnitude of this community. In doing so, employers must also focus on the rich diversity of distinct cultures within it.

Although Hispanic people make up a quickly growing proportion of the workforce, high unemployment remains a longstanding problem in the community. According to the Bureau of Labor Statistics, which has been tracking unemployment cycles since the 1970s, the Hispanic unemployment rate has always been at least 1.2 times the rate of non-Hispanic white Americans.

To remedy this, it is imperative that organizations demonstrate public support for the Hispanic workforce by finding more creative ways to source, hire, and embrace them.

Terms to use	What to know
Latinx Latina/o Hispanic	*Latinx is a term used to reference the community in a gender-inclusive way, but often resonates more with younger generations, while older generations may prefer to use Latina or Latino.* *About 50 percent of individuals with Hispanic/Latinx heritage prefer to be identified by their family's home country, (e.g., Colombian, Cuban, Mexican).*

Challenges Affecting the Hispanic Community

Top biases and challenges

- **Stereotypes and political stances.** Immigration has long been a divisive topic among Americans. Because of fraught political rhetoric, many Americans assume many Hispanic individuals are illegal or do not "belong" in this country.
- **Being misappropriated.** The Hispanic community is often misappropriated into national origins that do not actually reflect an individual's heritage (e.g., falsely referring to a person from Argentina as "Mexican").
- **Language.** As with refugees and immigrants, many Americans will falsely assume that their lack of English skills means they are unintelligent or uneducated.

Hispanic students face many challenges, partly due to inequities that the community faces regarding access to opportunities. "Don't presume the Hispanic community has been afforded the opportunities and resources you have," says Tom Savino, CEO of Prospanica, a nonprofit that focuses on the empowerment of Hispanic professionals. "In most cases they haven't."

- **Finishing a college degree.** Despite high numbers of Hispanic students enrolling in four-year degree programs, this population is the least likely to obtain a degree, often due to financial difficulties and lack of support at home, according to a 2020 UnidosUS study.

- **Immigration and upward opportunities.** Because many in the Hispanic community are immigrants, first in their generation to attend college, and often playing a key role in financially supporting family members who aren't afforded the same opportunities, the community often faces socioeconomic challenges.

- **Limited access to quality educational opportunities.** Many Hispanic students apply to low-cost, less selective institutions because of their lower socioeconomic status. This can limit their earning potential after graduation.

Looking more broadly at the community, other biases emerge.

- **Assimilation versus inclusion.** Many Americans expect the Hispanic community to completely assimilate into "American" culture. Even though this community is the largest ethnic cohort in the U.S., many non-Hispanic Americans continue to diminish Hispanic individuals' unique cultural identity.

- **Language barriers.** Many Americans believe that people living in the U.S. should speak English exclusively, and they make assumptions about the education and intelligence of those they hear speaking any non-English language. Forty-one million residents (13.5 percent of the U.S. population) speak Spanish at home. About 35 million Hispanics also identify as proficient English speakers.

- **Redlining.** Redlining is the discriminatory practice of denying financial services such as loans or insurance to buyers because they live in neighborhoods deemed to have residents who are more likely to default. The practice has been outlawed, but that hasn't stopped sellers, landlords, insurance companies, and banks from discriminating against the Hispanic community. According to Salud America!, a U.S.-based Latino-focused organization, 54 percent of Hispanic heads of household rent rather than own their homes, versus 28 percent for white heads of households.

Ways to Hire and Empower the Hispanic Community

1. **Community partnerships.** Connecting with organizations like the Association of Latino Professionals for America (ALPFA), Prospanica, or the Society of Hispanic Professional Engineers (SHPE) will help in recruiting more Hispanic job seekers.

2. **Sponsorship.** Establish sponsorships and senior-level advocate relationships to build belonging and mobility for Hispanic employees.

3. **Build opportunities for long-term wealth.** Hispanic Americans make up a large portion of Millennial and Gen X populations. It's imperative that organizations provide early and meaningful opportunities for long-term savings and retirement funds for all workers.

4. **Break down stereotypes.** Use your partnerships with Hispanic organizations or create training to combat negative stereotypes and perceptions about the Hispanic community.

5. **Celebrate your Hispanic employees.** Whether this is through a Hispanic ERG or by celebrating popular Hispanic holidays, find a way to bring Hispanic cultures into your workplace. Heritage Month programs (September 15 to October 15) are particularly useful.

First Step in Supporting the Hispanic Community

Because such a large percentage of the Hispanic population in the U.S. is bilingual, it makes sense that many of your employees may prefer to communicate in both English and Spanish. Make sure you have accessible Spanish language materials for your employees. Take it one step further by translating brand material to other languages as well. This will show potential candidates that your organization values their cultures and actively creates space for your Hispanic employees.

INDIGENOUS AND NATIVE AMERICAN COMMUNITY

"The reality is that there are so many thriving indigenous communities in North America that are beautiful for all sorts of different reasons despite the specific struggles that they have."

—Erica Tremblay,
filmmaker and member of Seneca-Cayuga tribe

Over the last 50 years, many countries that have historically mistreated their indigenous people have experienced an awakening, and younger generations have tried to make amends for the crimes of their predecessors. Yet many of these communities remain deeply misunderstood. This is at least partly due to outdated educational systems.

In the United States, for example, 87 percent of American schools do not cover Native American history beyond the 19th century, according to Illumi*Native*, a nonprofit initiative for Native Nations and peoples in the United States. This surely explains in large measure the reason that biases and misconceptions about Native Americans and other indigenous people persists today.

One of these misconceptions is about their modernity and daily life. At one time or another, most Native Americans have had to answer questions about living in teepees or working solely in agriculture on their tribal lands.

There are also misconceptions about how "Native" a person truly is, thanks to policies like blood quantum laws. The U.S. government establish 'blood quantum' laws to measure a tribal person's racial makeup. These laws have given rise to the concept that a person can be a "percentage" Native American, and many white-identifying people have attempted to engage by sharing a genealogical or historical connection to tribes.

This undermines the central role of the tribe, which is defined as a nation enrolling and claiming someone as a member. The decision to admit someone to the tribe does sometimes partly depend on blood percentage proof. But ultimately, tribal membership must be claimed through the tribe, not the individual trying to diversify their background.

To best support and empower Indigenous employees and candidates, we need to correct many of our assumptions and misunderstandings. First, it's important to know the truth about Native American representation in the U.S. population. According to the National Congress of American Indians, the American Indian population in the U.S. is expected to grow from 1.6 percent of the country's total population today to 2.4 percent by 2060. This is an increase from 3 to 10 million people in one generation.

This data, which seems to be relatively accessible for most demographics, was something the Native American community had to fight to publish. In the 2020 census, large groups of registered tribes and Native Americans pushed to get an accurate depiction of their representation in the United States. Historically, Native Americans have been undercounted in the national census, which has led to further underfunding and erasure of their experience as Americans. Today, there are over 570 federally recognized tribes in the United States, all of which should qualify for governmental financial assistance and recognition.

Many Americans yearn for more information about Indigenous peoples and their history. The Reclaiming Native Truth Project conducted a 2018 survey that shows that 78 percent of Americans want to better understand Native Americans as a collective and as individual tribes. Events such as the Standing Rock Sioux Tribe Pipeline protests of 2016 have shed light on Native American history and current experiences. It is up to us all to develop our understanding and awareness of American Indians so that we can best support and engage this underrepresented group. A few stats to keep in mind:

- **Thirty-three percent** of Native Americans report experiencing discrimination by not being paid or promoted equitably.

- The unemployment rate for American Indian and Alaska Native populations is **6.6 percent**, versus 3.9 percent unemployment for the total population in 2018.

- Of the American Indian population, **19.7 percent** has less than a high school degree compared to the 10.5 percent of the total population in 2018.

Terms to use*	Terms to avoid
Native American*	*Indian*
American Indian	*Eskimo*
Indigenous	*Powwow in place of meeting*
Alaska Native	*Up/down the totem pole*
First Nations (Canada)	

Preference is to use specific tribal name, as there is no single Native American tribe, culture, or language.

Challenges Impacting the Indigenous and Native American Community

- While most Indigenous people regularly interact with society beyond their tribal community, each tribe has its own culture and traditions to support. These diverse communities often have their own language and can be geographically isolated from other parts of the country. A lack of government support, along with language barriers, can lead to challenges in understanding and supporting them.

- In 2020, New Mexico state and local governments committed to producing audio recordings for several New Mexico tribes to guide them when filling out census forms. This was in response to the realization that of the 59-language census instructions available, only one was in a Native language—Navajo.

- Another challenge facing Native American communities is access to education, which naturally leads to a lack of employment opportunities. Some studies suggest that only 65 percent of Native Americans graduate from high school, which is the lowest graduation rate among any group in the United States. This fact alone highlights the disparities facing Indigenous Americans hoping to enter the workforce as young adults.

Top biases

- Native Americans can be falsely perceived as not modern or "civilized" because of their grounding in tribal cultures.
- American culture continues to perpetuate "Wild West" imagery, stereotypical costuming, and terminology.
- Non-Native Americans engage in significant cultural appropriation, whether that means ignoring the stereotyping of sports team mascots, referring to people or things as their "spirit animal," or wearing traditional tribal clothing as a costume.

Ways to Hire and Empower the Indigenous and Native American Community

1. **Advocate.** Engage in initiatives to spread accurate information about tribes, and build your local awareness through movements such as #LandBack and Reclaiming Native Truth.

2. **Connect.** Meaningfully connect with local tribal nations to recruit locally. Tribal Employment Rights Organizations (TEROs) are excellent resources for employers seeking to build community partnerships.

3. **Observe.** Commemorate American Indian Heritage Month with programs that educate and inform about history, abuses, broken treaties, achievements, needs, and more.

4. **Research the big picture.** Familiarize yourself with housing shortage trends in your area. The Department of HUD reports a lack of funding to build adequate housing for Native Americans. Housing and access to reliable transportation both affect individuals' ability to stay gainfully employed.

First Step in Supporting Native American Communities

One way to build your own local awareness about Native American tribes is to determine whose land you occupy, either at work or in your personal life. The app Native Land can be downloaded for free and uses your location to determine what tribes once did, or might still, inhabit your region. This will help you and your employees develop an appreciation for the sacrifices forced upon Native American people.

WOMEN

"Whether you are a male CEO or a female CEO, it [increasing the diversity of the team] is a business imperative because if you look at graduating seniors from colleges, more than 50 percent are women. More than 50 percent! And if you look at the best grades, they are being gotten by women. So if you really want companies to be successful, we have got to draw from the entire pool, not just try to say, 'Hey, we are going to exclude a portion of the population'."

—Indra Nooyi,
former Chairman and CEO of PepsiCo

Gender discrimination is perhaps one of the most recognized and broadly discussed examples of workplace bias, yet large-scale solutions remain elusive. As such, you may find yourself asking, "How can I, as a leader, contribute to solutions for such a pervasive, deeply rooted, and systemic problem?"

A 2020 United Nations study found that in 50 countries where adult women are more educated than men, they still receive, on average, 39 percent less income than men—despite devoting more time to work. As shocking as that might be, it is not all that surprising, given what we know.

While there are no easy answers, leaders who are willing to step up and take on the sometimes uncomfortable work of confronting gender bias will find that progress, even on a small scale, is achievable. Consider that women today make up nearly half the workforce. Just a few generations ago, that statistic would have seemed inconceivable. Massive inequities still remain, but the movement for women's equality has spawned a workforce full of women—and men—who are eager to see those injustices resolved once and for all.

There are always setbacks to big picture goals, and now more than ever, it is vital to address your own organization's blind spots. In December 2020, due to the COVID-19 pandemic, women lost 140,000 jobs while men gained 16,000 jobs. Looking at job loss through an intersectional lens, the same data shows that Black and Brown women were hit even harder because of the sectors in which they work, specifically hospitality and food service. As of 2021, the unemployment rate for Latinas was 9.1 percent. For Black women, it was 8.4 percent—the second highest rate overall.

A 2020 study from McKinsey and Lean In titled "Women in the Workplace" found that one in four women are now either considering leaving the workforce altogether or is willing to downshift their career. The most commonly cited causes included the emotional toll of repeated racially charged violence and the disappearance of support systems, like teachers and childcare, that helped women of color and working mothers take part in the workforce.

Even when these challenges don't force women to leave the workforce entirely, they can prevent them from advancing. According to a 2018 Catalyst study, women earned 57 percent of bachelor's degrees and 60 percent of master's degrees in the U.S. This trend has been steadily increasing since 1982, yet women still represent only a small portion of leadership positions at major companies. As of January 2021, only 31 companies in the S&P 500 had a female CEO.

Unfortunately, women do not need to be told that their gender could put them at a disadvantage when it comes to hiring. Fifteen percent of men believe their gender could be an obstacle to them, whereas 29 percent of women believe their gender presents challenges to their success, according to the aforementioned McKinsey and Lean In study.

Terms to use	Terms to avoid
Woman	*Girls, Ladies*
Female	*Terms of endearment (e.g., honey, sweetheart)*
	Woman as a modifier (e.g., woman CEO)
	Guys when referring to a mixed-gender group

Challenges Affecting Women in the Workplace

Women make up 46.8 percent of the labor force in the United States, yet the gender wage gap shows their earnings, varying by race, are only 53–85 percent of a white, non-Hispanic man's earnings. One of the strongest determinants of these disparities is the "broken rung" that exists between lower-level positions and promotions to management. The aforementioned "Women in the Workplace" study found that for every 100 men promoted to a managerial role, only 72 women received similar promotions. Despite making up nearly half of the labor force, women face limited opportunities for growth and advancement. This is widely known as the "glass ceiling" phenomenon. Furthermore, as we consider intersectionality, women of color are even less likely to be promoted. This is known as the "concrete ceiling."

Sponsorship and mentorship also disproportionately benefit men over women. According to the McKinsey and Lean In study, women are 24 percent less likely to be offered formal support from senior leaders, who are often men to begin with. Also, 64 percent of women have experienced microaggressions in the workplace, including gaslighting and people questioning their expertise. These frequent microaggressions are compounded for women, making it difficult for them to feel a sense of belonging in the office.

Top biases and challenges

- The false notion that women are more emotional and erratic and therefore unable to be in positions of power
- The perception that women will require more time off from work or can't travel due to childcare responsibilities
- Male-dominated work environments with a culture that caters to cisgender white men

Ways to Hire and Empower Women

1. **Evaluate and standardize pay.** Make your pay structures transparent and public. Conduct annual audits to ensure people working the same job are getting equal pay.

2. **Flexible work.** Offer flexible work options for all employees to ensure equal opportunity for participation across gender lines. This can drastically reduce the burden and pressure working mothers feel.

3. **Professional development.** Establish mentorship programs to encourage mobility in your organization.

4. **Advocate.** Speak up to actively combat gender discrimination in the workplace. Speak up when a woman gets interrupted in a meeting. Speak up when you notice your women colleagues want to give their two cents but don't want to interrupt. Speak up when you hear misogynistic comments passed off as jokes.

5. **Set hiring and promotion goals.** Establish a benchmark of where your organization is today in terms of its gender representation at all levels and in all departments. Then set clear goals to work toward equal gender representation.

First Step in Supporting Women

One way to assess whether your organization prioritizes a variety of voices is to consider how decisions are made and who is included in the process. Making sure that your female employees have a seat at the table when making decisions is a good way to signal the value you place on equality. This may require you to establish project committees or panels, but opening the door for more input will improve your business practices.

ASIAN AMERICAN AND PACIFIC ISLANDER COMMUNITY

"Many may believe the Asian community isn't underrepresented in the workforce. But it's important to know the community still faces bias and racism, not to mention a 'bamboo ceiling.' Although

Asian job seekers may be represented reasonably well at the entry level, the community is passed over for many leadership opportunities, leaving a visible gap at the top of most organizations."

—— John Yang,
Asian Americans Advancing Justice (AAJC)

The Asian American and Pacific Islander (AAPI) community faces unique challenges to obtaining full inclusion and equity—and silence and erasure intensify those challenges. One significant obstacle for this community is the model minority myth, a stereotype that paints Asian Americans as "A" students who are good at math, play the violin, and never get in trouble. While the stereotype may seem less destructive than those facing Black and Latinx people, it's still a harmful caricature that prevents employers from seeing Asian applicants and employees as unique individuals.

More than 20 million people who identify as Asian live in the United States, with Chinese, Indian, and Filipino Americans making up 60 percent of the Asian American population, according to the Pew Research Center. Yet Asian Americans have long been excluded from conversations about racial inequity in the United States. This makes it that much more crucial for allies and advocates to develop empathy for and understanding of the particular needs of the AAPI community.

A study conducted by the Anxiety and Depression Association of American (ADAA) shows that members of the Asian American community are three times less likely to seek mental health resources than any other group. With the stigma surrounding mental health in this community, organizations have the ability to make a life-changing difference for their employees by providing access to mental health services.

Terms to use	Terms to avoid
Asian American	*Oriental*
Pacific Islander	
AAPI	

Challenges Affecting the Asian Community

Asian American and Pacific Islander men make a few cents *more* per dollar than white men, according to a 2020 Payscale study. And typically, they are more highly represented than their Black and Latinx peers in higher-paying jobs. So at first glance, they may not seem to have significant inclusion and equity challenges.

Asian Americans make up about 6 percent of the labor force (though that number is growing rapidly) and have the highest levels of education and income in the country. Yet they make up only 2.6 percent of the corporate leadership of Fortune 500 companies, according to DiversityInc. Just as women operate beneath a proverbial glass ceiling that keeps them out of leadership positions, Asian Americans are said to struggle beneath a bamboo ceiling. Research suggests that there are three primary reasons that Asian Americans are overlooked for senior jobs. A few key factors that may lead to equitable career progression:

- The same stereotypes that help Asians succeed (e.g., being smart, competent, and hardworking) may actually hurt them by indicating a perceived lack of social skills, assertiveness, and overall leadership potential.

- Being excluded from informal power networks that sometimes are more influential than competency.

- A lack of Asian role models or mentors in the workplace.

These factors are also intertwined with deeply ingrained cultural traits. "Many Asian professionals arrive in the workplace with a set of culturally ingrained [ideas] of what is appropriate behavior, ways to relate themselves to superiors and to elders that may well be a recipe for invisibility," said writer Welsey Yang in a 2014 interview with NPR. To his point, leaders need to be aware of the cultural differences that members of the AAPI community bring to the workplace. Always be sure to establish your expectations clearly regarding employee feedback, and don't be afraid to solicit opinions from employees who may seem hesitant to offer it for cultural reasons.

Top biases and challenges

- Many non-Asian Americans believe in the model minority myth. Because of perceptions about educational attainment and success in the United States, many people don't view discrimination against Asian Americans as legitimate or valid.
- Asian Americans face the broadest income inequality within the same racial group. Asians in the top 10 percent of earners make 10.7 times more than the Asians in the bottom 10 percent of earners.
- The bamboo ceiling refers to barriers Asian Americans and Pacific Islanders face when trying to advance into leadership positions. This is similar to the glass ceiling that affects women.

Ways to Hire and Empower the Asian Community

1. **Circulate information in multiple languages.** Providing translations builds a more inclusive community and ensures all stakeholders are receiving the same information.

2. **Keep yourself and your workforce educated about anti-Asian sentiment.** Consider investing in unconscious bias or bystander effect training.

3. **Explicitly include Asian Americans in your organization's public DEI statements.** The model minority myth can discourage people from including AAPI employees in their understanding of diversity and inclusion.

4. **Understand the cultural differences** that make some AAPI individuals less likely to speak up or be vocal in ways that may hinder their ability to advance in the workplace.

First Step to Supporting the Asian Community

Just like any underrepresented group, the AAPI community includes many different cultures and stories. In order to promote a more inclusive understanding of the community, consider how to amplify the individual voices of your Asian American employees. Asia itself is a continent comprising 48 countries with myriad cultures within each. Start by familiarizing yourself with the different cultures of your AAPI employees and how they can have a direct impact on how they interact with you in the workplace. Are they actually timid or do they simply respect hierarchy?

If your organizational structure is flat, do your AAPI employees fully understand what that means for how they should interact with their colleagues? Help your employees make connections outside of their teams. Introduce a mentorship program or connect them with high-ranking AAPI individuals within your own network. If you want to take a look at your existing AAPI employees, assess their management potential and provide them with honest feedback on how they can improve themselves professionally to climb the ladder and break through that bamboo ceiling.

REFERENCES

Mackenzie, Lori Nishiura, and Melissa V. Abad. "Are Your Diversity Efforts Othering Underrepresented Groups?" *Harvard Business Review*. February 5, 2021. https://hbr.org/2021/02/are-your-diversity-efforts-othering-underrepresented-groups.

WORKING PARENTS

"Employment Characteristics of Families, 2019." Bureau of Labor Statistics News Release. April 21, 2020. https://www.bls.gov/news.release/pdf/famee.pdf.

"New Survey: COVID-19 & Employee Sentiment on Changing Workforce." Glassdoor. March 23, 2020. https://www.glassdoor.com/blog/new-survey-covid-19/.

Parker, Kim, and Eileen Patten. "The Sandwich Generation: Rising Financial Burdens for Middle-Aged Americans." Pew Research Center. January 30, 2013. https://www.pewresearch.org/social-trends/2013/01/30/the-sandwich-generation/

Pelta, Rachel. "FlexJobs Survey Shows Need for Flexibility, Support for Working Parents." Flexjobs. September 15, 2020. https://www.flexjobs.com/blog/post/flexjobs-survey-flexibility-support-parents-pandemic/.

OLDER AND EXPERIENCED WORKERS

AARP. "Insights from Global Employers: The Future of Work Is Living, Learning and Earning Longer." Accessed March 26, 2021a. https://www.aarpinternational.org/resources/global-employer-survey.

AARP. "Mentorship and the Value of a Multigenerational Workforce." Accessed March 26, 2021b. https://www.pwc.com/gx/en/diversity-inclusion/best-practices/assets/the-pwc-diversity-journey.pdf.

Brzezinski, Mika. *Comeback Careers: Rethink, Refresh, Reinvent Your Success—at 40, 50, and Beyond.* Hachette UK, 2020.

Eisenberg, Richard. "Senate Aging Committee Spotlights Aging Workforce Challenges." PBS. December 7, 2017. https://www.pbs.org/wnet/chasing-the-dream/stories/senate-aging-committee-spotlights-aging-workforce-challenges/.

Jenkins, Jo Ann. "The Future of Work Is Here." AARP. August 7, 2020. https://www.aarp.org/politics-society/advocacy/info-2020/jenkins-supporting-multigenerational-workforces.html.

Kita, Joe. "Workplace Age Discrimination Still Flourishes in America." AARP. December 30, 2019. https://www.aarp.org/work/working-at-50-plus/info-2019/age-discrimination-in-america.html.

"Median Employee Tenure Unchanged at 4.6 Years in January 2014." U.S. Bureau of Labor Statistics. September 25, 2014. https://www.bls.gov/opub/ted/2014/mobile/ted_20140925.htm

"Millennials: Confident. Connected. Open to Change." Pew Research Center. February 24, 2010. https://www.pewresearch.org/social-trends/2010/02/24/millennials-confident-connected-open-to-change/.

Pitt-Catsouphes, Marcie, et al. "The National Study Report." Center on Aging and Work at Boston College. March 2007. https://www.bc.edu/content/dam/files/research_sites/agingandwork/pdf/publications/RH04_NationalStudy.pdf.

PricewaterhouseCoopers. "The PwC Diversity Journey: Creating Impact, Achieving Results." Accessed March 24, 2021. https://www.pwc.com/gx/en/diversity-inclusion/best-practices/assets/the-pwc-diversity-journey.pdf.

Terrell, Kenneth. "Age Discrimination Common in Workplace, Survey Says." AARP. August 2, 2018. https://www.aarp.org/work/working-at-50-plus/info-2018/age-discrimination-common-at-work.html.

Terrell, Kenneth. "Employers Worldwide Often Exclude Age From Diversity Policies." AARP. August 5, 2020. https://www.flexjobs.com/blog/post/flexjobs-survey-flexibility-support-parents-pandemic/.

"Three Things Employers Need to Know About: Training and Development for Workers 50+." Center on Aging and Work at Boston College. Accessed March 26, 2021. https://www.bc.edu/content/dam/files/research_sites/agingandwork/pdf/publications/RH04_NationalStudy.pdf.

United States Senate. "America's Aging Workforce: Opportunities and Challenges." December 2017. https://www.aging.senate.gov/imo/media/doc/ Aging%20Workforce%20Report%20FINAL.pdf.

REFUGEES AND IMMIGRANTS

ENIC-NARIC Networks. Accessed March 26, 2021. https://www.enic-naric .net/usa.aspx.

"HRC Joins Forces with Tent Partnership for Refugees, More Than 20 Global Businesses to Support over 1,000 Refugees in North America." Human Rights Campaign. Accessed March 26, 2021. https://data .census.gov/cedsci/table?q=ACSST5Y2016.S0501&g=0100000US&tid =ACSST5Y2016.S0501.

Kallick, D. D., and Roldan, Cyierra. "Refugees as Employers: Good Retention, Strong Recruitment." Fiscal Policy Institute. Accessed March 26, 2021. https://live-tent-site.pantheonsite.io/wp-content/uploads/2018/05/ TENT_FPI-Refugees-as-Employees-Report.pdf.

Pearson, Matthew R. "How "Undocumented Workers" and "Illegal Aliens" Affect Prejudice toward Mexican Immigrants." *Social Influence* 5, no. 2 (2010): 118–132. http://www.communicationcache.com/uploads/ 1/0/8/8/10887248/how_undocumented_workers_and_illegal_aliens_ affect_prejudice_toward_mexican_immigrants.pdf.

United States Census Bureau. "Selected Characteristics of the Native and Foreign-Born Populations." Accessed March 26, 2021. https://data .census.gov/cedsci/table?q=ACSST5Y2016.S0501&g=0100000US&tid =ACSST5Y2016.S0501.

LGBTQ+ COMMUNITY

"Addressing Anti-Transgender Violence." Human Rights Campaign. Accessed March 26, 2021. https://assets2.hrc.org/files/assets/resources/ HRC-AntiTransgenderViolence-0519.pdf?_ga=2.19003068.589392774 .1592240536-208228424.1590700033.

"Corporate Equality Index 2021." Human Rights Campaign. Accessed March 26, 2021. https://www.hrc.org/resources/a-workplace-divided- understanding-the-climate-for-lgbtq-workers-nationwide.

"Discrimination in America: Experiences and Views of LGBTQ Americans." NPR. Accessed March 26, 2021. https://legacy.npr.org/documents/2017/ nov/npr-discrimination-lgbtq-final.pdf.

Ellsworth, D., and A. Mendy. "How the LGBTQ+ Community Fares in the Workplace." McKinsey & Company. June 23, 2020. https://www

.mckinsey.com/featured-insights/diversity-and-inclusion/how-the-lgbtq-plus-community-fares-in-the-workplace.

"Lesbian, Gay, Bisexual, and Transgender Workplace Issues: Quick Take." Catalyst. June 15, 2021. https://www.catalyst.org/research/lesbian-gay-bisexual-and-transgender-workplace-issues/.

Sawyer, Katina B., Christian Thoroughgood, and Jamie Ladge. "How Companies Make It Harder for Lesbian, Gay, and Bisexual Employees to Achieve Work-Life Balance." *Harvard Business Review.* Updated September 14, 2018. https://hbr.org/2018/08/how-companies-make-it-harder-for-lesbian-gay-and-bisexual-employees-to-achieve-work-life-balance.

Sawyer, Katina B., Christian Thoroughgood, and Jamie Ladge. "Invisible Families, Invisible Conflicts: Examining the Added Layer of Work-Family Conflict for Employees with LGB Families." *Journal of Vocational Behavior* 103 (2017): 23–39. https://www.sciencedirect.com/science/article/pii/S0001879117300817.

Sears, Todd, and Jane Barry-Moran. "AllyUp: Ally Is a Verb." Out Leadership. Accessed March 26, 2021. https://outleadership.com/wp-content//uploads/2020/06/AllyUpFinal2020_Web.pdf.

"Supreme Court Delivers Major Victory to LGBTQ Employees." NPR. June 15, 2020. https://www.npr.org/2020/06/15/863498848/supreme-court-delivers-major-victory-to-lgbtq-employees.

"2015 Hate Crime Statistics." FBI. Accessed March 26, 2021. https://ucr.fbi.gov/hate-crime/2015/topic-pages/victims_final.

"2015 U.S. Transgender Survey." National Center for Transgender Equality. Accessed March 26, 2021. https://www.ustranssurvey.org/.

"Workplace Divided: Understanding the Climate for LGBTQ Workers Nationwide, A." Human Rights Campaign. Accessed March 26, 2021. https://www.hrc.org/resources/a-workplace-divided-understanding-the-climate-for-lgbtq-workers-nationwide.

PEOPLE WITH DISABILITIES

"Banking Status and Financial Behaviors of Adults with Disabilities." National Disability Institute. Accessed March 29, 2021. https://www.nationaldisabilityinstitute.org/wp-content/uploads/2019/11/ndi-banking-report-2019.pdf.

"Disability and Health Overview." CDC. Accessed March 27, 2021. https://www.cdc.gov/ncbddd/disabilityandhealth/disability.html#:~:text=A%20disability%20is%20any%20condition,around%20them%20(participation%20restrictions).

"Disability Impacts All of Us." CDC. Accessed March 27, 2021. https://www.cdc.gov/ncbddd/disabilityandhealth/infographic-disability-impacts-all.html.

"EEOC Releases Fiscal Year 2019 Enforcement and Litigation Data." U.S. Equal Employment Opportunity Commission. Accessed March 27, 2021. https://www.eeoc.gov/newsroom/eeoc-releases-fiscal-year-2019-enforcement-and-litigation-data.

"Financial Inequality: Disability, Race and Poverty in America." National Disability Institute. Accessed March 27, 2021. https://www.national disabilityinstitute.org/wp-content/uploads/2019/02/disability-race-poverty-in-america.pdf.

"Guidelines for Writing About People with Disabilities." Americans with Disabilities Act National Network. Accessed March 27, 2021. https://adata.org/factsheet/ADANN-writing.

"Persons with a Disability: Labor Force Characteristics Summary." U.S. Bureau of Labor Statistics. February 24, 2021. https://www.bls.gov/news .release/disabl.nr0.htm.

"Why Employers Don't Hire People with Disabilities: A Survey of the Literature." CPRF. Accessed March 27, 2021. https://www.cprf.org/ studies/why-employers-dont-hire-people-with-disabilities-a-survey-of-the-literature/.

"Workers with a Disability by Detailed Occupation." United States Census Bureau. Accessed March 27, 2021. https://www.census.gov/data/ tables/2017/demo/disability/acs-17.html.

VETERANS

Adler, Lou. "New Survey Reveals 85% of All Jobs Are Filled Via Networking." LinkedIn. February 29, 2016. https://www.linkedin.com/pulse/new-survey-reveals-85-all-jobs-filled-via-networking-lou-adler/?trk=Yahoo_News.

"Employment Situation of Veterans Summary." U.S. Bureau of Labor Statistics. March 18, 2021. https://www.bls.gov/news.release/pdf/vet.pdf.

Rolen, Emily. "A Closer Look at Veterans in the Labor Force." U.S. Bureau of Labor Statistics. November 2017. https://www.bls.gov/ careeroutlook/2017/article/veterans.htm?view_full.

"Veterans Employment Toolkit." U.S. Department of Veteran Affairs. Accessed March 27, 2021. https://www.va.gov/vetsinworkplace/.

FORMERLY INCARCERATED INDIVIDUALS

Bronson, Jennifer, and Marcus Berzofsky. "Indicators of Mental Health Problems Reported by Prisoners and Jail Inmates, 2011–12." *Bureau of Justice Statistics* (2017): 1–16. https://www.bjs.gov/content/pub/pdf/ imhprpji1112.pdf.

"Issue and Impact." Women's Prison Association. Accessed March 27, 2021. https://www.wpaonline.org/issue-and-impact/.

Martin, Glenn E. "Why Ending Bias Against the Formerly Incarcerated Helps All Americans." Crime Report. December 19, 2017. https://thecrimereport.org/2017/12/19/why-ending-bias-against-the-formerly-incarcerated-helps-all-americans/.

"Mass Incarceration: An Animated Series." ACLU. Accessed March 27, 2021. https://www.aclu.org/issues/smart-justice/mass-incarceration/mass-incarceration-animated-series.

Sawyer, Wendy, and Peter Wagner. "Mass Incarceration: The Whole Pie 2020." Prison Policy Initiative. March 24, 2020. https://www.prisonpolicy.org/reports/pie2020.html.

"Understanding the Challenges of Prisoner Reentry: Research Findings from the Urban Institute's Prisoner Reentry Portfolio." Urban Institute Justice Policy Center. January 2006. http://www.urban.org/sites/default/files/publication/42981/411289-Understanding-the-Challenges-of-Prisoner-Reentry.PDF.

"Words Matter." Fortune Society. Accessed March 27, 2021. https://fortunesociety.org/wp-content/uploads/2020/12/final-humanizing-language.pdf.

BLACK COMMUNITY

Brundage Jr., Vernon. "Labor Market Activity of Blacks in the United States." U.S. Bureau of Labor Statistics. February 2020. https://www.bls.gov/spotlight/2020/african-american-history-month/pdf/african-american-history-month.pdf.

"Majority of African Americans Live in 10 States; New York City and Chicago Are Cities with Largest Black Populations." United States Census Bureau. August 13, 2001. https://www.census.gov/newsroom/releases/archives/census_2000/cb01cn176.html.

"Labor Force Characteristics by Race and Ethnicity, 2018." U.S. Bureau of Labor Statistics. October 2019. https://www.bls.gov/opub/reports/race-and-ethnicity/2018/home.htm.

"Race in the Workplace: The Black Experience in the US Private Sector." McKinsey & Company. February 21, 2021. https://www.mckinsey.com/featured-insights/diversity-and-inclusion/race-in-the-workplace-the-black-experience-in-the-us-private-sector.

Yuan, Karen. "Working While Black: Stories from Black Corporate America." *Fortune*. June 16, 2020. https://fortune.com/longform/working-while-black-in-corporate-america-racism-microaggressions-stories/.

HISPANIC AND LATINX COMMUNITY

Coulombe, Kathleen, and William Rafael Gil. "The Changing US Workforce: The Growing Hispanic Demographic and the Workplace." 2016. https://www.shrm.org/hr-today/public-policy/hr-public-policy-issues/Documents/15-0746%20CHCI_Research_Report_FNL.pdf.

"Employment Situation News Release." U.S. Bureau of Labor Statistics. February 24, 2021. https://www.bls.gov/news.release/archives/empsit_05082020.htm.

Flores, Antonio. "How the U.S. Hispanic Population Is Changing." Pew Research Center. September 18, 2017. https://www.pewresearch.org/fact-tank/2017/09/18/how-the-u-s-hispanic-population-is-changing/.

"Following Their Dreams in an Inequitable System: Latino Students Share Their College Experience." UNIDOS US Policy & Advocacy. Accessed March 27, 2021. http://publications.unidosus.org/bitstream/handle/123456789/2078/unidosus_followingtheirdreams_lr.pdf?sequence=4.

Gamboa, Suzanne. "Racism, Not a Lack of Assimilation, is the Real Problem Facing Latinos in America." NBC News. February 26, 2019. https://www.nbcnews.com/news/latino/racism-not-lack-assimilation-real-problem-facing-latinos-america-n974021.

Gonzalez-Barrera, Ana. "The Ways Hispanics Describe Their Identity Vary across Immigrant Generations." Pew Research Center. September 24, 2020. https://www.pewresearch.org/fact-tank/2020/09/24/the-ways-hispanics-describe-their-identity-vary-across-immigrant-generations/.

"Hispanics in the US Fast Facts." CNN. February 24, 2021. https://www.cnn.com/2013/09/20/us/hispanics-in-the-u-s-/index.html.

"Leading Hispanics in STEM." SHPE. Accessed March 27, 2021. https://www.shpe.org/.

Poston, Dudley L. "3 Ways That the U.S. population Will Change over the Next Decade." PBS NewsHour. January 2, 2020. https://www.pbs.org/newshour/nation/3-ways-that-the-u-s-population-will-change-over-the-next-decade.

Sukumaran, Pramod. "Redlining Is Illegal, But It's Still Hurting Latino Families." Salud America! May 31, 2019. https://salud-america.org/redlining-is-illegal-but-its-still-hurting-latino-families/.

Zamarripa, Ryan. "Closing Latino Labor Market Gap Requires Targeted Policies to End Discrimination." Center for American Progress. October 21, 2020. https://www.pbs.org/newshour/nation/3-ways-that-the-u-s-population-will-change-over-the-next-decade.

INDIGENOUS AND NATIVE AMERICAN COMMUNITY

"American Indians and Alaska Natives in the U.S. Labor Force." U.S. Bureau of Labor Statistics. November 2019. https://www.bls.gov/opub/mlr/2019/article/american-indians-and-alaska-natives-in-the-u-s-labor-force.htm.

"Changing the Narrative about Native Americans: A Guide for Allies."
  First Nations Development Institute. Accessed March 27, 2021. https://
  illuminatives.org/wp-content/uploads/2018/04/MessageGuide-Allies-
  screen-spreads.pdf?x18008.
Chow, Kat. "So What Exactly Is 'Blood Quantum'?" NPR. February 9, 2018.
  https://www.npr.org/sections/codeswitch/2018/02/09/583987261/so-
  what-exactly-is-blood-quantum.
Clift, Joey. "8 of the Biggest Misconceptions People Have about Native
  Americans." Insider. January 9, 2020. https://www.insider.com/mis
  conceptions-native-americans-usa-culture-2020-1.
"The Future Is Indigenous." Illuminative. Accessed March 27, 2021. https://
  illuminatives.org/nativenow/.
"Income and Poverty in the United States: 2016." United States Census
  Bureau. September 2017. https://www.census.gov/content/dam/Census/
  library/publications/2017/demo/P60-259.pdf.
"Indian Country Demographics." National Congress of American
  Indians. Accessed March 27, 2021. https://www.ncai.org/about-tribes/
  demographics.
"The Issues Surrounding Native American Education." Native Hope. Accessed
  March 27, 2021. https://blog.nativehope.org/the-issues-surrounding-
  native-american-education#:~:text=Recent%20statistics%20from%20
  the%20Bureau,the%207th%20and%2012th%20grades.&text=This%20
  means%20only%2065%20percent,graduation%20rate%20among%20
  American%20students.
Kesslen, Ben. "Native Americans, the Census' Most Undercounted Racial
  Group, Fight for an Accurate 2020 Tally." NBC News. December 29, 2019.
  https://www.nbcnews.com/news/us-news/native-americans-census-
  most-undercounted-racial-group-fight-accurate-2020-n1105096.
Mullan, Dillon. "New Mexico Cuts Census Barriers for Native Language
  Speakers." Government Technology. January 14, 2020. https://www
  .govtech.com/gov-experience/New-Mexico-Cuts-Census-Barriers-for-
  Native-Language-Speakers.html.
"The Native American Housing Needs Study." HUD USER. Accessed
  March 27, 2021. https://www.huduser.gov/portal/pdredge/pdr-edge-
  research-022117.html.
Neel, Joe. "Poll: Native Americans See Far More Discrimination in Areas
  Where They Are Majority." NPR. November 14, 2017. https://www
  .npr.org/2017/11/14/563306555/poll-native-americans-see-far-more-
  discrimination-in-areas-where-they-are-a-majo.
"Reclaiming Native Truth." Illuminative. Accessed March 27, 2021. https://
  illuminatives.org/reclaiming-native-truth/.
"Tribal Enrollment Process." U.S. Department of the Interior. Accessed
  March 27, 2021. https://www.doi.gov/tribes/enrollment.

Women

Clifford, Catherine. "PepsiCo CEO: Hiring More Women and People of Color is a 'Business Imperative.'" CNBC. October 17, 2016. https://www.cnbc.com/2016/10/17/pepsico-ceo-hiring-more-women-and-people-of-color-is-a-business-imperative.html.

"Earnings over Time." Women's Bureau. Accessed March 27, 2021. https://www.dol.gov/agencies/wb/data/earnings#earnings-ratio.

"Economic News Release." U.S. Bureau of Labor Statistics. Accessed March 27, 2021. https://www.bls.gov/news.release/empsit.t02.htm.

"Historical List of Women CEOs of the Fortune Lists: 1972–2020." Catalyst. May 28, 2020. https://www.catalyst.org/research/historical-list-of-women-ceos-of-the-fortune-lists-1972-2020/.

Kurtz, Annalyn. "The US Economy Lost 140,000 jobs in December. All of Them Were Held by Women." CNN. January 8, 2021. https://www.cnn.com/2021/01/08/economy/women-job-losses-pandemic/index.html.

Minor, Maria. "Women in the Workplace: Why They Don't Get Recognized as Much as Men." *Forbes*. December 5, 2020. https://www.forbes.com/sites/mariaminor/2020/12/05/women-in-the-workplace-why-they-dont-get-recognized-as-much-as-men/?sh=52a98c4557df.

"Tackling Social Norms: A Game Changer for Gender Inequalities." UNDP. Accessed March 27, 2021. http://hdr.undp.org/sites/default/files/hd_perspectives_gsni.pdf.

"Women in the Workforce: United States: Quick Take." Catalyst. October 14, 2020. https://www.catalyst.org/research/women-in-the-workforce-united-states/#:~:text=In%202019%2C%20there%20were%2076%2C852%2C000,of%20the%20total%20labor%20force.&text=57.4%25%20of%20women%20participated%20in, compared%20to%2069.2%25%20of%20men.

"Women in the Workplace 2020." McKinsey & Lean In. Accessed March 27, 2021. https://wiw-report.s3.amazonaws.com/Women_in_the_Workplace_2020.pdf.

Ziv, Stav. "7 Striking Facts about the State of Women in the Workplace." Muse. Accessed March 27, 2021. https://www.cnn.com/2021/01/08/economy/women-job-losses-pandemic/index.html.

Asian American and Pacific Islander Community

"Asian Americans/Pacific Islanders." Anxiety & Depression Association of America. Accessed March 27, 2021. https://adaa.org/find-help/by-demographics/asian-pacific-islanders.

Blackburn, Sarah-Soonling. "What Is the Model Minority Myth?" Learning for Justice. March 21, 2019. https://www.learningforjustice.org/magazine/what-is-the-model-minority-myth.

Budiman, Abby, Anthony Cilluffo, and Neil G. Ruiz. "Key Facts about Asian Origin Groups in the U.S." Pew Research Center. May 22, 2019. https://www.pewresearch.org/fact-tank/2019/05/22/key-facts-about-asian-origin-groups-in-the-u-s/.

"Bystander Intervention Training." Bystander Resources. Accessed March 27, 2021. https://www.ihollaback.org/bystander-resources/.

"Does the 'Bamboo Ceiling' Shut Asian Americans Out of Top Jobs?" NPR (Podcast). May 23, 2014. https://www.npr.org/2014/05/23/315129852/does-a-bamboo-ceiling-shut-asian-americans-out-of-top-jobs.

D'Onofrio, Kaitlyn. "Asian Divide in the C-Suite." DiversityInc. Accessed March 27, 2021. https://www.diversityincbestpractices.com/the-asian-divide-in-the-c-suite/.

Eligon, John. "Why the Fastest Growing Population in America Is the Least Likely to Fill Out the Census." *New York Times*. Updated February 15, 2020. https://www.nytimes.com/2020/02/14/us/asian-american-census.html.

Kochhar, Rakesh, and Cilluffo, Anthony. "Income Inequality in the U.S. Is Rising Most Rapidly among Asians." Pew Research Center. July 12, 2018. https://www.pewresearch.org/social-trends/2018/07/12/income-inequality-in-the-u-s-is-rising-most-rapidly-among-asians/.

Kwon, Danielle. "Confronting Racism and Supporting Asian American Communities in the Wake of COVID-19." Urban Institute. March 24, 2020. https://www.urban.org/urban-wire/confronting-racism-and-supporting-asian-american-communities-wake-covid-19.

"Labor Force Characteristics by Race and Ethnicity, 2019." U.S. Bureau of Labor Statistics. December 2020. https://www.bls.gov/opub/reports/race-and-ethnicity/2019/home.htm.

Lang, Cady. "Hate Crimes Against Asian Americans Are on the Rise. Many Say More Policing Isn't the Answer." *Time*. February 18, 2021. https://time.com/5938482/asian-american-attacks/.

"Memorandum Condemning and Combating Racism, Xenophobia, and Intolerance Against Asian Americans and Pacific Islanders in the United States." White House. January 26, 2021. https://www.whitehouse.gov/briefing-room/presidential-actions/2021/01/26/memorandum-condemning-and-combating-racism-xenophobia-and-intolerance-against-asian-americans-and-pacific-islanders-in-the-united-states/.

"The Racial Wage Gap Persists in 2020." Payscale. Accessed March 27, 2021. https://www.payscale.com/data/racial-wage-gap.

Tran, Van C., Jennifer Lee, and Tiffany J. Huang. "Revisiting the Asian Second-Generation Advantage." *Ethnic and Racial Studies* 42, no. 13 (2019): 2248–2269. https://www.tandfonline.com/doi/full/10.1080/0141 9870.2019.1579920.

Wong, Garyan. "Racism Against the Asian Community Has to Stop: Take Action Today." Salesforce. February 22, 2021. https://www.salesforce .com/blog/support-asian-community/.

CHAPTER 4

Designing an Inclusive Brand and Candidate Experience

In 2018, Splunk saw an opportunity to show job seekers just how committed the software company was to diversity. Splunk, whose slogan is "bring data to everything," had a diverse staff and a vibrant, inclusive culture. In fact, it was one of the first things new hires often noticed about the company. But job applicants, particularly those from underrepresented groups, had no way of seeing it from the outside.

"We had done all the usual things, like putting a DEI statement and photos of our team members on our careers page," says Splunk Chief People Officer Kristen Robinson. "But today, that stuff is just table stakes. None of it felt unique to our brand, which is this quirky blend of individuality and data obsession. We needed to do something to give diverse applicants a sense of how joyous it can be to work here."

Back in 2017, two of Splunk's employees (Splunkers), Sarah Harbin and Chris Russell, had been exploring a creative approach to share Splunk's commitment to inclusion and celebrate their coworkers' diversity in a way that was true to Splunk's work as a data company. The two came up with an ingenious storytelling solution they called "A Million Data Points" that centered on the unique qualities and multiple identities that make up each team member. They put their ideas into action and created a powerful campaign that allowed all Splunkers to share their personal stories.

It started with a fun, colorful video featuring Splunkers talking about themselves in terms of data points. "I am Black." "I am not straight." "I am a United States Marine." "I love sea turtles." "I went to college on a basketball scholarship. But it was an engineering college."

Some Splunkers spoke in their first languages or wore their native culture's ceremonial clothing. Others appeared with their pets or artwork. Some shared snippets of stories about their upbringing. One even sang opera.

It ended with a simple message, "You are a million data points."

As Robinson and the team were considering how to tell the diversity story to job seekers, they realized the Million Data Points campaign from the prior year could be the perfect vehicle. The video and narrative became the centerpiece of a new DEI page on Splunk's website, which included a downloadable report about the company's diversity data. The effects were immediately noticeable. Candidates would mention the video and the report in interviews, even offering their own personal "data points" and sharing why the message resonated with them. Suddenly, DEI was front and center in Splunk's recruitment process, and it was reflected in the kinds of people who were applying.

"A Million Data Points" is now the foundation of Splunk's talent brand, and it's even made its way to more broadly represent the brand to customers. This even shows up in initial meetings with candidates where they are invited to share their own personal data points. As Splunk learned, if you want candidates to come knocking, you need to lay out a welcome mat that says, "Come in, you are celebrated here!"

WHY AN INCLUSIVE BRAND MATTERS

You get one first impression with job seekers. In that brief moment, someone who could be a valuable member of your team might decide they would love to work with you—or that they'd rather work anywhere else. More often than not, that first impression is your organization's public brand.

Your organization's public brand can have dozens of touchpoints with job seekers: your website, advertising, social media, email messages, packaging, and, of course, public comments about diversity, all of which could inform a job seeker's decision. If potential hires from underrepresented or often discriminated-against populations look across the breadth of your brand collateral and find not a single positive or representative signal about diversity, you can bet they will get the message.

You may not think of all these things as recruiting tools, but for job seekers concerned about inclusion, they are all clues to how they'll be treated. That's why it's so important to build a brand that is not just nonracist or "colorblind." It has to be proactively inclusive.

Now consider the cross section of diverse communities we explored in the last chapter. How will you authentically stand out to each of them? Remember that even your most impressive internal diversity and inclusion efforts are not visible to your candidates if you're not actively sharing them. And at a time when diversity has become a corporate priority around the world, placing underrepresented job seekers in high demand, there is a lot of noise to compete with.

Too many organizations save their diversity and inclusion messages for their recruiting efforts. But your candidates see the same brand as your customers. They can view the same websites, get the same emails, and see the same ads. Today, you need to send a signal in every place your brand lives, and all of these signals must communicate that you're an inclusive organization that celebrates its employees' differences.

Your brand as it pertains to job seekers extends well beyond your controlled assets and career page, so consider where else that first impression could come from: feedback from previous employees, social media posts from customers, Yelp reviews, news articles. Fair or not, the signals sent by people outside the company often make the most memorable impression with candidates.

Research has consistently shown that candidates of all kinds are looking for employers who are committed to diversity and inclusion. A 2015 PwC study revealed that 86 percent of female millennials consider an employer's policy on diversity, equality, and workforce inclusion as a key factor when deciding whether to work for that organization.

That's why simply publishing stock photos of "diverse employees" on your career page with loose rhetoric on your values could actually do more harm than good. In today's hiring landscape, it's key that your brand authentically promises what you intend to deliver. Anything that falls short of this and comes across as inauthentic or exclusionary can be a turnoff to talented candidates from underrepresented communities.

ASSESSING THE INCLUSIVITY OF YOUR BRAND AND COMMUNICATION

For many organizations, one of the greatest obstacles to transforming their brand is figuring out who within the organization has ownership over it. Your marketing team may have designed your brand with customers and sales in mind, then allowed the HR team to own the recruiting page. Or maybe your HR team insisted that the "talent brand" be different from the rest of your corporate brand, resulting in talent outreach assets with their own messaging and imagery. Or maybe there's a specific executive at your organization who insists on owning the website because they have a vision for the brand experience, but that vision doesn't include marketing and HR perspectives.

Regardless, to job seekers and customers, the brand is the brand is the brand is the brand. Yes, they expect to see something different on the merchandise page of your site than they do on the careers page, but they are perfectly capable of connecting the dots. If your hiring website espouses values you clearly don't demonstrate in your manufacturing, they'll question the integrity of your whole organization. If they don't see diversity in your TV ads, they might not even apply.

When it comes to developing your brand, you may need alignment among your leadership, marketing team, and the HR team. No silos. No territories. Map it out for greater clarity, because it's all one story. As you figure out how to do that, use these questions to determine if you have an inclusive talent identity and candidate experience. Also consider who should be owning and supporting each of these:

- Have you looked at representation and imagery on your website and your other public materials?

- Have you created an authentic and inclusive brand identity outside of your talent brand alone?

- Have you taken steps to proactively communicate your diversity commitment in your public materials?

- Have you taken steps to ensure accessibility for all candidates?

- Have you been thoughtful about communicating inclusive hiring practices up front?

- Do you offer the option for informational interviews?

- Do you have systems to follow up with candidates to communicate feedback?

- Do you have a process in place to learn from candidates how you can continuously make your hiring process more inclusive?

For additional resources to assess your diversity hiring efforts visit: http://Mathison.io/Index.

If any of these areas aren't yet part of your efforts, your aligned teams have an immediate opportunity to develop more inclusive hiring practices. It's critical to continue reevaluating the internal decisions that have a direct impact on the process from the candidate's viewpoint. This will enable you to easily pinpoint areas of improvement and eliminate any biases that might exist in your hiring experience.

COMMUNICATING AN INCLUSIVE BRAND IDENTITY

Your brand identity acts as a litmus test for the authenticity of your diversity agenda. Getting this right sends a strong message to candidates from underrepresented communities. If your organization has already taken steps to clearly define your brand voice, values, and communication tactics, these can all be shared internally. It tells them that you strive to treat all communities fairly and respectfully and each person is equally empowered to pursue opportunities within your organization. However, fulfilling this commitment is not a simple undertaking. To do it well, you have to account for the wide range of diversity that makes up underrepresented communities and the distinct perspectives and challenges that each community brings when they enter your hiring process.

The external image you project to applicants should not be taken lightly, and finding your organization's authentic voice is essential. In a 2019 study by Yello, a talent acquisition software company, 83 percent of respondents said that diversity in the workplace is important enough to be a factor when deciding whether to accept a job. Ask yourself what these people are seeing when they investigate your commitment to DEI values.

Communicating Your Commitment to Diversity

The careers page of your website is a great place to demonstrate your commitment to diversity. But if you are really looking to diversify your talent pool, we suggest you create a separate diversity, equity, and inclusion page. Simply having such a page already stands out to job seekers that you are serious about diversity, and this becomes a channel you can use to keep candidates and stakeholders apprised of your progress.

A dedicated DEI page can contain a lot of things. Take Splunk's video, for example. That's a great example of how you can get creative while still communicating the seriousness of your commitment. But one essential item that needs to be on all DEI pages, or at least on your careers page, is a strategic diversity statement. It doesn't have to be much: just a handful of sentences that tell the world why your organization values diversity and what you are doing to encourage it. The only rules are that it should be heartfelt and it should sound like it came from your organization.

Take, for example, the diversity statement from software company Dataminr, which it posts on its public career profiles:

> *"At Dataminr, we believe that our differences give us strength. We hire talented, unique individuals who are encouraged to be their authentic selves and who support their team members to do the same. We serve a global community made up of many cultures and strive to reflect that diversity with a workplace built on merit and equity."*

That's a concise, authentic statement that leaves little doubt where Dataminr stands on the issue. Having a statement like that displayed prominently on your DEI page could go a long way toward establishing your talent brand with job applicants.

A WORD ON EQUAL EMPLOYMENT OPPORTUNITY (EEO) STATEMENTS

If your organization performs certain kinds of government work, you are required by law to carry an Equal Employment Opportunity (EEO) statement on your job postings. But all kinds of organizations have long used them to communicate their commitment to equal opportunity hiring (or to provide some perceived level of legal protection).

You've seen these statements before. "Mathison is an equal opportunity employer. We do not discriminate in employment on the basis of race, color, religion, or sex."

There may have been a time when EEO statements were sufficient to brand yourself as a company with progressive values. But today, candidates perceive EEO statements as something employers are legally obligated to include, and they do little to separate you from the pack or reassure underrepresented job seekers. By all means, include the EEO on your job listings—particularly if you are required to by law. But do not make the mistake of assuming it says anything of significance about your organization to potential hires.

COMMUNICATING YOUR DIVERSITY EFFORTS AND MAKING YOUR EQUITABLE HIRING PRACTICES TRANSPARENT

Anyone can write a nice-sounding diversity statement and stick it on a website. If you really want to communicate your organization's dedication to DEI hiring, you need to get specific. Use your dedicated page to share all the steps you are taking to create a more equitable hiring process for candidates.

Not sure where to start? The topic of each chapter in this book represents a clear story you can convey to candidates about the measures you are taking to improve access, reduce bias, and fairly advance candidates in the process. This level of detail not only tells job seekers that diversity matters to your organization, but it also lets them know specifically how they fit into your vision for the future.

Salesforce, for example, has a dedicated DEI page that contains its diversity reports, data, and goals. One such goal is for underrepresented groups to comprise 50 percent of its U.S. workforce by 2023. Citi also uses its website to share its goal to "increase representation at the Assistant Vice President through Managing Director levels to at least 40 percent for women globally and 8 percent for Black employees in the US by the end of 2021."

Here you also have a chance to showcase all the opportunities for team members to engage in your diversity and inclusion programs, whether formal, like (ERGs), or otherwise. For example, Citi's diversity page showcases its 10 affinity groups, including Black Heritage, Citi Salutes (Military Veterans), and Citi Women and Pride (LGBTQ). The fact that these groups are led by executives from the CEO's leadership team further accentuates Citi's commitment to this cause.

Your DEI section also gives you the perfect place to highlight community partnerships tied to your diversity efforts. First Republic Bank, for example, showcases its partnership with Management Leadership for Tomorrow (MLT), a nonprofit that helps high-achieving Black, Latinx, and Native American individuals secure "high-trajectory jobs." Featuring these types of partnerships gives strong evidence of your efforts at work.

Sharing Stories and Testimonials from Your People

It's good to tell the world you're committed to diversity. But it's far better to show them.

Nothing shows the world that you are dedicated to diversity quite like the stories and testimonies from your own team members. Just as Splunk found with "A Million Data Points," showcasing the perspectives of your people not only makes these stories real and personal for your candidates, but it also gives you a meaningful way to engage your broader organization. Medical technology firm Stryker features videos of employees talking about the company's inclusive hiring practices, why they chose to work for the company, and how it maintains an inclusive culture. Such personal stories are far more powerful than a company simply stating what it believes. Even if you don't have the means to produce a professional-looking video, you can start by collecting written statements from your team members. These can be posted to your website and even your social channels to help build your talent brand.

SHOWCASING IMAGERY OF UNDERREPRESENTED COMMUNITIES

Today's job seeker has a sixth sense for inauthenticity, so you need to be careful about the imagery you use on your careers or DEI page.

Your best bet is to showcase real images of your organization and your people. If for some reason that's not a good option, you can use stock photos. However, stock photo libraries are a minefield of racial and gender insensitivity. Many stock photos reinforce stereotypes, and some engage in barely veiled tokenism. For example, search "disability" on most stock photo libraries, and the results will likely be dominated by photos of smiling people in wheelchairs surrounded by able-bodied people (also smiling). Such imagery smacks of inauthenticity and could give job-seekers the opposite impression of what you intend. If you're going to use stock photography, take the time to search for images that look natural and don't reinforce stereotypes. This is also one of those times when it's especially important to seek the opinions of people with a wide range of perspectives to make sure you aren't missing something that might be offensive to someone.

Global image provider Getty Images has created collections of imagery focused on what they refer to as "Visual Representation," through which diverse people around the world are authentically and accurately represented through visuals. To that end, the company created a vast library of visual content that intentionally fills gaps and counters stereotypes to more authentically represent traditionally underrepresented or misrepresented groups. Getty Images recommends that organizations trying to be more inclusive begin by intentionally choosing images that not only speak to people in a broad sense, but which also welcome the community to engage and interact.

EXTENDING YOUR INCLUSIVE BRAND TO OTHER MEDIA

Your diversity brand extends well beyond your career or DEI page. In fact, diversity representation can be embedded within all other sections of your website and public materials. Your social media channels give you a dynamic way to reinforce your diversity commitment, build community, and engage with job seekers. Global consultancy McKinsey hosts live Q&A sessions on YouTube in which interested candidates can ask recruiters questions about the company's diversity and inclusion efforts.

Some companies have even incorporated their diversity principles into their products. American Eagle's loungewear and lingerie line, Aerie, is well-known in the clothing industry for pushing the bounds of diversity. Its #AerieREAL social media campaign, with a tagline of "Power. Positivity. No retouching," is part of a six-year initiative to foster inclusivity by featuring models of various abilities, shapes, races, and ethnicities—a stark contrast to traditional lingerie advertising. This has resulted in a lot of positive publicity and lured many underrepresented job seekers to the company.

ENSURING ACCESSIBILITY FOR CANDIDATES

Picture this: You're hard of hearing and you need a job. You follow a LinkedIn post to a corporate website with a prominent and robust DEI page. It contains a strong statement regarding the company's dedication to accommodating applicants with disabilities. Feeling good about the company, you begin the online application process—only to discover that it requires watching a video that offers no subtitles.

If you're going to publicly declare your commitment to diversity, you must make sure that your entire hiring process is accessible for people of all abilities. Applicants with disabilities can face a wide-ranging set of challenges, and it's vital that you remove those road-blocks to the best of your ability.

A study by Partnership on Employment & Accessibility Technology (PEAT) showed that 46 percent of applicants with disabilities have found an online application process "difficult to impossible" to use. Nine percent reported having dropped out of such a process due to usability problems with the application format or the careers page.

Taking intentional steps for accessibility is also key to ensuring your organization is meeting regulatory policies and processes. For example, the American Disabilities Act (ADA) prohibits discrimination against people with disabilities in the hiring process and states that any applicant who makes a request that enables them to perform the duties of the job must be honored as long as it does not cause significant difficulty or expense to the employer. It also requires employers who have 15 or more employees to provide reasonable accommodations on the job for people of all abilities, which extend to changing job tasks, improving accessibility, providing accessible equipment, and scheduling. Here are steps we recommend to cover all your bases on accessibility.

Communicate Your Accessibility Commitment

We recommend communicating your accessibility commitment up front so it is visible to job seekers early in the process. This not only demonstrates your commitment to accessibility, but it communicates key details about how candidates of all abilities should engage with you. This step also gives you the opportunity to ask candidates if they require specific accessibility accommodations. Global consultancy Accenture invites job seekers to request accommodations for each one of its active job postings with this statement:

Accenture is committed to providing equal employment opportunities for persons with disabilities or religious observances, including reasonable accommodation when needed. If you are hired by Accenture and require accommodation to perform the essential functions of your role, you will be asked to participate in our reasonable accommodation process. Accommodations made to facilitate the recruiting process are not a guarantee of future or continued accommodations once hired. If you would like to be considered for employment opportunities with Accenture and have accommodation needs for a disability or religious observance, please call us toll free at 1 (877) 889-9009, send us an email, or speak with your recruiter.

Ensure Your Career and Web Pages Are Accessible

It's key that applicants of all abilities can successfully access your career page and online application. The Web Content Accessibility Guidelines (WCAG) detail a set of standards to ensure web experiences are accessible. A 2019 study found that the career pages of 89 Fortune 100 companies failed at least one of the six standards outlined by WCAG.

- **Keyboard accessibility.** Be sure that candidates can easily tab through your website without the need for a mouse.

- **Screen reader compatibility.** Build website navigation that is consistent and easy to interpret so it will be compatible with screen readers for individuals who are blind or have low vision.

- **Video captions.** Include transcript and captions for all videos and online media in places such as your career page.

- **Alt tagging.** Ensure you have alternative text for images that describes the function of each image, in a way that isn't too long for each description.

- **Color contrasts.** Test the design of your site and materials for proper color contrast for individuals with color blindness using tools like the Chromatic Vision Simulator.

- **Using tables.** Table structure and information should have text descriptions so that it can be translated into print, braille, speech, and so on.

There are assistive technologies such as Userway, Audioeye, and accessiBe that can be integrated into your organization's website. These will improve your candidates' web experience by providing critical assistive options.

Offer Reasonable Accessibility Accommodations

With such a rich diversity of abilities across the disability community, it's important to understand where in your process candidates may face accessibility challenges and where you can offer reasonable accommodations. We recommend asking candidates early in the application process if they require any special accommodations. For example, if a candidate with a hearing disability requests the support of a sign-language interpreter, this should be a request you can accommodate by having preestablished resources available.

We also recommend extending virtual interview options to all candidates and using accessible video conferencing systems. For example, Zoom offers candidates screen reader support, automatically generated transcripts, third-party captioning, and rearranged video options to improve accessibility. If you do need to have onsite interviews, be sure to choose an accessible location for candidates with proper ramps, elevators, accessible parking, and accessible bathroom accommodations. Providing the option for written materials in accessible formats, such as large print, braille, or audiotape, should be a standard practice as well.

Educate Your Team on Accessible Hiring Practices

It's important that you meaningfully engage your team around your accessibility efforts by educating them on your commitment and the specific measures you are taking. Ideally, you should provide them with some training on how best to engage candidates with disabilities and alert them to available resources. For example, tell team members ahead of time if they will be interacting with an applicant who needs a special accommodation. Team members should know how to field these requests and where to easily direct candidates. Citi has developed a list of Disability Etiquette best practices, including reminders to shift perspective when speaking to or about people with mobility, hearing, or visual impairments, mental health illnesses or learning disabilities, or those on the autism spectrum.

DEVELOPING AN INCLUSIVE CANDIDATE EXPERIENCE

Building on the accessibility of your hiring process, you have a unique opportunity to create a human-centered experience that brings out the best in every candidate and ensures each person feels empowered. Much of this comes down to deliberately defining more inclusive policies and practices that your team will mobilize. Here are some areas where we recommend focusing attention:

Offer Flexible Scheduling Options

Many underrepresented job applicants have current (or several) jobs that already demand most of their attention, or they may be balancing obligations at home. You can ease a great deal of stress by letting candidates know that you can be flexible and make reasonable accommodations for their schedule. For example, during the COVID-19 pandemic, online personal styling service Stitch Fix shared this message with its applicants early in the process to signal flexibility and support:

> *Authenticity and Integrity are two of our guiding values at Stitch Fix, and we want all of our candidates to feel able to bring their best selves forward in our recruiting process. We recognize that interviewing can be stressful in and of itself, and that the events and challenges confronting our nation are hitting some of us in more personal and local ways. In that spirit, our team is prepared to reschedule interviews if you need more*

time to prepare or just need time to focus on and process the events around us. We are also open to discussing additional accommodations that help you participate confidently and fully in this process.

In addition to flexible scheduling, we suggest refraining from setting tight deadlines for candidate take-home projects or assignments that you may give them. It's best to allocate several business days for projects and not assume that candidates are free to complete assignments during weekends or evenings. For example, a working parent who has childcare responsibilities may not be able to turn around a case study assignment with a tight deadline.

Ensure Responsiveness to Candidates

Good jobs are worth waiting for, but no one can wait forever. If you ask candidates to sit for interviews weeks or even months apart, or simply take too long to get back to them, they will end up feeling frustrated and disrespected. When this happens, they are more likely to drop out of the process or move on to another opportunity, thus robbing your organization of a potentially valuable team member (not to mention the lost investment of time and money you put into finding and interviewing them).

In 2016, recruiter services firm MRINetwork conducted a study of employers and recruiters and found that 47 percent of job offers were rejected because applicants chose to go elsewhere. This is strong evidence that slow hiring timelines can end up costing you good prospects.

Establishing service-level agreements (SLAs) with anyone involved in recruiting for your organization is an effective way to address this problem. SLAs are informal contracts that spell out the responsibilities and deliverables that recruiters and hiring managers commit to in advance of recruiting. This ensures that important steps like resume review, interview scheduling, and final selection happen within a specific timeframe. It also reduces lag time and bottlenecks in the recruitment process and contributes to an improved and consistent experience for applicants.

Develop Inclusive Virtual and Onsite Interview Options

Following the mass shift to remote work brought on by the COVID-19 pandemic, there is no longer any excuse for failing to offer a remote interview option. For people with disabilities or travel issues, in-person interviews can be unnecessarily burdensome. Offering to conduct interviews over video conference or the phone eliminates a barrier that likely has nothing to do with performing the job.

If it is absolutely necessary that the applicant travel, be transparent about your reimbursement policies before asking them to make arrangements. If you aren't offering reimbursement for transportation or other expenses, or if your process for coordinating travel is cumbersome or involves a long delay, you could create financial or logistical burdens for candidates. We suggest facilitating as much of the coordination and direct expensing of the onsite interview as possible. Tools like Reimbi will help you process travel expenses for candidates within a day of the expenditure, and Pana will help coordinate travel bookings.

Offer Informational Interview Options

Smart job seekers know that the best insights into life at your organization come from the people who already work there. This is especially true for underrepresented candidates, who may have concerns about how they'll be treated once they're part of the team. In our 2021 Diversity Hiring Report, only 26% of job seekers from underrepresented communities reported that employers offered optional informational interviews. This represents a massively missed opportunity.

Rather than let these applicants get their information from anonymous review sites like Glassdoor, which can be unreliable and overly negative, many employers will now set up informational interviews between candidates and current employees (either someone from an ERG or someone who can speak to the applicant's concerns). This is a great way to build trust with potential coworkers and to show them you care about their concerns as part of an underrepresented community. Just be sure to let them know that the interview will be private and have no bearing on their candidacy.

LISTEN TO YOUR COMMUNITY AND GATHER FEEDBACK

Your engagement and follow-up with candidates at the end of the hiring process will leave the most lasting impression. Whether they got the job or not, what candidates will remember most vividly is how your hiring experience with them concluded. Any negative experience or lack of follow-up at the end of the process could influence how candidates think of you, how they talk about you to other potential candidates, and whether they choose to pursue another opportunity with you in the future.

Having your application rejected can be a painful experience, and you owe it to unsuccessful candidates to provide them with constructive feedback whenever possible, especially in the cases where they have invested a considerable amount of time and effort in the process. According to a 2018 survey by recruiting research firm Talent Board, close to 70 percent of candidates received no feedback after their candidacy was rejected during the screening and interviewing stages. These statistics point to a widespread hiring issue that candidates face every day.

Often, applicants are left wondering why they are no longer being considered for a position, and this can be even more frustrating if they were under the impression that everything was going well. Therefore, refusing to acknowledge their efforts not only damages your talent brand, but leaves candidates feeling dehumanized and unworthy. This is not what you want a candidate to take away from their time with you. Instead, a personal and kindly worded message can go a long way toward uplifting a discouraged job seeker. You can go beyond that by giving them a call, thanking them for their time, and sharing specific feedback that will help them improve on their application. This gives you an opportunity to deliver the bad news while providing valuable and encouraging insights.

You can make this process easier by putting a system in place that establishes who will follow up and within what timeframe. The Talent Board survey revealed that candidates who received feedback on the same day they interviewed were 52 percent more likely to continue a relationship with the employer by applying again or referring others to the organization. When you give candidates feedback, you can also use that opportunity to ask them about their overall experience and ways you as an employer can improve on your process.

You can also use ERGs and affinity groups in your organization to review your recruitment strategy. ERGs can be particularly useful for gathering anonymous feedback on how you can involve employees from different communities in the hiring process and understand the barriers of entry for candidates from certain groups. This will help hiring managers deliver tailored feedback that addresses specific issues in a candidate's application.

Home mortgage company Better has formalized the role of a Candidate Concierge dedicated to creating an inclusive experience for candidates. As part of its process, Better circulates a survey to collect feedback from every candidate, specifically asking what the company could do to create a more inclusive experience. Better has received tremendously valuable insights from its candidates on this question alone and has used this feedback to make specific improvements to the hiring process for future applicants.

FIRST STEP TOWARD IMPACT

Most companies these days put a lot of thought and intent into their brand but if you design it solely for customers of your product or service, you are missing out on a massive recruitment opportunity. Your brand is a larger part of what attracts—or repels—potential applicants. If diversity and inclusion aren't part of your brand, you will definitely run into trouble diversifying your talent pool. At the end of the day, building an inclusive brand and candidate experience goes back to the job seekers. Make this about them.

If there is one thing you can do as a first step, try asking for feedback from candidates from underrepresented groups, even if you don't hire them.

Did they feel respected and supported during the interview process? Did they have concerns about how they would be treated if they were hired? Was your organization's attitude toward DEI efforts part of their decision to apply?

Just as Splunk took decisive steps to make its upfront brand and candidate experience personal and real, you have the chance to do the same by asking these questions.

REFERENCES

"Disability Etiquette Awareness." Accessed March 22, 2021. https://www.citigroup.com/citi/diversity/assets/pdf/DisabilityAwareness Etiquette2.pdf?ie.

"Diversity in the Workplace Statistics: 2019 Job Seeker Survey." Yello. July 21, 2020. https://yello.co/blog/diversity-in-the-workplace-statistics/.

"The Female Millennial: A New Era of Talent." PricewaterhouseCoopers. Accessed March 19, 2021. https://www.pwc.com/gx/en/about/diversity/internationalwomensday/the-female-millennial.html.

"Global Diversity and Inclusion." Citi. Accessed March 22, 2021. https://www.citigroup.com/citi/diversity/our-approach.html.

"Infographic: The Accessibility of Online Job Applications." Peatworks. January 6, 2021. https://www.peatworks.org/digital-accessibility-toolkits/talentworks/make-your-erecruiting-tools-accessible/new-data-on-the-accessibility-of-online-job-applications/.

"Live Q&A with McKinsey & Company: Learn about an Exciting Career in Consulting." YouTube. 2018. https://www.youtube.com/watch?v=RSoRP0b4uPU.

Phenom People, Inc. "Phenom People Study Reveals 89 of Fortune 100 Career Sites Fail to Meet Digital Accessibility Requirements." Globe-Newswire News Room. Phenom People, Inc., October 1, 2019. https://www.globenewswire.com/news-release/2019/10/01/1923388/0/en/Phenom-People-Study-Reveals-89-of-Fortune-100-Career-Sites-Fail-to-Meet-Digital-Accessibility-Requirements.html.

"REAL Talk." #AerieREAL Life. February 25, 2021. https://www.ae.com/aerie-real-life/real-voices/.

Roberts, Terry. "A Message from Terry Roberts, Chief Inclusion & Diversity Officer." *AEO Inc.*, June 24, 2020. https://www.aeo-inc.com/2020/06/24/a-message-from-terry-roberts-chief-inclusion-diversity-officer/.

"2016 Recruiter & Employer Sentiment Study." MRINetwork. Accessed March 22, 2021. https://mrinetwork.com/media/303943/recruiter_sentiment_study_1st_half_2016.pdf.

"The 2018 Talent Board North American Candidate Experience Benchmark Research Report Now Available." Talent Board. February 7, 2019. https://www.thetalentboard.org/press-releases/the-2018-talent-board-north-american-candidate-experience-benchmark-research-report-now-available/.

CHAPTER 5

Writing Inclusive Job Descriptions and Candidate Communication

"We're looking for a dynamic, committed team player who will go the extra mile in a fast-paced environment."

This line from a job description might appear normal and welcoming, yet it has five problematic words and phrases. If you can't spot them, don't worry, because by the time you get through this chapter, you'll have a trained eye for sussing out—and eradicating—potentially exclusionary language from your job descriptions.

Writing inclusive job descriptions and candidate communication is an essential skill because many job seekers' first impressions of your organization will come directly from what they read in your posting. When you use exclusionary words and phrases, you not only tarnish your talent brand, but you inadvertently convince countless qualified candidates that this is not the job for them. Job seekers from underrepresented communities will infer what you don't really mean to convey and miss out on prime opportunities; your organization will lose the chance to bring in new people with needed capabilities and fresh ideas. Inclusive language is an important first step in setting the tone for inclusion and belonging to all potential job seekers.

Consider the case of Snagajob, an online staffing platform that specializes in hourly work. Because they serve a diverse workforce to begin with, the company's leaders felt strongly that Snagajob's staff should reflect that diversity. To help achieve that goal, the company decided to take a look at the data. Back in 2019, Snagajob reviewed its applicant pool, candidate slate, and new-hire demographic data and conducted internal employee surveys.

What the research revealed was that female employees felt underrepresented in the workforce, particularly in management positions. "We learned that there was a gap between how men and women felt about their representation and voice at Snagajob," says Candace Nicolls, Senior Vice President of People. Without representation at the top, there was no guarantee their needs would be heard or addressed. Candace also noted that for Black individuals, there was representation at the management level but none at director and above.

One of the first things Snagajob did was revamp its job descriptions to make them more inclusive and welcoming to all communities. The company developed guidelines that established objective language, eliminated gender-biased and exclusionary terms—such as the male-oriented "ninja" and "rock star"—and reduced the word count of job postings to ensure they were accessible. It also revised existing job postings and created templates to ensure hiring managers and recruiters could consistently apply the new framework to job descriptions in the future.

Today, all of Snagajob's job postings are created and analyzed through its new process, and the company has seen a visible difference in the representation of its applicant pool. For example, the percentage of new hires who identify as Black or African American has increased from 8 percent in 2019 to 13 percent in 2020. Snagajob also hit its 2020 goal and saw that 52 percent of employees at the manager level or above came from underrepresented populations. Female representation at the manager level has increased from 38 percent to 42 percent, and from 26 percent to 32 percent at the leadership level. Since releasing its first diversity, equity, and inclusion report in November 2020, Snagajob has continued to increase its workforce representation.

WHY INCLUSIVE JOB DESCRIPTIONS AND CANDIDATE COMMUNICATION MATTER

When it comes to diversifying your candidate pool, no single part of the process has more make-or-break potential than your job descriptions and communication with candidates. Job seekers rely heavily on what they read from you to determine whether the role—and your organization—is right for them. And they are making those decisions quickly. Depending on the candidate's interest, their average time reviewing your job description could be as low as 49.7 seconds, according to research from the job site Ladders.

With our digital devices almost always within arm's reach, it's easier than ever to pull up, and swipe through, job listings. Employers that don't make an immediate positive impression risk losing a candidate's attention. Worse yet, if your messaging is off, candidates can promptly form negative opinions about your culture and commitment to diversity.

While your talent brand makes a promise to underrepresented job seekers, your job description communicates how you'll fulfill that promise through an opportunity that matters to the job seeker personally.

It's important to be intentional about what message you want to send to job seekers—and not just through your words, but through length, formatting, tone, and more. If a description is too long, many applicants won't bother reading it. If it's too short, they may not take it seriously. If it was posted over a month ago, applicants might assume the role is filled. If the degree requirements or experience seem too lofty, candidates may feel unqualified. Any one of these reasons is enough to deter potential applicants from applying.

Beyond affecting the diversity of your candidate pool, job descriptions are an opportunity for organizations to ensure consistency and set the groundwork for fairness throughout the hiring process. Given the great deal of potential subjectivity in other parts of the process, the job description gives you the chance to build an equitable foundation from the onset. It is the common ground and unified reference point that everyone involved can refer to during points of ambiguity (which will inevitably arise).

What is written in your job description directly affects how you screen and qualify candidates, the questions you will ask in interviews, and the criteria on which you will ultimately base your hiring decision. The job description represents a commitment to job seekers. It showcases the opportunity you have to offer, your expectations, and whether your organization will provide them with a safe place to learn and grow. You prove your integrity by keeping your word.

Damage caused by inaccurate job descriptions can linger long after an employee is hired. One in five workers who voluntarily leave their positions cite a "lack of job fit," according to Gallup. The disconnect can stem from the expectations set the first time someone reads about a role. Candidates rely on the job description to determine if they have the right qualifications, as well as to decide if your organization will be a place where they will feel a sense of belonging and be able to thrive.

In the rest of this chapter, we'll guide you through the process of creating inclusive, well-written job descriptions.

Assessing the Inclusivity of Your Job Descriptions

It's easy to think that job descriptions are primarily the responsibility of the HR and talent teams, but in fact, team leaders and executive leaders are equally on the hook for what is written and who is hired. A lot of assumptions are made here, but this is an area where everyone needs to play a role and have buy-in to the process for it to really work.

Here are some questions to help you assess how inclusive your job descriptions and language are today. As you go through the following items, consider which team member should own or support each of these areas. Remember, it's not just up to management or hiring teams to attract underrepresented job seekers. You too can make a difference by keeping your team accountable.

- Is there an upfront process to ensure internal alignment around job descriptions before they go live?

- Are there steps in place to define objective candidate requirements and qualifications?

- Do you have a process to structure your job descriptions in an easy-to-understand format?

- Who defines salary ranges, and how are they communicated internally and to candidates?

- Do you take measures to remove or reconsider degree or experience requirements or enable substitutes for either?

- Do you communicate your diversity commitment in job descriptions?

- What steps are taken to identify and remove exclusionary language from job descriptions?

- Do you have systems or templates in place to sustain the development of inclusive job descriptions?

- Do you have systems to analyze your communication with candidates outside of the job description to ensure it's inclusive and accessible?

For additional resources to assess your diversity hiring efforts visit: http://Mathison.io/Index.

If the answer is "no" to any of these questions, you have an amazing opportunity to create meaningful change in your organization.

WRITING MORE INCLUSIVE JOB DESCRIPTIONS

1. Create Internal Alignment Around Your Job Descriptions

As you've likely experienced, team members can have vastly differing opinions on everything from the best project management software to what "casual Friday" means. These different views often arise when it comes to creating job responsibilities and qualifications for a new listing. Be careful not to ignore any issues; what can seem like small cracks initially can lead to larger crevices and fundamental problems later on.

You can head off potential headaches by creating a system for internal alignment among your decision makers. We recommend scheduling a meeting with stakeholders to define what success looks like, assign roles and duties, and determine what responsibilities and qualifications should be included in the job description. Get the specifics down, including details on who will be involved with screening and interviewing applicants. Also, note who has the final say if there are any conflicting beliefs.

Once you've gathered everyone's input, have a point person circulate a draft of the job description so team members have a chance to review and provide feedback. Before posting your listing, be sure to confirm that:

- All stakeholders have had the opportunity to provide feedback and feel included in the decision-making.

- There is no ambiguity in the job description that needs to be clarified.

- Everyone is clear on their roles and responsibilities in the hiring process for this role.

2.   Opt for a More Common, Understandable Job Title

A job title is often the first thing a candidate will see, and most use those few words to gauge if they will be a good fit for the role. It's important to have a concise, specific, easy-to-understand job title that will appeal to a large candidate pool. Trying to be creative by branding a marketing associate as a "marketing ninja," for example, can make a description exclusionary. Not only are words like "ninja" and "guru" culturally appropriated and potentially offensive to people of Asian and Hindu descent, but terms like these may be unfamiliar to job seekers or signal that an employer is looking for a particular demographic to fill the role.

Employers frequently use alternative or creative job titles to stand out among other similar postings, but this often does more harm than good. Nearly two-thirds of applicants wouldn't apply to a job with a title that was hard to understand, according to a Resumie.io 2020 study. The survey additionally shows evidence of generational divides among applicants when the job titles aren't streamlined. So the "wacky" titles are not only limiting your applicant pool overall, but particularly deter older and experienced workers from applying.

Ask yourself these three questions before committing to a job title:

- Will candidates search for this title?
- Does the title accurately reflect the role?
- Does the title include any exclusionary language? (For example, "ninja," "athlete," or "guru.")

3.   Use an Easy-to-Read Format

While job descriptions should be unique for each individual position, there are a few aspects that all effective, inclusive listings share. Each should be structured in an easy-to-understand format. Consider using subheads, which help applicants comprehend long descriptions. Also, ditch the long paragraphs and lengthy prose. When possible, incorporate bullets, which can make text easier to understand.

The use of specific font styles and sizes can make your posting more accessible for all, and especially for those with learning differences such as dyslexia. Minimalistic-looking sans serif fonts are often more legible than serif type, which tends to have more decorative features. The British Dyslexia Association recommends using sans serif fonts like Arial, Verdana, Tahoma, Century Gothic, Trebuchet, Calibri, or Open Sans. The association also suggests a font size of 12 to 14 point or equivalent. It's best to stay away from harder to read fonts like Haettenschweiler, Monotype Corsiva, or Comic Sans Italicized. We recommend putting words in bold to emphasize important messaging. Avoid italics and underlining as this may cause letters to run together visually for some candidates.

4.   Write in a Conversational Tone

A job description presented in a conversational voice will invite a broader audience to explore the role. Write as if you are explaining the position to a friend. Yet be careful not to make the language overly casual because this may lead candidates to question the posting's validity.

The best candidates are busy, so help them out by making your job posting simple to read. Be mindful of the length of words and sentences, the number of syllables, and the use of pronouns. We recommend writing to an eighth-grade reading level or lower to ensure readability and maximize attention. The Hemingway Editor App is a free online tool to easily check your reading level.

A few tips to keep in mind:

- Use short words and sentences.

- Use first person/second person instead of third person (We/Our or You/Your and not He/She).

- Make sure the opening paragraph grabs the reader's attention.

- Use understandable language that is not overly technical or specific to an industry or field.

5. Keep the Writing Concise

Many applicants will check job opportunities on their mobile devices, skimming through descriptions before deciding which ones to read fully.

Lengthy, gratuitous descriptions will deter some applicants from reading through the entire posting. SHRM research shows that postings below 250 words or more than 2,000 words receive significantly fewer job applications. Textio, an augmented writing platform that helps users write more inclusive job descriptions, recommends keeping descriptions from 300 to 700 words in length. Ideal length can also differ across industries. For example, education and legal jobs with longer descriptions get more clicks than social media manager jobs, which typically perform better with shorter descriptions. When you limit the length of a job posting, you're forcing yourself to reduce the number of candidate requirements, which ultimately benefits women applicants. Since women are more likely to self-select themselves out of jobs, this is one area where we have the ability to reduce that likelihood. We recommend keeping your descriptions specific and concise, not exceeding 700 words.

6. Define Objective Responsibilities and Qualifications

Most of us want to feel as though we are making a difference with the work we do. So, when creating a job description, it's essential to highlight how a candidate's contributions can directly benefit your organization. The job description's responsibilities section gives you prime real estate to describe the role in a captivating and inspiring manner. After reading this section, candidates should feel excited by the possibilities and motivated to apply.

Our recommendation: Begin your job description with a brief overview of how the position relates to your big-picture business objectives, mission, and vision. The purpose of a job description is to attract potential candidates, but the goal of an *inclusive* job description is to inspire the most underrepresented communities of job seekers to apply.

To ensure accurate, compelling descriptions, focus more on required outcomes than processes. Clearly state expected deliverables, what the person in this position will accomplish. Be transparent around the requirements and demands of a position to help candidates determine if the role is accessible to them. Try to avoid listing broad processes like "plan strategic events to strengthen business offerings." Take the guesswork out by being clear, concise, and to the point.

Describe the necessities to successfully get the job done. At times, job descriptions will include functions that are not truly required, which may deter some people from applying. For example, you've likely come across these qualities numerous times: detail-oriented, have good interpersonal skills, or proficiency in Microsoft Office. These skills are listed in so many job postings regardless of role, organization, or industry. They are thought to be the standard, the bare minimum that organizations expect of their employees. But these skills are not always needed. Adding unnecessary qualifications may exclude certain groups of candidates. A study by Hewlett Packard found that 78 percent of women have not applied for a job because they believed all listed qualifications were requirements, yet men will apply for a job even if they meet only 60 percent of the stated qualifications. We recommend you only add requirements that are truly required. Review the core job requirements, such as knowledge, skills, and responsibilities, to determine any nonessential material you can eliminate. And while many companies include a "Preferred Qualifications" section, we recommend against it. Qualified candidates may choose not to apply if they lack a capability referenced in that area.

And we know you are busy, so it may be tempting to copy generic templated job requirements from a past posting with similar requirements to the new opening. We recommend against that as well. Too often, past job descriptions have not been written with DEI best practices in mind. And because standards evolve quickly, it's good policy to always start fresh when posting a new position.

In 2017, German chemical company BASF was keen to expand its diversity hiring pipeline and took notice that lofty education and years of experience requirements deterred underrepresented communities from applying. In turn, BASF Vice President of People Ivory Harris led a new initiative called Impact-Based Hiring to explore ways to eliminate these requirements.

Ivory and her team consulted with customers and competitors to define specific skills they were successfully searching for in each job function. She also tested potential tactics with BASF's Employee Resource Groups. BASF used the combined lessons to create a plan for eliminating education and experience requirements and to instead focus on skills and competencies.

BASF educated its team members on what alternate skills and competencies in an applicant's profile were most valuable and explained how to look at a job candidate holistically. As a result, the company has seen a noticeable difference in the representation of its applicant pool, particularly among women and people of color.

7. Explore Alternatives to Degree and Experience Requirements

In recent years, more and more employers have reconsidered the necessity of including degree requirements and years of experience in job listings. George Walker, vice president of diversity, equity, and inclusion at nonprofit Planned Parenthood, says bias around where people went to school, what degree they earned, or their years of experience had seeped into his organization's hiring process. This occurred even though many of Planned Parenthood's senior leaders didn't finish college.

"As soon as we noticed the risks of this potential bias, we eliminated degree and experience requirements from our job postings altogether," Walker says. Degree requirements most commonly appear in job descriptions where employers require a bachelor's degree, even though most fail to explain why this is a requirement or how it is applicable.

Global management consultancy Ernst & Young (EY) conducted a study in 2015 and found that individual strengths and future potential were greater indicators of success than degrees or academic performance. As a result, EY removed the degree requirement from all of its UK hiring the following year.

Rigid educational requirements can create a barrier to finding and employing qualified candidates. A highly talented individual who can't afford to go to college may choose an alternative educational path, such as a boot camp or a certificate program—routes that can provide just as much value as a college education in preparing people for success, according to many hiring experts. For instance, according to a 2019 webinar published by Wiley, about two-thirds of hiring managers are willing to hire candidates with certifications instead of a four-year college degree. By adjusting expectations and credentials, hiring managers can broaden their pool of candidates and diversify their potential workforce.

Including a minimum (or maximum) requirement for years of experience can also be problematic. Quantity of years in experience doesn't always translate to the quality of a candidate. Besides, many employers provide training to equip employees with the tools they need to be successful, making "years of experience" less of a critical factor for every position.

Whenever possible, avoid the use of an experience range in your posting. A more inclusive approach is to highlight skills that will lead to a candidate's success.

Embedded analytics platform Sisense instituted a process to assess a candidate's accomplishments throughout their career rather than focusing on education and years of experience. It did this by removing the candidate requirements section from its job postings altogether. Instead, Sisense creates job *advertisements* that focus on describing the team the applicant would be a part of and the job responsibilities themselves. This encourages candidates to think more about the company and the job duties, rather than spending time wondering if they are good enough even to apply. Hiring teams have undergone inclusive hiring trainings that emphasize the importance of structured interviews and objective scorecards to reduce bias. They are also taught not to pay attention to degrees and years of experience but rather home in on an individual's accomplishments.

For example, instead of requiring "5+ years of marketing experience," consider asking for experience with specific tasks, such as updating multiple social media accounts or writing company blog posts. Think about the specific experiences or accomplishments that may come with years of relevant employment and reword the qualifications to focus on that. Specificity will help candidates understand what the role truly requires. This will help save time on both ends.

This chart can help you determine transferable skills.

Barriers to job seekers	Potential substitutes
Degree requirements	Knowledge or experience in a given area Acceptable alternatives such as certificates from training programs
Years of experience	Specific skills or accomplishments
Proficiency in *xyz*	Willingness to learn and ability to adapt to new programs and tools

Barriers to job seekers	Potential substitutes
Desired or preferred skills	Focus instead on the necessary qualifications needed for this role

8. Identify and Remove Exclusionary Language

The job description speaks volumes about your organization's values. Your choice of wording shows a candidate how inclusive your organization is to certain underrepresented groups.

As mentioned earlier, certain words and phrases can be problematic. For example, masculine-coded words such as "ninja" or "rock star" could signal that your organization has a male-dominated culture, potentially alienating female candidates. One thing to keep in mind is that many masculine-coded words can be attributed to how the media uses and portrays them. Using acronyms or corporate jargon can also create an unintended barrier. For instance, saying that you are looking for a candidate who can "give 110 percent and wear multiple hats" can indicate that the role has long hours and a lack of work-life balance. We must be intentional with our words and weed out possible misinterpretations.

Exclusionary Terms (Microaggressive Terms)

Coined in 1970 by psychiatrist Chester Pierce, the term "microaggression" refers to seemingly innocent terms or uses of language that negatively affect underrepresented groups. Unfortunately, microaggressions surface relatively frequently in job descriptions. The most glaring examples are gender-coded, but isolating language can negatively affect candidates of any underrepresented group.

Stela Lupushor is the founder and chairperson of Amazing Community, a nonprofit organization devoted to helping women age 45 and older navigate the work world. "When microaggressive or exclusionary terms show up in a job description," she says, "it can be extremely harmful to underrepresented job seekers. It signals: *You aren't understood or embraced here.*" Stela, who has decades of work experience, says that any woman over 45 automatically disqualifies herself when reading a job description that describes its ideal candidate as someone who is "young and energetic who can give 110 percent." Such women would infer that the company is looking for someone younger with few obligations who can work long hours. Such a listing would also imply that the organization isn't keen on flexible work schedules or accommodations to those with families or caregiving responsibilities. It could also expose the organization to claims of potential age discrimination.

The key takeaway here is to keep your language simple and transparent; your description should be inclusive of people from all backgrounds. Here are some examples of exclusionary terms to avoid in your communications:

Examples of Exclusionary Terms

Hacker	Athlete
Ninja*	Fast-paced
Energetic	Gives 110%
Preferred or Desired Skills	Young
Rock star*	Master
Has a good sense of humor	His/Her

* = also classified as jargon

Jargon, Corporate Cliches, and Buzzwords

You've likely seen jargon and buzzwords in job listings. The telltale sign: after carefully reading a job description, you still have no idea what the position actually entails. For example, an employer seeking a "laser-focused coding guru with out-of-the-box thinking to strategically optimize their business offerings" will leave many people scratching their heads.

Jargon often takes the form of acronyms commonly understood by people who work in a specific industry—and only that industry. The intent may be to sound professional, but instead, the result can be far fewer applicants. Job seekers may feel like they aren't good enough to apply because they are intimidated and unsure of what the role entails. To broaden your applicant pool, use commonly understood language.

In a 2019 study conducted by Milkround, a career site for graduates, 7 in 10 respondents said jargon could discourage them from applying to a job. And just over 6 in 10 felt they couldn't apply for a role if they didn't understand every part of the job description. Nearly half (47 percent) said they've gone to an interview without fully understanding the job responsibilities.

Here are some examples of wording to avoid in your job postings:

Examples of Jargon, Corporate Cliches, and Buzzwords

World-class	Proficient in (Don't use unless absolutely necessary.)
Expert	Move the needle
Game changer	Disruptor
Self-starter	Optimize
Synergy	Dynamic
Guru	Wizard

Gender-Coded Terms

Gender-charged terminology is a type of exclusionary language that is all too prominent in job postings. Many of the adjectives and descriptors we use in daily interactions are coded as masculine or feminine, and including these words in a job description can discourage potential candidates from applying. Terms such as aggressive, superior, or competitive can be associated with societal masculinity norms and indicate a more male-dominated environment. Many female applicants may not identify with these descriptors. Although we acknowledge that individuals who do not identify as male can also be aggressive and competitive in nature, we want to focus on words that are likely to exclude groups from applying. This is especially important for job postings within largely male-dominated industries, such as tech. For related reasons, LinkedIn found in 2019 that women apply to 16 percent fewer jobs and even fewer senior roles on its platform.

It's also important to be mindful of using any terms or language that could potentially isolate or exclude certain job-seeker communities.

For example, referencing "maternity" leave instead of "parental" leave could send an exclusionary signal to non-gender binary parents or LGBTQ+ parents who do not identify as working mothers.

Feminine-coded words may pose barriers to candidates who identify as introverts or may have conditions that affect their social skills. Such candidates may be less likely to apply to roles where the language heavily emphasizes team-oriented, approachable, or compassionate individuals.

A 2016 study from the job board platform ZipRecruiter found that job listings with gender-neutral wording got 42 percent more applicants than listings that contained words associated with feminine or masculine stereotypes. Here are a few examples of masculine- and feminine-coded words to avoid:

Masculine	Feminine
Aggressive	Compassionate
Dominant	Pleasant
Superior	Approachable
Competitive	Modest
Dominating	Empathetic
Champion	Team-oriented

9.   Proactively Communicate Your Commitment to Diversity

The job description gives you the chance to authentically communicate your diversity commitment to candidates and go beyond your Equal Opportunity Employer (EEO) statements. While the EEO statement is often the only place where diversity is referenced in job descriptions from a compliance perspective, we recommend using the job listing to highlight your dedication to diversity. For example, in its job descriptions, professional services company Accenture says, "Our rich diversity makes us more innovative, more competitive, and more creative, which helps us better serve our clients and our communities."

While most organizations highlight traditional perks such as a 401(k) and paid time off in the benefits section, you also can use this area to highlight diversity programs such as ERGs, diversity councils, and diversity-focused training and events for team members.

10.   Disclose the Salary Range

Although most job postings do not include a compensation range, providing this level of transparency can be a draw for underrepresented candidates. In sharing a clear salary range, you signal that your firm values pay equity. This can give a job seeker added comfort and assurance to get involved with your organization.

"Pay transparency removes the distrust people have," says Leslie Miley, a tech industry engineering manager and equality advocate, in a 2019 LinkedIn article. "As an African American, I'm always distrustful because all the data supports that I'm going to be paid less. If you come out and say, 'This is what our salary is, these are the ranges,' that's going to build trust."

Pay transparency is especially beneficial when trying to recruit women and people of color. Studies show that pay inequity is hardly something of the past: According to a 2020 study published by the World Economic Forum, North America has made little to no progress in closing the gender gap. To the contrary, at the current rate of policy change, it would take 151 years to achieve full pay equity between men and women. However, many Western European and Latin American countries are likely to close their gender gaps within the next 60 years.

This level of transparency is a telling sign about your organization's culture and commitment to diversity. Nearly seven in ten job seekers say salary is the top factor when considering applying to new positions, according to a 2018 study by the Harris Poll on behalf of the career site Glassdoor.

We will dig into establishing pay equity and compensation ranges in Chapter 9.

11. Repost Your Job Posts Every 30 Days

Review any existing listings to check the date when it was published. The job description for an open role may not have changed since you created it, but if it was posted months ago, applicants might think it's outdated, or the role has been filled. You can combat these assumptions by reposting job descriptions after 30 days.

12. Create Systems to Manage Inclusive Job Descriptions and Candidate Communication

It's much easier to consistently ensure inclusive job descriptions and candidate communication when you have a system in place to monitor it. After applying the previously described practices to your existing job openings, it's essential to develop systems for all the future jobs you create. Here are a few tactics to make this sustainable:

1. **Use automated scanners.** Automated tools or scanners like Mathison's bias scanner, Diversity Sidekick app for teams, or Kat Matfield's Gender Decoder can analyze your job descriptions for exclusionary terms and recommend changes. You simply paste your job description into a web interface and it assesses your posting for exclusionary terms with recommended replacements.

2. **Create your unique job templates.** You can create your own job description by creating one general comprehensive template that can be repurposed broadly, or specific templates by job types or job families.

3. **Train your team in writing inclusive job descriptions and communication.** You can lead training to teach the techniques and methodologies for writing inclusive job descriptions.

4. **Apply these insights to other candidate and employee communication.** Consider all the other communication that candidates and employees might read and apply the same lens of inclusive language; from candidate emails and interview

questions to the offer letter and even performance reviews, everything should ultimately be assessed for inclusive and accessible language.

Your job descriptions are an ideal place for you to convey your organization's values and commitment to an inclusive culture. We recommend empowering your whole team to be part of this process. It makes the process so much more manageable and can lead to greater success when everyone shares in the responsibility.

Now, let's revisit that typical line from a job description that opened the chapter. Can you spot the five problematic words and phrases? It's not so hard once you learn to read from the perspectives of underrepresented job seekers. It's that perspective we all need to write from when composing those all-important job descriptions.

> *"We're looking for a <u>dynamic, committed, team-player</u> who will <u>go the extra mile</u> in a <u>fast-paced environment</u>."*

First Step Toward Impact

Job descriptions have the power to welcome an untold number of talented underrepresented people into your company, or to ensure they keep their distance. Bearing in mind the lessons above, you now have a remarkable opportunity to ensure a more inclusive hiring process by evaluating and rethinking your job descriptions. Taking even one small step to make it more objective and accessible to all candidates will go a long way.

Here's an easy first action to take: Scrutinize just one job description—to the extreme. Look at one of your most important job descriptions—something high level and high stakes, where underrepresented job seekers considerations are important—and dissect it with decision makers on your team.

Examine the job description and circle any potential jargon, gender bias, and terms that may be exclusionary or subjective. Note what you would change and spend a couple of minutes writing a more objective and inclusive version. Then share your observations with other team members at your organization so your action can translate into broader improvements. While this is just one small step, it will give you and your team a powerful foundation for all your other jobs.

For additional resources and to download the tables and charts from this chapter visit: http://Mathison.io/Book.

REFERENCES

Bax, Rolf. "Part-Time Wizards: The US Cities Home to the Weirdest Job Titles." *Resume.io* (blog). March 12, 2021. https://resume.io/blog/the-usa-cities-home-to-the-weirdest-job-titles.

"4 Reasons It Pays to Share Salary Ranges, According to Companies That Do." LinkedIn Talent Blog. Accessed March 19, 2021. https://business.linkedin.com/talent-solutions/blog/trends-and-research/2019/4-reasons-it-pays-to-share-salary-ranges-according-to-companies-that-do.

"Global Gender Gap Report 2020." Accessed March 22, 2021. http://www3.weforum.org/docs/WEF_GGGR_2020.pdf.

Ignatova, Maria. "New Report: Women Apply to Fewer Jobs Than Men, But Are More Likely to Get Hired." LinkedIn Talent Blog. Accessed March 22, 2021. https://business.linkedin.com/talent-solutions/blog/diversity/2019/how-women-find-jobs-gender-report.

"Junk the Jargon." Milkround. Accessed March 26, 2021. https://www.milkround.com/insights/job-ad-jargon-decoder/#/.

Lam, Bourree. "The Best Job Candidates Don't Always Have College Degrees." *Atlantic*. September 24, 2015. https://www.theatlantic.com/business/archive/2015/09/ernest-young-degree-recruitment-hiring-credentialism/406576/.

Mohr, Tara Sophia. "Why Women Don't Apply for Jobs Unless They're 100% Qualified." *Harvard Business Review*. March 8, 2021. https://hbr.org/2014/08/why-women-dont-apply-for-jobs-unless-theyre-100-qualified.

"Removing These Gendered Keywords Gets You More Applicants." *ZipRecruiter* (blog). August 21, 2018. https://www.ziprecruiter.com/blog/removing-gendered-keywords-gets-you-more-applicants/s.

"Salary and Benefits Are Most Important for U.S. Workers and Job Seekers Looking at Job Ads." Harris Poll. August 1, 2018. https://theharrispoll.com/salary-and-benefits-are-most-important-for-u-s-workers-and-job-seekers-looking-at-job-ads/.

"Shedding Light on the Job Search." Ladders. October 10, 2019. https://www.theladders.com/career-advice/shedding-light-on-the-job-search.

Walsh, Jeremy, and Dan Schawbel. "Closing the Skills Gap 2019." Wiley, On-Demand Webinar. January 29, 2021. https://edservices.wiley.com/on-demand-webinar-closing-the-skills-gap-2019/.

Zielinski, Dave. "Study: Most Job Seekers Abandon Online Job Applications." SHRM. August 16, 2019. https://www.shrm.org/resourcesandtools/hr-topics/technology/pages/study-most-job-seekers-abandon-online-job-applications.aspx.

CHAPTER 6

Diversity Sourcing

Nearly every employer we speak with believes that the success of their diversity recruiting depends primarily on their ability to source candidates from underrepresented communities. If only they could get this part right, everything else would fall into place. Somewhere out there is that magic diversity job board or silver-bullet sourcing solution they believe will solve this problem indefinitely, once and for all.

We wish it were that simple. Diversity sourcing is challenging for every employer we know. We have yet to find a single organization that has definitively and permanently figured it out. There isn't a single stakeholder at your organization who can achieve it on their own, and there's no magical tactic that does the trick for every role. Josh Bersin, a leading expert in talent management and industry research, recently conducted a study that showed 12 percent of leaders hold their hiring managers responsible for diversity sourcing. However, the same study also shows that only 11 percent of recruiters are assessed for their diversity sourcing. These statistics alone demonstrate the dissonance between intention and impact in the diversity sourcing space.

To really make your diversity sourcing solutions effective, you need to assess the representation among each of your existing teams and be realistic about the potential applicant pools. Consider role-specific strategies that account for the unique challenges of every open position. It's important that diversity sourcing does not just fall on the shoulders of a few recruiters but instead becomes an organization-wide mandate and activity.

Inevitably, your approach will be iterative, collaborative, and based on collective learning. Most important, remember that advancing your diversity sourcing, like your diversity recruiting efforts overall, is about making progress, not achieving perfection.

UNDERSTANDING WHY DIVERSITY SOURCING MATTERS

It's not what you know, it's who you know.

The old truism about job hunting may seem old fashioned, but it's as true today as ever. Referrals are still the number one way that people get new jobs, according to LinkedIn. Even in the age of ZipRecruiter, Indeed, and countless industry-specific job boards, 50 percent of people say they got their job through friends, and another 37 percent say they hear about jobs through their professional networks, according to research from recruiting software company Jobvite.

Referrals are one of the many insidious ways that the traditional hiring process is set up to perpetuate racial, ethnic, and gender imbalances. People tend to refer their friends, and our friends tend to look like us. Even with a total absence of malice or conscious racism, the "who you know" system tends to produce teams with very little diversity.

But the problem goes deeper than that. Even when we go searching for the most qualified people, we tend to look in the same places: the best schools, the usual job fairs, or our biggest competitors. And when we post jobs online, we use industry-specific job boards that outsiders don't know about, or use the sort of exclusionary language we discussed in Chapter 5.

It's easy for employers to think this is purely a diversity pipeline problem. And it's true that some industries struggle more than others to attract underrepresented candidates. But we also need to acknowledge that the pipeline isn't always the issue. According to the Pew Research Center, women now outnumber men on college campuses. And according to the Current Population Survey, Black Americans now graduate high school at roughly the same rate as the general population, and they are rapidly approaching the national average for college degrees. For jobs that don't require special degrees or training, there is very little excuse today for not finding non-white or women candidates.

Some employers say they lack the resources to find underrepresented candidates, or that they are a victim of geography. But an in-depth assessment of an organization's recruitment strategy will likely reveal that a huge part of the challenge is due to outdated hiring practices—practices that were originally created without consideration of diversity or a narrow view of diversity at best.

You can't hire someone if they don't know about your job, and you won't find many nontraditional candidates if you wait for them to come to you. It's not enough to be open to hiring people from underrepresented groups (URGs); you need to take active steps to bring them into your candidate pool. Employers need to consciously make these changes or systemic transformation will never happen.

Deciding to diversify your workforce means divorcing yourself from those old systems and mindsets and embracing new ones, even when it takes work—which it will. Let's take a look at how to get started.

RETHINK YOUR APPROACH TO DIVERSITY SOURCING

There are some common pitfalls to watch out for when assessing your organization's struggles with diversity sourcing.

As we explored in Chapter 3, many organizations lack an inclusive definition of *diversity* itself, which means their diversity recruiting efforts have a narrow focus that leaves entire communities out of the equation.

Another common misstep is placing the onus for finding underrepresented candidates solely on recruiters or HR, which puts undue pressure on professionals who typically lack the tools, connections, or support for sourcing candidates by themselves.

And many organizations make the mistake of eliminating underrepresented candidates based on an overly stringent set of job requirements. As we explored in the last chapter, take a look at your job descriptions and ask yourself whether someone in that position really needs that degree or certificate or that many years of experience. How many of those skills can be learned on the job?

Finally, don't make the mistake of focusing solely on external hires when you have the opportunity to first look within your own existing team. Sometimes, a sourcing issue can be alleviated by looking at your own team for people you can promote.

Underrepresented job seekers face their own challenges. Many have been conditioned not to see themselves as viable candidates in particular fields, even when they are perfectly qualified. This is a conditioned response to decades of exclusion, and it takes work to overcome. Mathison's 2021 Diversity Hiring Report found that 50 percent of underrepresented job seekers directly see being from an underrepresented community as a disadvantage in the hiring process. As a result, organizations need to go the extra mile to welcome and empower underrepresented groups and help change this internalized narrative, showing them that they have as good a chance as anyone with the right qualifications.

Overall, whether you are launching or rebooting a diversity sourcing strategy, there needs to be an intentional, well-planned internal and external plan if you want to have the best chance at success. This starts with assessing where you are now.

ASSESSING WHERE YOU ARE WITH DIVERSITY SOURCING

It's easy to declare that diversity sourcing is the responsibility of a select few in the organization. But this is one of the biggest obstacles to reform in this area. We all have a role to play in finding and reaching new communities that can grow diversity in our organizations, from the leadership down to junior staff. If it's a mission that matters to you, it's important to do your part and try to get others to come along with you.

If you're struggling to improve your organization's diversity sourcing, try drawing a map of how you believe sourcing works and sharing it with your coworkers. Ask them for their constructive feedback and corrections. That will help confirm what you know and reveal where you may be mistaken.

As you embark on improving your diversity sourcing strategy, here are some questions to gauge where you can best focus your efforts.

- Does your team have a holistic and inclusive definition of diversity?

- Where do you believe you are currently lacking representation in your organization?

- Do you consistently review the demographics of your applicant and new-hire pools?

- Have you explored a role-specific strategy for how you will grow diversity in your organization?

- Do you have a process to consider internal candidates for all of the roles that you are hiring for, first and foremost?

- Do you use any tools or systems for finding, sourcing, and tracking underrepresented job seekers for your roles?

- Do you have partnerships in place to source from underrepresented groups?

- Have you engaged your broader team outside of recruiters for diversity sourcing and referrals?

For additional resources to assess your diversity hiring efforts visit: http://Mathison.io/Index.

DEVELOPING A ROLE-SPECIFIC DIVERSITY SOURCING STRATEGY

Part of where many organizations fall short in diversity sourcing is assuming that the strategies that work well in one role or function will apply to all roles and functions. In reality, for each of the roles you are hiring for, you are starting with a team already in place and a pool of candidates ready for hire, each of which will have their own degree of diversity. To do this right, you need to develop a role-specific analysis and strategy that doesn't approach the work in broad strokes. Event management and ticketing platform Eventbrite develops a miniature diversity hiring action plan for every role the company is recruiting for because it found that the diversity hiring tactics that work well for one role may not apply to another. For every role you are seeking to fill, we recommend attempting to answer these three questions:

1. How diverse and representative is this team now, and where is there room for improvement?

2. How diverse is the pool of likely candidates? If it's largely homogenous, why?

3. What tactics, tools, and resources can you use to find and attract more underrepresented candidates?

Global meal kit company HelloFresh set up a system to assess the diversity representation of each of its roles and functions to determine where it needed to expand its sourcing efforts and specifically where underrepresented candidates were dropping out. Candidates self-identify at the moment they apply, so the company is able to chart every stage of the hiring process to pinpoint exactly where the issues arise. This gives the company very specific insights into where it lacks representation for each role and where it needs to diversify hiring efforts.

TACTICS TO APPLY FOR DIVERSITY SOURCING

As you begin to mobilize role-specific strategies for diversity sourcing, there are three things that we recommend you do along the way to ensure you are constantly learning and improving:

1. **Apply an iterative and experimental approach to your sourcing tactics.** Attempts to diversify your talent pool won't be perfect out of the gate. Be patient, learn as you go, and you will soon start to make progress.

2. **Continuously measure what tactics are working and what is not.** Just as we explored in Chapter 2, you can't manage what you can't measure. As you experiment with

different tactics, try to measure what is making a difference, both in your pipeline and your hires.

3. **Capture all that you learn in your own "Diversity Sourcing Playbook."** As you learn from tactics that do and do not work, take the opportunity to create your own internal playbook for diversity sourcing that is role-specific. This will ensure that the outcomes of the strategies you employ for each role become institutional knowledge that can lessen the learning curve for your team in future hiring.

The following sections explore tactics you can apply in the process.

Apply a Framework or Rule to Require Diverse Representation

As diversity sourcing has become a priority for organizations around the world, several common frameworks or rules have gained popularity. It's important to note that what works well for one role may not work for another. Just as we recommend a role-specific strategy, we don't recommend a universal framework to be applied to all roles.

As mentioned in Chapter 2, the Rooney Rule is a policy aimed at boosting Black and POC representation among head coaches in the NFL. The rule requires league teams to interview at least one minority candidate for leadership vacancies. Its high profile has inspired other organizations and industries to adopt similar measures to ensure a diverse slate of applicants when hiring for leadership roles. But it should be noted that, even in the NFL, the Rooney Rule's success has been dubious at best, suggesting that simply interviewing underrepresented candidates is inadequate if other biases remain.

Another popular approach is the Mansfield Rule, which was designed to address the diverse leadership gap in the legal industry. It requires law firms to consider at least 30 percent minority candidates, including women, LGBTQ+ people, and people with disabilities for leadership and governance roles as well as equity partner promotions, formal client pitch opportunities, and senior lateral positions. Unlike the Rooney Rule, which is enforced across the NFL, the Mansfield Rule is optional, but its growing popularity among law firms suggests it is making a difference.

There are some cautionary tales when applying these tactics, particularly in cases where the requirement is to have at least one minority candidate in the final pool. Studies have shown that because our unconscious biases tend to preserve the status quo, the lone diverse underrepresented candidate in the pool of finalists can often be labeled as outside the norm, and statistically, that individual would have almost no chance of getting hired. For instance, one study featured in the *Harvard Business Review* revealed that survey participants preferred hiring a man when two of the three finalists for a job were men. Similar results were achieved when the experiment was conducted with a finalist pool of one Black candidate and two white candidates, with participants favoring a white candidate.

Inversely, the same research found that when there were at least two women or minority candidates in the final candidate pool, the odds of getting hired increased significantly. It was nearly 79 times greater for female candidates and 194 times greater for a minority candidate. This is known as the "two in the pool effect," and it's worth bearing in mind as you compile your list of finalists.

Build Community Partnerships

Many organizations have successfully diversified their pipelines by building community partnerships with organizations that serve underrepresented groups. For example, according to the National Association of Colleges and Employers (NACE), the two most common sources of underrepresented candidates are Historically Black Colleges and Universities (HBCUs) and Hispanic Serving Institutions (HSIs). Building a relationship with such organizations in your area or field of expertise can go a long way toward helping you find more diverse underrepresented candidates.

You can also partner with multicultural fraternities and sorority organizations that cater to specific diverse communities. The

National APIDA (Asian Pacific Islander Desi American), Panhellenic Association (NAPA), and the National Multicultural Greek Council (NMGC) are three umbrella organizations that have a combined membership of 30 fraternities and sororities. When you add to those the nine Black Greek Letter Organizations (BGLOs) that form the National Pan-Hellenic Council (NPHC), collectively known as the Divine Nine, that's a total of 39 organizations where you can source underrepresented job seekers from a wide range of ethnicities.

Other examples include Alpha Lambdu Mu (ALM) from the University of Texas, the Mu Delta Alpha (MDA) sorority for Muslim-interest students, and the Jewish fraternity Alpha Epsilon Pi (AEPi), which operates chapters on more than 175 campuses in seven countries. By collaborating with any of the Greek organizations, you tap into their networks and gain access to students and alumni who might be job hunting or looking to switch jobs.

Looking beyond educational groups, there are countless professional and advocacy groups that regularly partner with companies looking to diversify. These groups can be industry-specific or tailored to a particular ethnic group. Food service giant Aramark, for example, partners with Out & Equal Workplace Advocates, an organization that works exclusively for LGBTQ individuals, and the American Corporate Partners for Veterans. Likewise, global accounting firm KPMG has a productive and mutually beneficial relationship with the National Black MBA Association (NBMBA).

Formerly incarcerated people are one of the most commonly overlooked populations for potential hires, but many companies have found great success—both in diversifying their workforce and in simply finding great employees—by partnering with organizations that help them find jobs. One such group, nonprofit startup Refoundry, places formerly imprisoned people in jobs within their preferred career track and even helps them launch their own businesses. Employers of any size are likely to find such groups to be eager and accommodating partners.

Veterans are another frequently overlooked pool of applicants that employers can access through several nonprofit organizations. For example, the Veterans Employment Network of Massachusetts provides training and reintegration programs for formerly incarcerated or homeless veterans.

Because there are so many distinctions among community partnerships, it can be difficult to identify exactly which type and size can best support your sourcing needs. Below is a table that highlights the differences among these partner organizations while providing a few examples of each. It is important to note that these tactics are relevant to organizations of all sizes and will yield results as long as you are putting in the time and resources necessary. We've included a full roster of diversity-focused organizations by community in the appendix as well.

Type of Partner Organization	Description	Examples
Professional membership associations	Members all work in the same industry or job field and meet other professionals in their field through this connection.	• Society of Hispanic Professional Engineers • American Nurses Associations • Muslim Urban Professionals
Workforce development agencies	Training programs that provide existing and potential employees with the necessary skills to succeed in their organization.	• Upwardly Global • ProjectBASTA • National Association for Drug Abuse Problems (NADAP)
Advocacy groups	Special interest groups that work to influence public opinion and policy.	• America Working Forward • New York City Education and Training Center (NYCETC) • Jobs for the Future (JFF)
Alumni associations	Many larger alumni associations are broken into smaller, more focused interest groups.	• Boston College AHANA • USC Black Alumni Association • Texas Exes Hispanic Alumni Network

Type of Partner Organization	Description	Examples
Diverse chambers of commerce	Local group of organizations and businesses that work together toward a common goal; many are beginning to focus more heavily on DEI work.	• National Gay and Lesbian (LGBT) Chamber of Commerce (NGLCC) • State Vocational Rehabilitation Services • US Veteran Chamber of Congress (USVCC)
Education and training organizations	Alternative pathways of earning credentials or certifications for specific needs of their field or organization.	• Management Leadership for Tomorrow (MLT) • Workforce Professionals Training Institute (WPTI) • International Accreditors for Continuing Education and Training (IACET)
Colleges or universities dedicated to underrepresented communities	Historically Black Colleges and Universities (HBCU), Hispanic Serving Institutions (HSI), as well as universities focused on underrepresented groups	• Howard University (HBCU) • University of California, Riverside (HSI) • Gallaudet University (dedicated to the education of the deaf and hard of hearing)
Technical training organizations	Alternative pathways of earning credentials or certifications for specific needs of their field or organization.	• Girls Who Code • Per Scholas • ChickTech

Create Diversity Pipeline Programs

Diversity pipeline programs are training, mentorship, and community service programs that offer real-world experience for job-seekers from underrepresented groups. For many organizations, such programs provide a steady stream of talent that is not only diverse but already familiar with your organization. These include internship programs, apprenticeship programs, and mentoring partnerships. Whether these programs are internal or external, recruiting directly from colleges and universities, or partnering with nonprofit organizations, they can all assist with building a pool of entry-level talent.

As with any recruitment effort, it can be a challenge to create truly diverse internship, mentorship, and apprentice programs. Many such programs are overwhelmingly white and male, largely because they rely on the same recruitment strategies that exclude diverse communities from the general workforce. Partnering with community groups, educational institutions, and other nonprofit organizations can help you create programs that help solve your diversity challenges rather than reinforce them.

Abbott, a global medical devices and healthcare technology company, created a pipeline program focused on diversity by offering high school students from underrepresented communities internship opportunities in science, technology, engineering, and math (STEM). The students are all paid and given real, quality STEM-related work. The program has made a significant difference in the trajectory for these students—97 percent of them go on to study STEM in college. Of the students that have come back to work full-time as engineers at Abbott, 73 percent are women. Abbott went so far as to share the "Shaping the Future of STEM" blueprint of its STEM program externally so other organizations could follow suit. Mary Moreland, Executive Vice President of Human Resources for Abbott, said, "We not only saw the high school STEM internship create diversity in our pipeline when so many of these talented students went on to work for us as college interns and full-time employees, the program also had a positive impact on our workplace culture when it brought us such rich backgrounds and varied perspectives. Even if students didn't come to work with us after the program, we knew it was bringing the world much-needed STEM talent."

Global advertising firm Publicis Groupe wanted to build a strong early-career diversity pipeline and recognized that many students from underrepresented communities were not always afforded mentorship or professional development opportunities. The company created the Ad Fellows Program and worked with a cross section of community partners to source and screen entry level candidates from underrepresented communities. Each fellow was placed in a cohort to have experiential learning through project work. The program engaged senior executives from Publicis Groupe as mentors, and provided professional learning opportunities, including nonverbal communication training and even etiquette for fine dining experiences with the company's clients. At the end of the program, the company held a job fair where the fellows could find full-time opportunities.

Apprenticeships are very similar to internships, but with some important differences. Internships tend to involve students or entry-level workers, last only a couple of months, and—infamously—sometimes provide little actual job experience. On the other hand, apprenticeships tend to involve workers that already have some relevant skill or experience. They also last longer—usually at least a year—and involve valuable on-the-job training. An apprenticeship program may require a larger investment of time and resources from your organization, but it creates a sturdy pipeline of well-trained potential candidates who are prepared to make an easy transition to full-time employment.

Unfortunately, the available race and gender representation data for apprenticeship programs is not very encouraging. In 2019, the Department of Labor reported that 88 percent of new apprentices coming into federally registered programs were male; 56 percent were white, according to national nonprofit JFF (Jobs for the Future). And female representation in these programs has barely improved over time. In 2017, only 7.3 percent of registered apprentices were women, a meager 1.1 percent increase over 2008.

Because apprenticeship programs usually require some level of training, they are susceptible to the same kinds of bias and exclusion that infect the general workforce. Creating a diverse apprenticeship program may therefore require a greater degree of effort and mindfulness than creating a diverse internship program. In a 2018 HBR article, Ryan Carson, CEO of EdTech company Treehouse, explained how his company broke the mold to create a diverse apprenticeship program.

For years, Treehouse had been trying to diversify its workforce but had little to show for it. "Even though we were following the typical playbook—posting open positions on job boards that specialize in attracting candidates from underrepresented groups, sponsoring events, giving scholarships, and training our employees on inclusion and hidden bias—we weren't seeing progress," Carson wrote. To figure out what Treehouse was doing wrong, Carson interviewed people from diverse communities who had succeeded in tech, asking them why they hadn't applied for his company's open positions. What he found was that the company's overwhelmingly white, male workforce was sending the wrong signal to underrepresented candidates.

"My community does not trust companies that are majority white and male," the interviewees told Carson. "We do not see people like us succeeding in those companies. Why would we apply for your jobs?"

To overcome its problem, Treehouse established an apprenticeship program in partnership with a local Boys and Girls Club (BGC). Unlike tech companies, the BGC is a trusted organization within the community and had no trouble recruiting local youth for the program. Rather than require years of tech experience, Treehouse looked for candidates who had a strong work ethic and an interest in the industry, then provided the necessary training, including "online courses teaching necessary job and technical skills, like computer science fundamentals, complex problem solving, group collaboration, agile methodology, effective written communication, and so on." The company paid the apprentices a minimum of $15 per hour for 40 hours per week, and even created a six-month onboarding program specifically designed for women and people of color who had no previous tech experience.

Though the program initially involved only a handful of apprentices, 80 percent ended up with full-time jobs at Treehouse or one of its hiring partners. And while saving money was not one of the program's goals, Treehouse estimates that compared to the typical recruitment and onboarding process for engineers, the program saved the company over $1.3 million, a staggering ROI of close to 900 percent.

Use Technology to Facilitate Diversity Candidate Sourcing

From faxed resumes in the 1980s to job sites like Monster.com in the 1990s, technology has long played a transformative role in recruiting. Today, search engines driven by artificial intelligence are revolutionizing how employers build talent pipelines, and digital communities allow candidates of similar backgrounds to pool resources and employers to post hyper-targeted job listings. As is usually the case with technological solutions, results may vary, so proceed with caution.

AI-Powered Sourcing Solutions

A new generation of artificial intelligence recruiting tools are helping employers find underrepresented candidates. Employers input the attributes they are looking for in a candidate, and the system performs an extensive search of talent networks and public data to find matches. These systems help employers build diversity pipelines of both passive and active job seekers and have the flexibility to source from many underrepresented communities. If employers are struggling with finding underrepresented candidates, these tools can prove very helpful. Mathison uses AI technology to source candidates from a vast partner network based on an employer's diversity priorities, presenting curated candidate lists to save recruiters on top-of-funnel sourcing. Tools like GEM and TopFunnel provide candidate sourcing and engagement resources that include diversity filters.

Community-Specific Talent Marketplaces

Community-specific talent marketplaces allow employers to advertise job openings to a particular subset of underrepresented people. These are two-sided platforms where job seekers create profiles and apply to jobs and employers post opportunities and directly engage job seekers.

- **Jopwell.** A job site for Black, Latinx, and Native American students and jobseekers.

- **PowertoFly.** A recruiting platform for women in tech, sales, and marketing.

- **FairyGodBoss.** A community and networking hub where women can not only find jobs, but share stories and find support from other members of the community.

- **MyGWork.** A UK-based recruiting platform designed to support and connect LGBTQ+ professionals.

- **70 Million Jobs.** An employment platform for people who were formerly incarcerated. The site helps former inmates prepare for job interviews and connects them with organizations that are willing to hire people with criminal records.

Because these platforms attract active job seekers, employers who use them will typically see higher engagement from users. But given their limited scope, they are less useful for providing large numbers of applicants and are typically more centered around entry-level roles.

Diversity Job Boards

Diversity job boards have been around the longest of these three solutions. These sites are advertised as allowing employers to post job opportunities to job seekers from underrepresented communities—as well as employment agencies and other diversity sites—by posting open roles to a community feed. Some examples include Circa and Direct Employers.

The widespread sentiment from employers in our experience is that diversity job boards don't yield many measurable results. While these sites may seem cost-effective, many employers typically report they don't produce a steady flow of quality applicants. Some employers engage diversity job boards simply to help satisfy the Equal Employment Opportunity Commission (EEOC) compliance requirements. We recommend never relying on diversity job boards alone for diversity sourcing.

Apply Diversity Search Tactics on Professional Networks

Search engines are often the first stop for employers who have decided to actively seek out diverse candidates. But internet searches can quickly end in frustration if you're not using the right approach. Professional recruiters will often rely on Boolean search strings to help them more narrowly target their desired candidates. A Boolean search string is a type of search that combines multiple keywords using "and," "or," or "not" to produce more relevant results. Though it may sound simple, crafting the perfect Boolean search string for your job opening will likely require some trial and error. You can download a full table of Boolean search terms for diversity at: http://Mathison.io/Book.

ENGAGE YOUR TEAM MEMBERS IN DIVERSITY SOURCING AND REFERRALS

Your existing team can be your secret weapon to advancing your diversity hiring. Many employers overlook the opportunity to empower and incentivize their team members to refer underrepresented candidates for open roles. If you consider the possible reach you have when you add up collective networks of your entire team, it's immense. Unlocking diversity referrals among your full team enables you to cast a much wider net for your hiring. Not only can referrals help you grow diversity at your organization, according to research by Jobvite, but they can help you reduce hiring costs and increase retention rates. Referrals are far more likely to get hired than other kinds of candidates.

To mobilize an effective diversity referral approach across your team, you first want to be sure that your team has a clear sense of how you see diversity and where you want to increase representation of your referrals. We recommend spending time articulating all the underrepresented communities you are trying to reach so your team is fully aware; any gap in awareness here could mean a missed referral opportunity. Feel free to lean on what we wrote in Chapter 3 when sharing these insights with your team.

We recommend having a clearly communicated system for your team to manage referrals. Many employers have a dedicated internal website or form that gives them an accessible and easy way for employees to refer candidates. Google created an internal referral portal linked to its open roles that enables team members to code in specific referral feedback and track the hiring status of the candidates they recommend. Other employers have opted for a more informal system where referrals are managed through a simple email alias. Whatever the system is, be sure it's clearly communicated and understood.

You have a great opportunity to invite your existing underrepresented team members to play an active role in your diversity referrals. Many employers develop targeted communication to invite their existing diversity councils or ERGs to refer candidates to open jobs the organization is hiring for. While this targeted strategy can be effective, it's important such communication doesn't come across as tokenizing but instead is framed around a genuine desire to have everyone be part of growing diversity at the organization.

To keep your full team actively engaged in diversity referrals, we recommend having targeted internal communication around your referral program and open positions. Consider posting links in internal newsletters and messaging boards. Remind your team of your referral program in internal meetings and town halls and empower your frontline managers to bring it up in their meetings with the team. You can also pursue an event-based approach to referrals by scheduling dedicated time to review open positions with the entire team and ask them for diverse referrals. This is something you can also extend as an opportunity to your ERGs or diversity council. Dataminr, the leading real-time information discovery platform, began to schedule a series of Diversity Sourcing Events that enabled them to engage ERGs and team members across the company to play a more active role in referrals. They witnessed these events both drastically increase the engagement within the company's referral program, and widen the pipeline of referrals from underrepresented communities.

You might consider creating incentive programs that give your team members an incentive for their referrals. This could be in the form of a cash bonus, extra vacation days, or other perks when candidates are hired. However, we strongly suggest not tying such incentives to underrepresented candidates referrals only. This can send the wrong signals about how your organization values its workers, so we recommend applying incentives to all referrals or none at all. Some of the employers we engage are introducing new models to make a community donation to a cause of the team member's choice following a successful referral. An incentive program coupled with strong messaging about your specific diversity goals ("We are committed to hiring 50 percent more women this fiscal year!") can be a powerful combination.

FIRST STEP TOWARD IMPACT

Changing your diversity sourcing methods is a long-term undertaking that will likely hit some roadblocks before coming to fruition. But that's no excuse not to get started now. One way you can immediately get started on diversity sourcing is to take the next, most important role that you are hiring for and gather your team to answer these three questions:

- What is the current representation on the team for this role and what communities would we like to see more of?

- What does the pool of potential candidates realistically resemble today?

- What tactics, tools, and resources related to diversity sourcing can we introduce to our team today?

It's okay if you don't know the answer to any of these. Starting the conversation is a major step and will ensure you and the team are on the path to casting a wider net in your hiring.

To access additional resources and download the tables and charts from this chapter visit: http://Mathison.io/Book.

REFERENCES

Bernstein, Heylee. "The Rooney and Mansfield Rules: Diversity Programs in Structurally Different Industries." Onlabor. April 3, 2019. https://onlabor. org/the-rooney-and-mansfield-rules-diversity-programs-in-structurally-different-industries/.

"Black High School Attainment Nearly on Par with National Average." United States Census Bureau. August 18, 2020. https://www.census.gov/ library/stories/2020/06/black-high-school-attainment-nearly-on-par-with-national-average.html.

"Changing the Face of STEM." Abbott U.S. Accessed March 24, 2021. https:// www.abbott.com/women-in-stem.html.

"Data and Statistics." U.S. Department of Labor. Accessed March 24, 2021. https://www.dol.gov/agencies/eta/apprenticeship/about/statistics.

Dishman, Lydia. "Why Your Single Minority Candidate Has Statistically No Chance of Being Hired." Fast Company. April 28, 2016. https://www.fast-company.com/3059352/only-interview-one-woman-theres-statistically-no-chance-shell-be-hired.

"Diversity, Equity, and Inclusion in Apprenticeship & WBL." JFF. Accessed March 24, 2021. https://www.jff.org/what-we-do/impact-stories/center-for-apprenticeship-and-work-based-learning/diversity-equity-and-inclusion-apprenticeship-wbl/.

"Elevating Equity: The Real Story of Diversity and Inclusion." Accessed March 22, 2021. https://ss-usa.s3.amazonaws.com/c/308463326/med ia/7667603358a676268833124902210463/202102%20-%20DEI%20 Report_Final_V2.pdf.

Fry, Richard. "U.S. Women Near Milestone in the College-Educated Labor Force." Pew Research Center. August 7, 2020. https://www.pewresearch. org/fact-tank/2019/06/20/u-s-women-near-milestone-in-the-college-educated-labor-force/.

"How My Company Created an Apprenticeship Program to Help Diversify Tech." *Harvard Business Review*. November 2, 2018. https://hbr. org/2018/11/how-my-company-created-an-apprenticeship-program-to-help-diversify-tech.

Hudson, Kristen. "4 Reasons to Invest in Employee Referrals." Jobvite. February 1, 2019. https://www.jobvite.com/blog/sourcing-and-nurturing/4-reasons-to-invest-in-employee-referrals/.

Johnson, Stefanie K, David R Hekman, and Elsa T Chan. "If There's Only One Woman in Your Candidate Pool, There's Statistically No Chance She'll Be Hired." *Harvard Business Review*. February 7, 2019. https://hbr. org/2016/04/if-theres-only-one-woman-in-your-candidate-pool-theres-statistically-no-chance-shell-be-hired.

"Mansfield Rule 4.0." Diversity Lab. Accessed March 23, 2021. https://www.diversitylab.com/mansfield-rule-4-0/.

"NFL Expands Rooney Rule Requirements to Strengthen Diversity." NFL. December 12, 2018. https://www.nfl.com/news/nfl-expands-rooney-rule-requirements-to-strengthen-diversity-0ap3000000999110.

"2021 Diversity Hiring Report." Mathison. Accessed March 23, 2021. mathison.io/2021DiversityReport.

"The Ultimate List of Hiring Statistics." Accessed March 22, 2021. https://business.linkedin.com/content/dam/business/talent-solutions/global/en_us/c/pdfs/Ultimate-List-of-Hiring-Stats-v02.04.pdf.

CHAPTER 7

Minimizing Selection Bias

A few years ago, the management team of a well-known global bank met to review the company's latest diversity data. Many leaders around the room took notice of the significant lack of representation among the disability community, and there was consensus that people with disabilities should be front and center in the company's hiring priorities. Soon after, the bank embarked on a large-scale effort to hire more people with disabilities. It worked through disability partner networks and employee referrals to successfully identify and source more than 600 individuals with disabilities across a wide variety of roles.

Yet in spite of the bank's honest intentions and hard work, it ended up hiring not a single one of those 600 people.

What went wrong? When the bank (which has requested to remain anonymous) went back to assess its missteps, it discovered that nearly every recruiter and hiring manager had decided early in the hiring process not to move forward with these candidates. Despite being aware of the bank's laudable goals, many of them decided these candidates were either unqualified or would not be successful in their preferred roles because of their disabilities. Others passed over candidates with disabilities early in the process or chose to advance other candidates they felt were more qualified later on. Despite the fact that the overwhelming majority of these candidates would have been able to perform the job duties as stated and were interested in the job, the unconscious bias among the team was so deeply ingrained that it prevented the bank from making any progress on its good intentions.

This story illustrates just how difficult it can be, even for organizations with the best intentions, to overcome selection bias in the hiring process. It also shows the significant risks that selection bias can pose to your organization. In a couple of instances for the bank in this case, people with disabilities raised concerns about potential discrimination in this process.

Even the most successful diversity sourcing efforts can be stifled by bias that is present at the critical juncture of first discovering and screening qualified candidates. The problem is that few people typically *think* they are susceptible to bias. But in the majority of cases, they're simply not aware of the bias that shows up in their early hiring decisions. Even in the cases where individuals are aware of their biases, they often struggle to make any changes to address bias in their decision-making.

This makes it all the more important that we become aware of our own biases, are intentional about the systems we develop to minimize bias in the selection process, and avail ourselves of the many tools now available to combat biases and learn how to overcome them.

WHY MINIMIZING SELECTION BIAS MATTERS

For some companies, the decision to prioritize diversity in hiring requires a decades-long journey. Other organizations are founded with diversity and inclusion baked into their mission statement. For either kind of company, and every one in between, those good intentions are routinely sabotaged in less than eight seconds.

That's how much time the average hiring manager or recruiter spends with a resume or professional profile before deciding to pass on a candidate. (To be exact, it's 7.4 seconds, according to research from job site Ladders.) While many legitimately unqualified candidates are no doubt eliminated in that time, research shows that many more are being discarded because of unconscious bias: hasty conclusions made based on someone's name, age, alma mater, address, and countless other details that ultimately have no bearing on someone's ability to do the job.

Those 7.4 seconds are where the rubber meets the road between your organization's desire to diversify and its deeply ingrained selection bias. Any serious effort to reduce the homogeneity of your hiring pool needs to start with those 7.4 seconds.

ASSESSING WHERE YOU HAVE BIAS IN THE SELECTION PROCESS

Assessing your brand probably feels like an exercise in integration. Formalizing inclusive job descriptions probably felt like building a more efficient assembly line. Improving your sourcing may have felt like drawing a map, to understand where you've been looking for treasure.

This step may, in relation, feel like a minefield. The more personal we get—moving from macro process to individual decisions—the more people will have sensitivity around their personal biases. Again, we all hold and we all apply bias; seldom do any of us acknowledge that. If we look at every final hiring selection we've ever made, we'd probably immediately say, "I simply made the best decision for the company," and never question it beyond that. But we have to ask questions, and we have to explore what drives our personal decisions. Throughout this chapter, we'll talk about a formalized way to explore decision-making criteria.

The following questions are a good place to start when evaluating your hiring process for areas where you can make an immediate difference. As you go through these items, consider who should be owning and supporting each. Some answers will be intuitive, and where you don't have answers, you'll know where to engage other leaders and stakeholders in discussion:

- Are your team members aware of unconscious bias and where it can show up in the candidate selection process?

- Do you have a process or strategy to address upfront candidate selection bias?

- Do you have systems to help ensure anonymous candidate profile or resume review?

- Have you instituted representative review panels and training for reviewers?

- Do you utilize any objective hiring assessments?

- Do you take steps to build awareness and understanding of personal bias?

- Do you have measures to reinforce awareness of bias in your team's daily work and hiring decisions?

- Do you have systems to independently collect and report candidate feedback?

For additional resources to assess your diversity hiring efforts visit: http://Mathison.io/Index.

If the answer to any of these is no, you have some immediate opportunities to take action and make progress. Let this audit be your guide to addressing what's broken and replace it with bias-free procedures.

How to Minimize Candidate Selection Bias

Years ago, Etsy, the e-commerce company focused on crafts and homemade goods, was greatly expanding its global hiring efforts to accommodate its rapid growth. The mission-driven company was always proud of its casual culture, which encouraged team members to be comfortable. There was no dress code, even for the company's board and leadership team meetings. Most employees showed up to work each day in jeans and T-shirts, sometimes even flip-flops.

However, Etsy's casual precedent led to an unexpected snag in its hiring process: Candidates who showed up to interviews in formal attire stuck out. Not only were such candidates often visibly uncomfortable during interviews, but Etsy found that some interviewers were raising concerns that these people might not thrive or fit in at the company.

Recognizing potential selection bias in the process, Etsy quickly devised a creative solution: Give every candidate coming in for an interview a lab coat. This provided an equalizing mechanism that enabled interviewers to focus on the conversations with the candidates rather than getting distracted by what they were wearing, and it created a more comfortable, casual setting for candidates who might have otherwise feared they presented too formally. Etsy used the opportunity to raise awareness across the organization about the risks of selection bias, and the lab coats greatly leveled the playing field for new candidates.

ANONYMIZING CANDIDATE INFORMATION

Like Etsy, you can explore creative ways to anonymize parts of candidate profiles to reduce selection bias. While Etsy did this with lab coats, you can determine what's best for your organization. Before engaging in this process, we recommend ensuring your team is aligned around the purpose and intentions of anonymization. This will help you distill what information can be screened out and how the process may be cleanly crafted.

A popular 2018 study identified some major advantages of anonymous candidate screening:

- **Job offers.** Increased number of job offer rates for individuals from underrepresented groups

- **Efficiency.** Streamlining application materials for long-term and frequent use

- **Expanding opportunities.** Comparability among candidates possibly increases

- **Attraction.** A wider base of applicants because of the strong message of commitment to diversity and equitable practices

Although it is easy to understand the benefits of anonymizing candidate profiles, there is some conflicting evidence of its efficacy. According to education and organizational psychology professors Eva Derous and Marie Ryan, hiring managers still pick up on subliminal clues about a candidate's identity, which can lead to continued discrimination and bias.

Here are some challenges to anonymous screening that leaders should be aware of.

Anonymized selection:

- Does not reduce discrimination across the board, but mostly where it is already prevalent

- Limits measures taken to ensure affirmative action

- Removes context, so some information could be misinterpreted without knowing the candidate's background

- Encourages colorblindness when differences can and should be celebrated rather than overlooked

- If not combined with other measures, can simply postpone discriminatory practices until further into the hiring process

As a way to combat selection bias, many organizations and HR teams take steps to anonymize aspects of candidate profiles through a series of measures, whether formally throughout their own applicant tracking system (ATS), or informally at the beginning of their hiring process. In an effort to better understand selection bias during resume screening, Associate Professors of Business Economics and Public Policy at Wharton Judd Kessler and Corinne Low created their Incentivized Resume Rating system. The system asks hiring managers to quantify and rate aspects of a resume with a fake identity attached to it. Then, once the manager has ranked the resumes, a real candidate's resume with a similar profile is forwarded to the hiring manager. Creating an entirely new mechanism for anonymizing resumes may not be a realistic goal for your organization at this time, so we've included some ways you can anonymize applicant profiles without making sweeping changes:

1.   Ask Candidates to Remove Identifying Information from Their Materials Before Submitting

To streamline your anonymization process, you can ask candidates to simply remove key indicators themselves. Katherine McNamee, hiring manager for the Society for Human Resource Management, applied this strategy by asking candidates to remove all identifying information before applying (name, graduation date, address, education). She then assigned each candidate/resume a number to keep track of the profiles. Global risk consultancy Control Risks recognized that in Latin America, it's standard for applicants to include their photos and marital status in their resumes, so it built into its process a step to ask candidates to remove that identifying information before applying.

2. Obscure Candidate Information

Perhaps the easiest way to remove identifying information from resumes is to institute some process to simply cross it off manually. If possible, have someone who is not a part of the hiring process redact the applicant's name, graduation year, and any other information that could potentially trigger a hiring manager's unconscious bias. Mathison offers technology that can help you to anonymize candidate profiles automatically.

3. Standardize Candidate Qualification Entry and Skip Resume Submission

Because it can be difficult to anonymize or limit what a job seeker presents in their resume, and since such information can be subject to bias, many organizations have stopped requesting resumes altogether. Instead, they ask an extremely specific set of questions pertaining to the role's requirements and daily objectives. This allows candidates to share only pertinent information in their application, which helps level the field.

TRAINING YOUR TEAM AND STRUCTURING YOUR PROCESS TO REDUCE BIAS

Selection bias tends to rear its head in multiple spots throughout the hiring process, so mitigating it requires a combination of training and structure. Your goal is to create systems that encourage objective reviewing and independent feedback. Following are three steps to take.

1. Assemble a Panel of Resume Screeners

Having a limited number of initial resume screeners can lead to unintentional selection bias. Most organizations typically have one or two people sifting through applications, deciding whether to advance or pass on candidates in the process. Because we all operate with our own unique recipe of unconscious biases, having so few decision-makers up front can lead to gaps in the selection process. To close some of these gaps, establish a resume-screening panel in which multiple individuals assess each candidate profile. This will ensure resumes and applications are seen through many diverse eyes.

2. Train Your Panel to Assess Materials Objectively

Establish clear guidelines regarding the details your reviewers should be looking for in candidate profiles. By telling your reviewers which specific skills, job titles, or competencies to look for, you increase their chances of finding the best-qualified person and not getting distracted by personal information that has no bearing on qualifications or job performance. You can also use this step to educate your reviewers on the common types of selection bias and how to overcome them.

3. Establish a System for Collecting Feedback Independently from Your Team

Conformity bias—our natural tendency to follow the herd—can be a powerful force when providing candidate feedback as part of a group. To avoid this, establish a process in which reviewers can submit their feedback about a candidate before hearing what the rest of the team has to say. This is a common feature of many applicant tracking systems (e.g., Greenhouse, Workable).

It's important to acknowledge that these steps are not the final stop in eliminating screening and selection bias. Even removing name, graduation date, and other candidate information does not guarantee unbiased and anonymized results. Often the clubs, memberships, or hobbies included in additional resume sections can give enough information about a candidate for a screener to forge unconsciously biased opinions about them. Ultimately, these suggestions should constitute only part of your ongoing anti-bias training.

Using Objective Hiring Assessments

Many organizations committed to reducing bias in the hiring process rely on some form of hiring assessment. Common hiring assessments include knowledge tests, cognitive ability tests, situational judgment tests (SJT), personality tests, or even just requests for a work sample. The idea is to assess a candidate's qualifications for the job independent of their formal education, work history, or personal background.

Large companies with massive hiring needs often use assessments to fill multiple positions at scale, but they can be just as beneficial to smaller companies looking to get a better sense of their candidates' actual skills.

The good news about assessments is that there are many to choose from. Whatever job you are hiring for, it is probably not hard to find an existing knowledge test specifically designed for it. And there are several well-established assessments that focus on more general attributes, such as personality type or judgment. But that abundance can quickly become a burden if you aren't clear about your requirements. Before putting a hiring assessment in front of a candidate and investing time and money in analyzing the results, make sure you clearly understand the priorities for that position. Identifying the knowledge, skills, abilities, and other characteristics for every open role will give you a better idea of what to assess and how. This is one reason why it's so vital that you take the time to craft accurate, thoughtful job descriptions (see Chapter 5 for more information).

When using any pre-employment assessment, there are a few things to keep in mind to ensure you are taking an inclusive and accessible approach:

- Ensure you're using the same test under the same conditions for all candidates for a given position. Make sure whatever test you use is job-related and an accurate predictor of performance in the job (should be valid and reliable).

- Be accommodating to applicants with disabilities by modifying the test or testing conditions or eliminating the testing requirement altogether.

- Make sure pre-employment tests are not the only deciding factor in the hiring process.

Here are a few examples of areas to assess and their respective hiring assessments:

Area	Skills to measure	Example assessments
Personality and behavior	1. Behavioral fit 2. Attitudes and motivation 3. Work style	**Situational judgment tests** (SJT) illustrate how an employee may respond to certain workplace situations. Berke personality test captures a candidate's thinking style and disposition by measuring a group of traits.
Cognitive and aptitude	1. Problem-solving skills 2. Adaptability 3. Interpersonal communication	**Criteria Cognitive Aptitude Test** (CCAT) measures an individual's ability to solve problems, digest and apply information, learn new skills, and think critically. **Cognitive ability test** is broken into five subtests that measure spatial awareness, numerical reasoning, and other such skills.

Area	Skills to measure	Example assessments
Skills assessment	1. Data analysis 2. Specific program skills (Microsoft Office, programming languages, etc.) 3. Computer literacy	**Codility** tests programming and coding skills of tech applicants, reducing the need to include years of experience or degree requirements on a job posting. **eSkill computer skills assessments** can be tailored to your role's needs, which means they can assess basic computer literacy skills like email and internet proficiency or more advanced topics such as hardware.
Sales assessment	1. Emotional intelligence 2. Interpersonal skills 3. Basic sales skills	**Emotify** is a useful assessment for sales positions and managerial roles. It assesses a candidate's ability to read and understand emotions. **Employee Select Sales Skills Assessment** places applicants in common sales scenarios. Results are then tabulated and recommendations are made for training.
Leadership and supervisory	1. Management style 2. Delegation approach	**Employee Personality Profile (EPP)** was created by CriteriaCorp and assesses leadership qualities through managerial questions. **Pymetrics** is a unique assessment platform that gamifies hiring assessments. It doesn't have traditionally "correct" answers but builds a candidate profile based on their process.

Building Awareness to Personally Address Bias

We surveyed a group of recruiters to find the 10 most common reasons that candidates are disqualified at the onset of the hiring process. These were the top responses:

- Age

- Gender

- Gaps in employment

- Unimpressive LinkedIn profile

- Education or institutions attended

- Too much time at one employer

- Too little time at any employer, "jumpy" record

- Lack of industry experience

- Not visibly diverse

- Need for visa sponsorship

It is shocking, if not surprising, to see that the two most commonly cited reasons are also among the most problematic. Clearly, stereotypes and assumptions about age and gender are still actively preventing people from even obtaining interviews for jobs that they are qualified to hold.

Less obvious is the implicit bias that leads some recruiters to disqualify people who have spent too much or too little time at one employer. The truth is, working parents and other underrepresented groups often have to change jobs frequently, or stay in a job longer than they would prefer, for reasons that have nothing to do with their qualifications or competence. Though the recruiter may have the best intentions, focusing on such aspects of a candidate's profile perpetuates the systemic bias that keeps such groups from advancing in the workforce.

Likewise, the preference for candidates who don't require a visa sponsorship likely has nothing to do with personal animosity against refugees or immigrants. The sponsorship process adds a layer of expense and complexity that most employers would rather avoid. Nonetheless, that preference represents a significant obstacle for marginalized communities—and prevents organizations from achieving their diversity and inclusion goals.

Immigrants and refugees also face an unfair obstacle when it comes to education. Employers may place less value on educational institutions they've never heard of, even those that may be academically superior to more familiar American universities. This also affects millions of candidates who, for purely financial or family reasons, have pursued higher education through more affordable state colleges, bootcamps, or certificate programs.

These misguided preferences are just a few of the more than 150 types of biases that eliminate qualified people during the initial screening process. For now, we will focus on twelve biases that most commonly show up in the selection process and how to address them.

Affinity Bias

Despite being widely known and documented, affinity bias remains one of the most insidious types of unconscious bias in the workplace. Put simply, affinity bias is the very human tendency to *favor people who share similar interests, experiences, or backgrounds as ourselves*. But however innocent this urge may be, the result—replicated countless times by innumerable decision makers—is an organization, or even an industry, that is made up almost entirely of demographically, ethnically, and socioeconomically similar people.

Overcoming affinity bias is hard enough when we focus on our own individual decisions. But over time, affinity bias has become institutionalized; hiring teams today look to hire or advance people who are a "culture fit" or who "share our core values." Too often, that translates into someone who shares similar interests, experiences, or backgrounds as those on the hiring team, such as going to the same university or growing up playing the same sport. This sort of bias rears its head any time we deem something non-work-related to be a determining factor in a candidate's suitability. This type of bias can be especially challenging for hiring managers to combat, because they will be the ones working directly with this person.

Recommendations:

- When interviewing, stick to your script. Resist the urge to bond with candidates over non-work-related activities, experiences, or preferences.

- Use predetermined evaluation criteria.

- Keep a pad nearby to jot down any similarities you share with the candidate. When making decisions, be aware what role those similarities may be playing in your judgment.

- Instead of "culture fit," think in terms of "culture add." Rather than looking for someone who shares your core values, consider what desirable values a candidate could introduce.

Affect Heuristics

One of us (we're not saying who) once had a boyfriend named Dan. Things did not end well with Dan, so now, when we meet someone named Dan, we have an instant negative reaction. We know it's nonsensical, and we're not proud of it. But we're willing to bet that you, too, know someone who forever spoiled a particular name for you.

Sometimes, we characterize these knee-jerk preferences as "following our gut." In reality, it's our brain taking mental shortcuts, making associations from subtle or peripheral cues instead of doing the hard work of getting to know someone. For example, the woman with the forearm tattoo isn't executive material. Or worse, the overweight man is lazy. We call this affect heuristics and, left unchecked, it can disqualify all sorts of perfectly qualified individuals and contribute to a homogenous workplace.

To overcome this bias, it's important that you rely on evidence and reasoning—not your gut—to support any negative feedback you may have about a candidate's suitability.

Recommendations:

- Assess your gut: Write down the reasons why you don't like the candidate. Forcing yourself to write it down may reveal how silly the reasons are.

- Use a scorecard to assess candidates so you're only assessing areas related to the job.

Attribution Bias

When someone cuts you off in traffic, do you assume they are rude and selfish, or consider that they might be experiencing a medical emergency? For most of us, the answer is the former. The truth is, we are quick to judge the actions of others harshly without knowing the whole story. Attribution bias occurs when you judge someone's behavior based on your own assumptions and experiences. This can cause recruiters and hiring managers to decide that a candidate is not suitable for a job purely because of something peculiar or unusual that the candidate did. For example, if a candidate shows up late to a video interview with a wrinkled shirt and messy hair, attribution bias may lead you to conclude that they lack personal hygiene, or didn't prioritize the meeting. But the reality could be that they are a working parent who was rushing to fix lunch for their children before joining the call.

Recommendations:

- Instead of making assumptions, give candidates the benefit of the doubt.

- Ask clarifying questions. Interviewees are likely nervous and may stumble over their words. Asking clarifying questions will help them share the whole story.

Confirmation Bias

We all have preconceived notions about what makes a person hard-working, or tough, or sophisticated, or even worthy of respect. People who went to Harvard are smart. Military veterans are gritty. Dog owners are gregarious; cat owners are introverts. New Yorkers are rude; Californians are laid back. Confirmation bias occurs when we look for clues to confirm our assumptions rather than try to see past them.

When we review resumes, we are essentially reading the timeline of someone's life. We can't help but pick up on subtle cues, like what college they attended or where they were born, that we use to create an image of this person in our head. This is a prime reason that 60 percent of interviewers will make a decision about a candidate's suitability within fifteen minutes of meeting them, and 26 percent do so in just the first five minutes.

Once this happens, an interviewer may spend the rest of the interview asking questions designed to elicit answers that support their initial judgment about that person. This is confirmation bias in action. Frequently, it's an unconscious attempt to preserve our concept of intelligence, to seek details that promote our initial assumptions and prove our ability to see the truth. But it ultimately prevents us from seeing the whole person sitting in front of us.

Recommendations:

- Create a list of predetermined, standardized questions ahead of time.

- Create questions that are skills-based, behavioral, or situational.

- Stick to a consistent script that's used for all candidates applying for a given position.

Conformity Bias

It's an inevitable aspect of any group setting: Some people will voice their opinions more loudly and forcefully than others. Conformity bias is the natural tendency of others to agree with those people—or people with more authority, or simply with the majority—due to fear of confrontation. This is more casually known as succumbing to peer pressure.

Now, think about how people in your organization share their feedback about job candidates. Is it in a group setting? Are some people in that room consistently more talkative than others? Do some people in that room report to other people in that room? If so, your organization may be unnecessarily subjecting itself to conformity bias.

Conformity bias can be particularly detrimental when some people in the room have not had a chance to even meet the candidate yet. Hearing their colleagues' opinions will almost certainly prime them to approach the interview with preconceived notions about the candidate, potentially excluding a qualified person through no fault of their own.

Recommendations:

- Ask interviewers to submit their feedback immediately, and privately, after the interview.

- If possible, set up your applicant tracking system (ATS) so that interviewers are not allowed to view feedback until they've written their own.

- Avoid group settings when sharing feedback on candidates until everyone has formed their own opinion, and then take pains to encourage quieter people in the room to share their previously stated opinions.

Contrast Effect

Rarely do we (or should we) interview just one person for a job. But once you are considering more than one candidate, you will inevitably fall prey to the contrast effect. Rather than judging each candidate on their own merits, you judge them primarily in contrast to the other candidates—particularly those whose interviews came immediately before or after theirs. Thus a candidate who interviewed after a weak interviewee on Tuesday will seem like a better option than an identical candidate who interviewed after a strong interviewee on Wednesday.

Recommendations:

- Space out your interviews so they aren't back to back and write down feedback as soon as you complete the interview.

- Make sure you have an objective scorecard with predetermined evaluation criteria in place so you aren't rating candidates against each other but rather against the job itself.

Type of bias	Definition	Example	Tactics to address
Affinity bias	To favor those who share similar interests or background to you	The candidate and I went to the same school. I like this candidate because we have XYZ in common.	Physically jot down any similarities you share with the candidate. Look for "culture add" versus "culture fit."
Affect heuristics	Taking mental shortcuts, aka going with your gut feeling	I have a gut feeling on this candidate. I glanced at the candidate's profile and am concerned about XYZ.	Assess your gut—write down the reasons why you don't like the candidate. Use an objective scorecard.
Attribution bias	Using an observation to determine a candidate is unfit for the job	The candidate didn't make a great first impression.	Don't make assumptions, and ask clarifying questions.
Confirmation bias	Drawing conclusions based on your personal beliefs and prejudices rather than merit	The candidate has a negative quality that is exactly what I'd expect from a New Yorker.	Create a list of predetermined, standardized, skills-based questions ahead of time.

Type of bias	Definition	Example	Tactics to address
Conformity bias	To act similar to the people around you regardless of your own beliefs—aka succumbing to peer pressure	It looks like the group all prefers one candidate so I'll hold off on sharing feedback.	Ask interviewers to submit their feedback immediately after the interview. Don't allow interviewers to view feedback until they've written their own.
Contrast effect	Comparing candidates to one another, instead of measuring their skills and potential for success	I prefer this candidate over the one we just interviewed.	Space out your interviews and write down feedback as soon as you complete the interview.

Below are a few more examples of common hiring biases to be aware of:

Type of bias	Definition	Example	Tactics to address
Name bias	Favoring those with certain kinds of names—typically Anglo American	Choosing *not* to give interviews to individuals with ethnic-sounding names	Anonymize profiles by removing names via Google Chrome extensions.
Beauty bias	The belief that attractive people are more successful, competent, and qualified	When you're more likely to choose the candidate you find more attractive regardless of their skills	Stick to phone interviews in the initial screening and first-round interviews.

(continued)

Type of bias	Definition	Example	Tactics to address
Anti-immigrant bias	To view immigrants as unqualified due to language and cultural barriers	Not moving forward with a candidate due to a perceived lack of American workplace etiquette or social skills	Evaluation criteria is especially important here so we don't let bias influence our perception of a candidate.
Stereotype bias	To filter information in a way that reinforces the stereotypes we unconsciously believe in	Asking candidates questions only related to a community they appear to identify with	Educate yourself on the most common stereotypes to actively avoid this way of thinking.
Halo effect	Using a positive trait to overshadow everything else	Favoring a candidate of dubious qualifications because they are familiar with an important client of yours	Assess the candidate without the one attribute that makes them a "unicorn" and see if you still feel the same way about them.
Horn effect	Using a negative trait to overshadow everything else	Disqualifying a candidate because they are unfamiliar with software your company relies on	Focus on the objective skills and qualifications of the candidate profile.
Anchor bias	Relying too heavily on one initial piece of information to make a decision	Overlooking a candidate's flaws because you discovered early on that they interned at an impressive company	Focus on the complete scorecard to assess the full candidate profile and how well they meet the requirements.

ADDRESSING BIAS THROUGH TECHNOLOGY AND RISKS WITH AI

An applicant tracking system (ATS) can be a useful tool for maintaining best practices in hiring policies. Once you've selected and implemented the ATS that best meets the needs of your organization, it's important to consider how the tool can be used to remove bias from your hiring process. It's just as vital, though, to consider any potential areas of bias in the tool that may be disadvantageous to some candidates.

Many applicant tracking systems anonymize candidate profiles by default. If yours doesn't, we strongly recommend enabling this feature. Most systems can mask the following candidate attributes until they have made it to the interview round: name, date of birth, address, university/school, gender, ethnicity, email address, and social media links. These anonymization measures allow hiring managers to focus on the candidate without being influenced by their own innate biases.

As mentioned in the previous section, implementing an independent feedback system is vital to eliminating conformity bias in the hiring process. Luckily, many ATS platforms already include independent feedback tools for members of a hiring committee to gather their thoughts individually about a candidate before risking groupthink in deliberative conversations.

Algorithmic hiring programs have recently entered the conversation with regard to risks of addressing bias. Originally intended to eliminate human bias, algorithms in the hiring process still have a long way to go in terms of reducing selection bias. According to recent research, algorithmic hiring processes eliminate human biases to an extent. However, it is extremely important to create and maintain algorithmic programming with a diverse set of inputs. If you train an algorithm on homogenous data samples, the program will operate under these rules and not help to diversify the process. Data and people analytics scientist Bo Cowgill refers to this phenomenon as "unrepresentative training data." Some studies even suggest that some uses of machine learning and hiring algorithms actually promote further discrimination.

Amazon's machine learning team had been building systems to streamline their recruiting process. The goal was to identify the top 5 percent of applicants from a large application pool. Despite their well-intentioned efforts, they discovered a major problem: The system's screening cues were based on historical job performance data that represented a pattern of bias against women workers. When sourcing candidates for a software developer role, the artificial intelligence (AI) recruiting tool used a data-based algorithm model to examine data patterns of the previous applicant pool and successful hires to determine selection cues for future hires. Because the technology profession is a male-dominated industry, the pattern showed that successful hires were typically men, so the tool detected this pattern and began to place a higher preference for men applicants than women applicants. It even went the extra mile and disregarded candidates that had the word "women" on their resume (e.g., "president of the women's coding team"). This meant applicants who attended all women's colleges were also at a disadvantage.

After attempting to fix these mistakes, Amazon scrapped the tool altogether, accepting that there was no guarantee that the AI system wouldn't find other ways to be biased against underrepresented groups. Unfortunately, Amazon may not be the only company that experienced limitations with automation and AI. To work toward diverse and equitable selection, your hiring team should be more diverse (not from the same background or team). Using an external auditor can help screen for biased information fed through software or a program, as well. Hiring software is not a prescriptive solution but should be supplemented with further research and evaluation throughout the hiring cycle.

FIRST STEP TOWARD IMPACT

To reduce bias in the hiring process, leaders must be willing to step back and take an honest assessment of their organization's full hiring process, including the drivers behind each decision. Only by doing this hard work can you develop a full roadmap to minimizing pervasive bias in your process, thereby unlocking opportunities to ensure greater fairness.

One action you can take immediately is to schedule time after your next few hiring decisions to conduct a post-mortem with the hiring team on the drivers behind their decisions. If everyone feels good about their choices, it's logical and helpful to ask them how they landed there.

Was there any bias that presented itself in the team's decision—or yours—to pass on a candidate? Creating the space for this sort of analysis will be illuminating for your future decisions. And the exercise will inevitably spark dialogue among stakeholders to make sure you're all moving forward with aligned intention, versus simply assuming the motives behind teammate decisions. The time you invest in these discussions should clear out a lot of cobwebs, expose vulnerabilities, and provide a cleaner slate for fairness.

To access additional resources and download the tables and charts from this chapter visit: http://Mathison.io/Book.

REFERENCES

Bortz, Daniel. "Can Blind Hiring Improve Workplace Diversity?" SHRM. August 16, 2019. https://www.shrm.org/hr-today/news/hr-magazine/0418/pages/can-blind-hiring-improve-workplace-diversity.aspx.

"Confirmation Bias—Definition & Examples." Decision Lab. February 26, 2021. https://thedecisionlab.com/biases/confirmation-bias/.

Cowgill, Bo, and Catherine E. Tucker. "Algorithmic Fairness and Economics." Columbia Business School Research Paper. February 14, 2020. Available at SSRN: https://ssrn.com/abstract=3361280 or http://dx.doi.org/10.2139/ssrn.3361280.

Dastin, Jeffrey. "Amazon Scraps Secret AI Recruiting Tool That Showed Bias against Women." *Reuters.* October 10, 2018. https://www.reuters.com/article/us-amazon-com-jobs-automation-insight/amazon-scraps-secret-ai-recruiting-tool-that-showed-bias-against-women-idUSKCN1MK08G.

Derous, E., and A. M. Ryan. "When Your Resume Is (Not) Turning You Down: Modelling Ethnic Bias in Resume Screening." *Hum Resour Manag J.* 29 (2019): 113–130. https://doi.org/10.1111/1748-8583.12217.

Frieder, R. E., C. H. Van Iddekinge, and P. H. Raymark. "How Quickly Do Interviewers Reach Decisions? An Examination of Interviewers' Decision-Making Time across Applicants." *J Occup Organ Psychol* 89(2016): 223–248. https://doi.org/10.1111/joop.12118.

"Pre-Employment Personality Assessments." Berke. Accessed March 24, 2021. https://www.berkeassessment.com/solutions/personality-testing? utm_source=adwords&utm_medium=cpc&utm_campaign=nonbran ddyanmicsearch&utm_term=&utm_content=111704167593&gclid= CjwKCAiAz4b_BRBbEiwA5XlVViufkBX98g7aTExchqQVmTL8 HvytcEF9DHS9zebhIQl7IpF5YJLnLhoCRaYQAvD_BwE.

"Research: How Companies Committed to Diverse Hiring Still Fail." *Harvard Business Review*. February 11, 2021. https://hbr.org/2021/02/research-how-companies-committed-to-diverse-hiring-still-fail.

Varshneya, Rahul. "Do Hiring Algorithms Prevent Bias or Amplify It and How to Get It Right?" Sourcing and Recruiting News. August 17, 2020. https://recruitingdaily.com/do-hiring-algorithms-prevent-bias-or-amplify-it-and-how-to-get-it-right/#:~:text=Hiring%20algorithms%20 optimize%20results%20for,data%20being%20fed%20to%20it.

"Visual Capitalist Cognitive Bias Codex." Visual Capitalist. Accessed March 24, 2021. https://www.visualcapitalist.com/wp-content/uploads/2017/09/ cognitive-bias-infographic.html.

"Why Do Recruiters Spend Only 7.4 Seconds on Resumes?" Ladders. October 7, 2020. https://www.theladders.com/career-advice/why-do-recruiters-spend-only-7-4-seconds-on-resumes.

CHAPTER 8

Developing Fair Interviews

There is no part of the hiring process to which we dedicate more time, energy, or scrutiny than interviews. They are the focal point for most hiring decisions and often the most stressful part of the process for candidates. They also present the greatest risk for potential bias across the entire hiring process.

When home audio manufacturer Sonos set out to advance its diversity recruiting efforts in 2020, the company immediately recognized a need to overhaul its interview process. The company's GC and Chief Diversity and Inclusion Officer, Alaina Kwasizur, and her team assessed Sonos's full hiring process, revealing an unstructured and largely improvisational approach to interviews that left team members feeling unsupported. Employees who were tasked with interviewing candidates were routinely asking for guidance on how to navigate interviews so they could more confidently make decisions they knew would be consistent with the company's values, culture, and expectations.

Kwasizur and her team knew that a lot was riding on getting the interview process right, not only to create a more equitable experience for job seekers, but to give team members the support and confidence they needed to know that they were making the right decisions.

But they also knew that their new approach would have to leave room for creativity. They didn't want interviews to feel stiff or for interviewers to feel boxed in by overly burdensome strictures. Like Sonos itself, they wanted the interviews to feel unique, reflecting the passion and vision that helped define the pioneering brand.

Kwasizur and her team developed a new interview process structured around the company's core behaviors: *Respect, Ownership Collaboration, and Transparency*. Dubbed *Inclusive by Design*, the new process gave Sonos team members a consistent method to guide their interviews, with a set of questions designed for each of the company's focus areas. But it also allowed for creativity, giving interviewers the freedom to make up their own questions depending on the unique circumstances of each role and candidate. As the final step of the process, Sonos made room for the qualitative evaluation of candidates so interviewers could factor in candidate behaviors rather than be confined to a rigid numerical scale.

Kwasizur's group educated the team on the purpose of the new process and saw immediate improvement for candidates and team members alike. In assessing the benefits, she noted, "Our new structure for inclusive interviews enabled candidates to immediately get a feel for Sonos and our values while giving our managers a more consistent and objective way to avoid pitfalls of abstract judgements."

WHY FAIR INTERVIEWS MATTER

The selection bias that we explored in Chapter 7 often comes to bear most visibly during the interview process, and interviews will largely determine the success or failure of your diversity hiring initiatives. If you are serious about diversifying your workforce, you owe it to yourself to take a hard look at how your organization conducts interviews.

Interviews are your "main event" in the hiring process, that moment when you and the candidate will have the most meaningful opportunity to learn what it's like to work together. Interviews encompass the greatest amount of time you will spend with the candidates and represent the most critical variable to influence hiring decisions. The interview experience is also one of the most influential factors for job seekers when they decide whether to accept your job offer.

However, for most organizations, interviews also represent the least structured and most subjective part of the hiring process. Many recruiters and hiring managers report feeling confident improvising their approach to interviews and not establishing a consistent interview structure, in part because they've been doing it that way for so long. This commonly translates to interviewers not taking the time before interviews to review the candidate profiles, determine what they're looking for in a candidate, or even decide what questions they will ask.

Not only does the improvisational approach leave significant room for bias, but it disrespects the candidate. Think back to a time that you really wanted a job and how much preparation you did for that interview. Now picture the interviewer barely bothering to come up with any questions before you arrived, or ushering in a competing applicant before you were out the door. How would that have affected your feelings about the job? Or the organization? It's important to remember that candidates are interviewing you just as much as you are interviewing them, and unprepared, meandering, or disorganized interviews reflect poorly on your organization.

Although many leaders prefer the informal approach to interviews, multiple studies have shown that this style of interviewing elicits little useful information about future work performance and increases the likelihood of biased decision-making. Unstructured interviews ultimately create inconsistency and ambiguity, which makes it difficult to fairly assess candidates. Taking time to establish a more deliberate and structured interview process will greatly reduce your susceptibility to bias in the long run.

Developing fair interviews at your organization should be a group project. Think of this as an opportunity to galvanize your team around your diversity goals. Remember, no one likes to be told what they can or can't say. But by engaging your team, getting their input, and determining an approach that works for everyone, you will give them a sense of ownership over the process, and they will be more likely to embrace it. There's no point in developing a structured interview format if your interviewers resist using it, or are visibly uncomfortable with it, when they're alone with the candidate.

ASSESSING HOW FAIR AND STRUCTURED YOUR INTERVIEWS ARE

Conducting job interviews can be a bit like driving: everyone thinks they are better than average.

We all like to think that we have our own, unique interview style, and that it's more effective than most everyone else's. We think that when we walk into that room, we know what we are looking for, whether it's a strict adherence to the job description or some intangible inner quality. We also tend to have our own ideas about which candidates will fit best with the company's culture and how much weight we should give to factors like diversity. One reason the improvisational approach has proved so enduring is that most people—especially those for whom conducting interviews is central to their career—don't think they need any help.

The results suggest this is simply not the case. If we were all as good at interviewing as we like to believe, we would all be meeting our diversity and inclusion goals. Still, bear in mind when assessing your interview process that, for your stakeholders, this may be a very personal issue. Take care to approach the assessment as a necessary and constructive procedural step, not a rebuke of anyone's performance.

At most organizations, it should be pretty clear who your stakeholders are here. Usually it will be hiring managers with HR providing support and guardrails. Given their central role, it's vital that hiring managers are given a voice in developing a new approach, which should then get solidified by leadership and clearly communicated back to those hiring managers.

As you assess your existing process to explore where you have an opportunity to create a more fair and structured experience, consider these questions:

- Does everyone in your organization have a clear sense of what your interview process is today?

- Do you schedule time before and after interviews to prepare and review?

- Do you predetermine what criteria you will use to assess candidates?

- Have you scripted your interview questions?

- Have you developed an interview scorecard with some level of objective ratings?

- Have you created mechanisms for independent interview feedback?

- Are your interview panels diverse and representative?

- Do you have a process in place to follow up with all interviewees to give them feedback afterwards?

- Do you take steps to ask interviewees how inclusive their interview experience was and ways you can improve your process?

For additional resources to assess your diversity hiring efforts visit: http://Mathison.io/Index.

If you've answered no to anything here, you have the beginnings of a roadmap for reducing bias and creating a more equitable interview experience. Even if you aren't in a position to directly influence your organization's interview practices, you can still make changes to the way you personally approach interviews.

Whatever changes you set out to make, you are hopefully excited about incorporating more structure and formality to your interviews. Applicants are dressing up and stepping up to show you their best selves; you now have the chance to do the same, with the same intentionality and open mind as them.

How to Structure Your Interview Process

There is no universal template for a structured job interview. Your approach to interviews should authentically reflect your organization. Interviews are a direct representation of your organization's culture, values, and team, so you should make sure you are happy with what they are saying—intentionally and otherwise—about your organization.

Remember, this is a process that you will ultimately depend on your team members to implement, so it's important to take the necessary steps up front to make sure it feels right for them. That means striking a balance between providing enough structure to ensure consistency and leaving enough room for creativity.

As you prepare for your structured interviews, keep in mind that effective structured interviews include the following three components:

- **Structuring your time.** Use the same relevant interview script and assessments for all candidates for a particular role to ensure fairness. Don't deviate!

- **Relevant assessment.** Look at the job description and prepare an assessment approach directly related to the responsibilities.

- **Evaluating your candidates.** Avoid bias by developing a scorecard that allows you to evaluate each candidate for a particular role using the same criteria.

Scheduling Your Time

We've all done it. We rush into an interview in the middle of a hectic day, barely thinking about it beforehand, and immediately running to another, unrelated meeting afterwards. Then, when we revisit that candidate later—hours, days, even weeks in the future—our memory of the interview is faded and inexact.

Though this pattern is common and understandable—for most of us, hiring is just one of many responsibilities—it ultimately does you, your organization, and the candidate a disservice. Good candidates take time to prepare for interviews; as employers, we owe them the courtesy of our full attention and consideration. More important, rushing into an interview without preparation, or not leaving time to finalize feedback, can lead to inconsistency and leave you vulnerable to bias.

To make your hiring process as consistent and structured as possible, we recommend having every interviewer schedule time *before* the interview to finalize the structure, questions, and script, and *afterwards* to evaluate the candidate and provide feedback while it is all still fresh and top of mind. An easy tactic to implement is to block off 15 to 20 minutes before and after each interview to allow for prep and feedback time.

It's also tempting to schedule interviews back-to-back, but we highly recommend against this. Seeing candidates one after another, with few breaks in between, increases your chances of succumbing to comparison and contrast effect bias. By intentionally spacing out interviews and leaving time to finalize feedback before preparing for the next interview or meeting, you are allowing yourself to evaluate candidates independent of one another, ensuring a more objective process.

Sample Interview Schedule

Interview component	Actions	30-minute interview slot	60-minute interview slot
Interviewer preparation	Review job posting and create a list of questions, as well as some predetermined probing questions. Familiarize yourself with questions and script. Determine your evaluation criteria and create the scorecard. Review candidate's application materials.	15–20 minutes before interview	15–20 minutes before interview
Opening/ introduction	Introduce yourself; allow candidate to do the same. Go over the interview schedule/plan.	3 minutes	5 minutes
Explanation of role and company	Clarify the need for the role and how it relates to the business. Emphasize the key functions and responsibilities of the position. Briefly describe the company if you feel there is time.	4 minutes	5–7 minutes

(continued)

Interview component	Actions	30-minute interview slot	60-minute interview slot
Behavioral questions	Ask questions as written and in their intended order. Take notes as the candidate answers so you can refer to this when completing the scorecard later.	8 minutes	15 minutes
Situational questions	Same as previous step	8 minutes	15 minutes
Time for candidate to ask questions	Close by thanking the candidate and providing them with the opportunity to ask you any questions.	5 minutes	15 minutes
Closing/exit	Thank the candidate for their time. Explain the timeline and next steps (what to expect). *Optional:* Provide the candidate with feedback.	2 minutes	2 minutes
Interviewer evaluates and completes independent feedback form	Dedicate some time after the interview to fill out the candidate's scorecard. Write down any remaining thoughts and impressions. Do not discuss feedback with other interviewers until it's time.	15 minutes after interview ends	15 minutes after interview ends

Deciding What You Want to Assess

Your first step in designing an interview is deciding what you want to get out of it. What qualities are you looking for in a candidate? What sort of temperament, skills, and aptitudes are required for success in the role? The better your questions are designed to elicit the insights you need, the greater the likelihood they will help you make the right decisions.

Luckily, you're not starting from scratch here. Remember that beautifully inclusive and specific job description from Chapter 5? Let your own job description be your guide when preparing for the interview. When deciding what to assess, keep that list of responsibilities and expectations in front of you. That should help keep you on track to look for the most important behaviors and competencies during the interview.

But we do not suggest doing this alone! We all have our individual blind spots and biases. Establishing interview criteria as a group helps to avoid those pitfalls and to make sure you're not inadvertently favoring particular backgrounds or perspectives.

And be careful not to create an assessment list composed entirely of experiences, skills, and education. Personality traits and temperament are also an important part of success in any job. If you're unfamiliar with how to assess such qualities, we recommend consulting the BARS (Behaviorally Anchored Rating Scales) method, which will give you a concrete method for analyzing behaviors. For example, you may be wondering whether your candidate has a positive attitude. Instead of relying on your intuition, BARS shows you how to look for indicators in the candidate's actions (e.g., does the candidate smile and make eye contact? When asked about challenging scenarios, do they remain optimistic in their answers?).

Selecting Your Interview Questions

Most interview questions can be divided into one of two kinds, situational and behavioral. Behavioral questions focus on how the candidate handled themself in previous real-world situations. Situational questions ask how the candidate would handle a hypothetical future situation.

As you prepare for your interview, you should have a fair mix of behavioral and situational questions. Interviewers typically prefer behavioral questions, but situational questions can be more specific measures for a role's responsibilities and daily functions.

Type	What question assesses	Example
Behavioral	Teamwork: allows candidates to show how they work through challenging circumstances with coworkers	"Give me an example of a time you faced a conflict while working on a team. How did you handle that?"
	Client-facing skills: shows how interviewees handle working with clients in an external facing role	"How do you go about prioritizing your customers' needs when you're working with a large number of clients?"
	Adaptability: determines how a candidate engages with an organization dedicated to creativity and innovation	"Describe a time when your team or company was undergoing some change. How did that affect you, and how did you adapt?"
	Motivation and values: provides candidates with the chance to share what drives them and makes them tick	"Tell me about your proudest professional accomplishment."
Situational	Time management: gives interviewees the opportunity to share their strategies for prioritization	"Sometimes it's just not possible to get everything on your to-do list done. What do you do when your responsibilities become a little overwhelming?"
	Communication: asks applicants to consider their communication style and strengths	"If you were going to give an effective presentation, how would you know it was successful?"

Critical thinking: shows how candidates process large amounts of information, data, and details and organize their plan of action	"You notice an error in a communication that has already been sent out to clients. How would you handle this?"

Ensuring Your Interviews Are Compliant

One of the dangers to improvised interviews is the potential for asking inappropriate questions. By adhering to a thoughtfully vetted script, you can avoid questions that might offend the applicant or even run afoul of the law.

Below is a list of topics that are not relevant to employment and therefore have no place in a professional job interview. We have included examples of common questions that fall under these topics, but please remember that these are questions to *avoid*. Instead, consider the alternative suggestions, which can build rapport without violating common standards of diversity and inclusion.

Topic	Don't ask	Try this question instead
Race, color, national origin	"Where are you originally from?"	"I see you work/live in [city]. What's your favorite thing about working/living there?"
Religion	"What are you doing for Christmas this year?"	"Do you have any interesting plans for this week or next?"
Sex, gender identity, sexual orientation	"Do you have a spouse? What does he/she do?"	"What are your pronouns?"
Pregnancy status	"Do you plan on having children?"	"Do you anticipate having to take time off upon starting this role?"

(continued)

Topic	Don't ask	Try this question instead
Disability	"Do you have a disability or any medical conditions?"	"Will you need any accommodations to work here?"
Age or genetic information	"When did you graduate from college?"	"What is the highest level of schooling you've completed to date?" "What interested you in [field of work]?"
Citizenship	"Are you a U.S. citizen?"	"Are you currently authorized to work in the U.S.?"
Marital status or number of children	"Do you have kids?" "Are you married?"	"Are you able to work during our company's regular hours?" "Travel is required for this position. Do you have any responsibilities that may make that challenging for you?"

Developing an Interview Scorecard

An interview scorecard is the most valuable tool you can have at hand during the interview process. Putting in time up front to develop this scorecard will help structure your thinking and evaluation of candidates in a way that is fair and efficient.

Additionally, developing a checklist with preferred (as well as problematic) answers to your interview questions can help you distill exactly what you're looking for.

When used together, both of these tools can help you avoid bias when assessing candidates. They will make it easier for you to evaluate everyone using a common metric instead of your gut feelings or emotional responses.

Below is an example of an interview checklist. As you can see, it accounts for a range of possible answers and includes specific desirable and undesirable responses.

Example Question

Give me an example of a time when you did not meet a customer's expectation. What happened, and how did you attempt to rectify the situation?

Response checklist

Looking for:

❑ Listened
❑ Validated the concern
❑ Explained the reasons/policy
❑ Provided options
❑ Found a creative solution

❑ Asked questions
❑ Managed personal emotions
❑ Found a creative solution

Red flag: Used blaming language

Below is an example of a scorecard we've adapted from the *Harvard Business Review*. Columns 1 and 2 will likely vary depending on what role you're interviewing for, but the structure can remain the same. First, begin with identifying what work habit you're rating the interviewee on. Next, to help you organize your responses, write down questions that correlate to each habit. The third column encourages the hiring manager to quantify a candidate's responses on a predetermined Likert scale. The rating can be adjusted to be numerical or qualitative (e.g., response checklist above). We also encourage leaving a column open at the end for independent interview feedback (see discussion below).

Interview scorecard

Candidate:
Role:
Interviewer:
Date:

Work habit	Question that assesses this habit	Rating on 1–5 scale	Comments/ notes
Time management			
Teamwork			
Communication			
Adaptability			

Strengths: **Opportunities for Growth:**   **Other:**

_____   _____   _____
_____   _____   _____
_____   _____   _____
_____   _____   _____
_____   _____   _____
_____   _____   _____
_____   _____   _____

Ensuring Independent Interview Feedback

Once you've finished the interview, it's important to make a record of your honest impressions quickly and clearly. As discussed in Chapter 7, waiting to give your feedback until you're in a group setting leaves you vulnerable to conformity bias (the tendency to go along with the crowd). And waiting until after you've interviewed other applicants opens the door to the contrast effect (analyzing candidates in relation to one another rather than on their own merits).

Taking time immediately after the interview to record your independent feedback allows you to synthesize and collect your thoughts, to draw your own conclusions about candidates, and—most essential—to have a physical record of those conclusions that you and other stakeholders can refer to as the interview fades from memory. This is an essential step in conducting fair, inclusive interviews.

Writing and reflecting independently can feel cathartic and is an important processing tool for many of us. While this should hold true as you work through your feedback, be sure to write fairly and objectively while maintaining your own voice. Some experts even suggest writing as if your candidate may potentially read your feedback someday. Would they find it fair and objective?

To make sure the interviewer doesn't skip this step, we recommend including an independent feedback section in your interview timeline.

Once you've recorded your thoughts, you can submit your feedback for a debriefing among the hiring committee. This debriefing should take place only after everyone has completed their feedback. Refraining from discussing candidates with your colleagues until after that formal debrief session can make a huge difference in how that applicant is perceived further down the line. Luckily, many applicant tracking systems already possess tools for tracking feedback.

FAIRLY EVALUATING CANDIDATES

After you've conducted your interviews, filled out your independent feedback forms, and distilled your findings in your scorecards, it is time to assess which candidates are the strongest and will move forward. This is often when many of the comparisons and muddled memories come to light, so relying on the recorded feedback will be key. You can choose between a qualitative or quantitative rating system, based on what you believe is best suited to your organization:

> **Qualitative rating** consists of the interviewers' observations of the candidate. While this provides interviewers more freedom to share nuanced opinions, it can make it harder to rank candidates against one another, assess candidates across cohorts, or make a final decision among a candidate group.

Quantitative rating uses a numerical scale to grade the candidates. This makes it easier to compare applicants, which can be useful in the final decision-making process. However, some interviewers find the quantitative scale to be too confining, reductive, or subjective, particularly if the criteria are not clearly defined.

Example assessment area	Qualitative rating	Quantitative rating
Collaboration with Others: Tell me about a time when you effectively collaborated with a team.	**Look for:** Involved others Sought feedback **Red flags:** Attempted to solve problem alone Did not effectively communicate	**How effectively did they collaborate with others?** (1–5)

One method for reducing bias in the evaluation step is to evaluate candidates horizontally. In other words, instead of evaluating a candidate's entire interview before moving on to the next person, evaluate every candidate's answer to question one, then go on to question two, and so forth. This helps reduce extraneous noise and sidestep distracting assumptions like whether candidates "look the part."

ENSURING DIVERSE INTERVIEW PANELS

Imagine going through weeks of interviews for a job you really want and never once seeing someone on the other side of the table who looks like you. Maybe you don't have to imagine.

When interviewers themselves don't represent the communities you are trying to hire, job applicants from underrepresented groups get the message loud and clear: The people deciding your fate do not share your perspective. And maybe this organization doesn't place a high value on hiring underrepresented people. For the company, allowing interviewers to be homogenous means reinforcing blind spots and accepting a less-than-equitable decision-making process.

You can create a more inclusive interview experience for candidates and a fairer decision-making process in your organization by ensuring diverse representation among your interviewer panels. This will help ensure diversity of perspectives and will send an inclusive signal to your candidates. And candidates do notice. Our research shows that 76 percent of underrepresented job seekers have observed a lack of diversity on interview panels, a clear sign that more needs to be done. In 2017, technology company Cisco took up the challenge and launched a Diverse Talent Accelerators Initiative, which created structures to mandate diverse interview panels. This included using inclusive language to minimize bias and prioritizing the gender and ethnic diversity of the recruiting teams for all functions and across all regions of the company. Cisco found that its new diverse interview panels increased the likelihood of Hispanic women advancing through the interview process by 50 percent and African American women by 70 percent.

In 2017, global chemical company BASF Corporation noticed that despite intentions to hire the best candidates from the diverse regional talent market, there was a tendency to hire from the same narrow talent pools. To address the problem, the company implemented a new strategy and practice that required at least 50 percent diversity on both interview panels and candidate slates. To reinforce the new approach, BASF instituted the rule that no interview takes place until they have achieved that 50 percent threshold. Their processed included drawing interviewers from other departments and engaging a robust sourcing strategy to enrich the candidate pool. "We saw a number of instances where our diverse hiring attempts were breaking down at the point of selecting candidates for interview," says BASF VP of HR Ivory Harris. "Having diverse panels and slates were key to turning that around."

Instituting Values-Based Interviews to Advance Diversity

As a company that is built on a foundation of cross-cultural harmony, Airbnb, the online vacation marketplace, has always prioritized diversity in its hiring. But the company found that it struggled to maintain diverse interview groups as the business expanded rapidly around the globe. This was a particular challenge in its technology groups, which were less diverse than the company overall.

The solution was a new values-based interview segment. The company implemented a policy that allowed interview panels to select anyone throughout the organization to serve as "values interviewer," a sort of guest who would come into an interview to ask two questions based on the company's values (belonging, entrepreneurial spirit, and being a great host). Airbnb specifically made an effort to engage members of its existing diverse employees in its ERGs as values-based interviewers.

Each values interviewer would select one or two of Airbnb's values and ask:

- What does this value mean to you?
- What is an example when you have lived by this value?

Airbnb's candidates (as well as the interviewers) now rate this feature as their favorite part of the interview process. Even better, it has improved representation and strengthened Airbnb's culture.

CHANGING DYNAMICS FOR INCLUSIVE INTERVIEWS

Job interviews have been such an integral part of the hiring process for so long that it can be hard to imagine life without them. But today, plenty of forward-thinking companies are finding alternative ways to evaluate potential hires that, depending on the role and organization, might be a better indicator of how someone will actually perform on the job.

Virtual and augmented reality experiences are adding a new dimension to the interview process. Some companies are finding ways to use VR so candidates can experience their company's culture and daily routines without leaving home. This technique can be particularly useful when public health, weather, or disability issues make in-person meetings unfeasible.

If technology is not your thing, one simple way to shift your interview process is to change the scenery. Meeting at a coffee shop instead of your office can put applicants at ease, which may allow them to be more present and engaged in the interview. This is likely to leave a positive impression on a candidate, who, after all, is a potential coworker.

Reengaging Candidates for Feedback after Interviews

Nobody likes to be the bearer of bad news, so too often we avoid calling former candidates to let them know they didn't get the job. Indeed, according to a study Mathison conducted in 2021, 67 percent of underrepresented job seekers said they had completed a job interview and never received feedback.

It's a common misconception that candidates would rather not hear from employers if they didn't get the job. To the contrary, candidates typically feel disrespected and frustrated when they don't hear anything. Remember, you have both invested a lot of time and effort in the process, so it's just common courtesy to share your decision. We've heard countless positive stories from candidates who didn't get the job but still received closure and feedback. And taking the time to reach out could pay off in goodwill if you decide to reengage that person for another job down the road.

Following up with candidates also gives you a chance to get their perspective on your interview process and uncover specific ways you can make it more inclusive. When you make that call, take time to ask the former applicant their feedback on the interview, what their experience was, and what specific ways you could make the process more inclusive and accessible. By continuing to ask, you can continue to refine your approach.

First Step Toward Impact

Job interviews are as important as they are stressful. For applicants, the interview performance can be the difference between a better life or a devastating career setback. For employers, the interview is often where you first catch a glimpse of that dream employee—or make a very expensive mistake. Given that kind of pressure, it's no surprise that the interview is where so many well-meaning diversity initiatives go off the rails.

The single action you can take to make your interview process more conducive to diverse hiring is to relieve some of that pressure. Schedule time before your interview to properly prepare questions and reflect on what you are looking for. And schedule time afterwards to collect your thoughts about the candidate and write down your unvarnished impressions.

This scheduled time will ensure you have a more deliberate experience with the candidate and your insights from the conversation are captured while they are still fresh. And it will allow you to enter the next interview with a clear head, ready to judge each individual applicant on their own merits.

No one expects job interviews to be fun, lighthearted affairs. But the anxiety of interviewing should never include the fear of being judged based on someone's unconscious bias. Taking steps now to remove that toxic element will mean a better experience for candidates and a stronger, more diverse workforce for your organization.

For additional resources and to download the tables and charts from this chapter visit: http://Mathison.io/Book.

REFERENCES

Bohnet, Iris. "How to Take the Bias Out of Interviews." *Harvard Business Review*. April 18, 2016. https://hbr.org/2016/04/how-to-take-the-bias-out-of-interviews?utm_campaign=harvardbiz&utm_source=twitter&utm_medium=social.

Dattner, Ben. "A Scorecard for Making Better Hiring Decisions." *Harvard Business Review*. October 25, 2017. https://hbr.org/2016/02/a-scorecard-for-making-better-hiring-decisions.

"Diverse Talent Accelerators." Accessed March 24, 2021. https://www.cisco.com/c/dam/en_us/about/inclusion-collaboration/diverse-talent-acceleraTor.pdf.

Sassoon, Josh. "How to Write Great Interview Feedback." *Medium*. Thumbtack Design, May 23, 2018. https://medium.com/thumbtack-design/how-to-write-interview-feedback-28d49be8f975.

"2021 Diversity Hiring Report." Mathison. Accessed March 23, 2021. Mathison.io/2021DiversityReport.

CHAPTER 9

Ensuring Equitable Job Offers

Cindy Robbins, Chief of Employee Success at Salesforce, approached CEO Marc Benioff in 2015 with some troubling news. Her team had discovered a deep pay equity gap, specifically among women. Benioff, having focused so much of his energy on creating equity at Salesforce, was shocked, and he committed himself on the spot to addressing the disparity.

Benioff launched an effort to make pay equity adjustments to Salesforce's employee salaries, dedicating more than $3 million to the initiative. He then began speaking publicly about the necessity of addressing pay inequities, sharing his story and showing people how they could drive this change.

But, a year later, Robbins returned to Benioff to report that the very same pay gaps had somehow reemerged. Benioff was stunned. Hadn't they just fixed this issue? How could it be happening again, and so quickly?

It turns out that $3 million and the goodwill of a CEO are no match for the unconscious bias that infiltrates everyday decisions. Robbins and her team discovered that, while leadership was focused on adjusting the salaries of current employees, new job offers and promotions over the last year had quietly rebirthed the very pay equity gaps that existed before.

Benioff knew that, as a company that provides systems to other companies, Salesforce had to address the issue holistically. He and the team hatched a plan that included establishing new job codes, each tied to predefined salary ranges that spanned the full company and fed directly into a fair and consistent process for constructing job offers.

The plan included specific changes to the performance and promotion process to ensure consistency in daily pay-level decisions. After three rounds of auditing, Salesforce had committed more than $8.7 million to leveling the playing field, not just for women, but for people of color as well. Today, Salesforce has a system in place that ensures equitable job offers, and Benioff has learned a valuable lesson: pay equity is an ongoing process that is never truly "solved."

Like Salesforce, many organizations have the best intentions regarding pay equity, but that doesn't always translate to meaningful change. Even after completing an upfront audit to identify the need and performing a reset, pay equity isn't always guaranteed. If initial pay ranges are tied to market rates, but the market itself is inequitable, these ranges can follow the same pattern. Pay equity is ultimately influenced by hundreds of decisions every year regarding job offers and promotions, where lingering bias could quickly widen the gap.

Salesforce taught us that a single-step fix is not enough. To achieve true and lasting pay equity, it must be established from the very start through equitable job offers, and it must then be reinforced intentionally through day-to-day systems and strategies. As with any deeply ingrained systemic issue, meaningfully taking action on pay equity starts with understanding the root of the problem and its impact on society.

UNDERSTANDING THE PROBLEM OF PAY EQUITY

To address the systemic pay inequity that exists today requires understanding its deep origins. If you can grasp the enormity of pay inequity as a problem for the affected communities, as well as society as a whole, you can then better understand how much really hinges on inequitable job offers.

To sum it up simply: Underrepresented communities bear the brunt of pay inequities, and this remains a key indicator of injustice in the workplace. Pay inequity is the most systemic issue of the hiring process, directly influencing how opportunities are created for underrepresented groups and how diverse representation is ultimately reflected in our organizations.

Although much of the media discourse has been focused on pay discrimination between men and women, the pay gap issue goes beyond gender and is very evident when we look at average wages across communities. In 2020, the U.S. Bureau of Labor Statistics reported that the weekly median full-time earnings of Black and Hispanic workers were anywhere from $200 to $600 less per week than white and Asian workers. This culminates in a staggering pay gap of anywhere from $10,000 to $30,000 per year.

Pay inequity is not simply a paycheck-to-paycheck issue; it directly influences the economic divide that exists in society. When women, people of color, and older workers earn less than their colleagues for equal work, these groups are left with fewer assets to buy property, invest in higher education, save for retirement, and pass on wealth to the next generation. This perpetuates a wealth disparity gap and makes it extremely challenging to break the cycle.

The Brookings Institute found that the net worth of an average white household in 2016 was $171,000, nearly ten times greater than that of a Black family ($17,150). And the gap widens even further. Statistics suggest that the intersectionality of race, gender, ability, and age directly translate to greater pay inequity, so underrepresented job seekers, especially women of color, face an uphill battle for equitable pay.

Equitable pay across your organization is the single most quantifiable indicator of inclusion. Not only can inequity in pay perpetuate a cycle of systemic disparity that exists in the workforce at large, but it can also have a devastating emotional effect on your people. When workers are underpaid, they feel unseen, underappreciated, and disempowered. Getting this right means making your people feel that they are respected, treated fairly, and valued by your organization.

UNDERSTANDING THE GENDER PAY GAP

A visible example of income inequality is the enduring gender pay gap in the U.S. Research from Lean In—the women's empowerment organization founded by Facebook COO Sheryl Sandberg—shows that on average, women in the U.S. earn 18 percent less than men in the workplace. This translates to an annual income gap of about $10,000 for working women, which can accumulate to nearly a million dollars over the course of a career. Even more notable is the geographic range of this gender gap: Women living in Wyoming make 63 percent of what men make in the same state. And this gender wage gap goes well beyond the United States: The same study reveals that women around the world collectively make 23 percent less than men. When we account for other factors such as workforce participation and access to credit, it is estimated that it would take a staggering 257 years to reach full gender parity.

One concerning factor in the gender pay gap is the influence of education level. Over the past few decades, women have consistently been graduating from college at higher rates than men. But surprisingly, research shows the higher a woman's degree, the deeper her earnings gap becomes relative to men with the same credentials. For example, women with a bachelor's degree earn 24 percent less than men, while women with an advanced degree earn 27 percent less. This not only disincentivizes women to pursue higher education, but it undoubtedly fuels a level of frustration for women who have invested years in their education.

Women's pay inequities are also greatly influenced by the way they are perceived and the unconscious bias they face within organizations. The *New York Times* found that women's attempts to negotiate salaries or pursue pay raises can often be met with an unfounded perception that they are overly demanding or unlikable. This often dissuades women from making any such attempts in the first place. Meanwhile, men, who are not bound by any such biased perceptions, continue to ask for and receive pay increases. Furthermore, bias and pay inequity often mount for women as they leave and reenter the workforce due to childcare responsibilities or seek lower-paying jobs that offer more flexibility to manage a family.

The gender pay gap is also influenced by the perception women have of negotiation, shaped largely by racial and cultural norms. For example, women from collectivistic cultures (including many East Asian and Latin American countries), where values such as respect for social hierarchy and self-sacrifice are more pronounced, may be less comfortable engaging in negotiation compared to women from individualistic societies like the U.S. or Canada.

UNDERSTANDING THE RACIAL PAY GAP

While the gender wage gap is arguably the most discussed example of workplace pay inequity, the disparity becomes even greater when we factor in race. Workplace racial bias remains rife in corporate America, and it continues to place people of color at an economic disadvantage over their white counterparts at every level. Data scientists have found that for every dollar earned by a white man, Black and Latinx men made only $0.51 and $0.73, respectively. When taking into account the proportionately larger number of incarcerated and unemployed Black men, the wage gap today between Black men and white men is just as wide as it was in 1950.

As significant as the pay gap is for women, it's far worse for women of color. A study by Payscale, a compensation and data software company, shows that a Black woman with the same job and qualifications as a white man would need to repeat 2020 2.2 times to catch up to that man's lifetime earnings. Overall, Asian men and women earn higher than their white, Black, and Latinx counterparts. However, a significant wage gap exists among Asian Americans, with Indian and Chinese Americans earning more than their Korean American and Vietnamese American counterparts.

The table below provides insight into the wage disparities among underrepresented communities and can serve as a starting point for discussions in your workplace.

Race	Women's % of earnings relative to white men	Men of color % of earnings relative to white men	Details
Latinx	55%	73%	This 55% figure accounts for an average of $1.1 million lost over a lifetime.
Native American	60%	87%	This 60% figure is an average across many different tribes. The gap is inconsistent across tribes; some women make 31% of a white man's earnings.
Black	63%	51% *Takes into account disproportionate incarceration rates among Black men.*	Four out of five Black women are the main earners in their family. This disparity further deepens long-term wealth disparities.
White	78%	N/A	This figure could cover 14 months of the median U.S. cost of rent.
Asian	87%	115%	Overall, Asian workers have a higher median income than white, Black, and Latinx workers. However, the income gap among Asian workers is the widest within any single racial group.

PAY EQUITY FACING OTHER COMMUNITIES

Communities defined by race, gender, and ethnicity are not the only ones facing a steep and rising pay inequity.

Research has shown that incarceration alone reduces a person's access to a steady job and income and is also correlated with slower-than-average wage growth. But for Black and Latinx individuals, the consequences can be even more dire. Based on current trends and rates of the U.S. criminal legal system, one in three Black men and one in six Latino men will be incarcerated over the course of their lifetime, seriously limiting their chances of establishing healthy and equitable pay patterns upon release. We must also acknowledge that these statistics are largely attributed to systemic racism that continuously puts Black and Latinx individuals at a significant disadvantage, making them much more likely than their white counterparts to end up in the prison system.

While there is little data on age as a standalone predictor of pay inequity, many statistics show that gender wage gaps expand as workers get older. For every dollar earned by a man, women between the ages of 54 and 65 make only 69 cents, while those 65 and older earn even less. This has long-term economic consequences according to AARP; women over 65 have a poverty rate of 11.6 percent, compared with men's rate of 6.8 percent.

The LGBTQ+ community is negatively affected as well. Lesbian women, in particular, are on the receiving end of significant pay inequity. According to the National LGBTQ Task Force, female same-sex couples earn a median income of around $38,000 versus a $47,000 median income for male same-sex couples. These figures are staggeringly low when compared with the median household income of white families, which is almost $72,000. Most unsettling is the fact that those who identify as transgender are four times more likely than the general population to earn less than $10,000 annually.

We know that generational wealth and systemic inequity drive gaps further, so it may not be surprising to learn that first-generation students and graduates are behind in earnings as well. Unfortunately, according to a report from the National Association of College and College Employers, first-generation graduates earn a starting salary 12 percent lower than their peers. Controlling for differences in college attendance and accounting for similar socioeconomic backgrounds does not eradicate the gap; first-generation men and women still earn up to 6 percent less than their peers who have a family history of college attendance.

WHY EQUITABLE JOB OFFERS MATTER

Now that we understand the problem and its consequences, let's look at the forces under our control that perpetuate these pay disparities in the workforce.

The greatest single source of long-term pay inequity is the job offer. If we are committed to addressing pay inequity in our organizations, we have to start there.

Let's say you have three candidates of mostly equal qualifications pursuing three identical positions at your organization: Jordan, Prisha, and Bari. You prepare three equal job offers with a starting salary of $100,000 each.

But just before you go to make your offers, someone on your team notes that Jordan is the only candidate who went to an Ivy League school—and besides, he is the breadwinner in his family. Afraid that Jordan might not accept, the team agrees to add another $10,000 to his offer—and his alone.

You extend your offers, and Jordan negotiates. After a few exchanges, you agree to increase his offer by another $10,000. Prisha doesn't negotiate at all. Bari does not negotiate, and then has a baby shortly after joining your organization. She asks to take a one-year leave of absence on top of her paid maternity leave, and you offer to extend the same original offer when she returns.

Fast forward 20 years. Even assuming that promotions and raises were given out equitably, Jordan has now made $400,000 more than Prisha and $500,000 more than Bari. Let's consider the role your organization played. Seemingly small early decisions—one informed by bias and another that was merely reactive to an aggressive candidate—led to a sizable pay equity gap.

The job offer process is rife with potential bias, intentional and otherwise. And if your job offers are inequitable, your entire organization will end up inequitable, with disparities compounding year upon year. Syndio, an HR analytics company focused on pay equity, has found that the initial job offer is the single most significant factor in long-term pay equity. Get that wrong, and the hopes of maintaining equitable pay across your organization are all but lost.

Inequitable offers can also be devastating for culture and morale. When we extend a job offer, we want the candidate to feel welcome and empowered. But the intricacies of that offer—how it's structured, how it's negotiated and finalized, how it compares to others—can leave a candidate feeling undervalued. "If, for some reason, people receive a job offer and feel they are being paid less, it is incredibly distracting," says Mita Mallick, Head of Inclusion, Equity, and Impact at software company Carta. "They don't feel valued. It impacts their psychological safety." Getting this right means empowering the people you are hiring from the start.

ASSESSING YOUR ORGANIZATION'S CURRENT PAY INEQUALITIES

Once you've committed to assessing and resolving pay discrepancies in your organization, it can be hard to know where to start. Making that kind of sweeping change is an enormous challenge with very high stakes, so it's not unusual to feel a bit paralyzed at the outset.

As always, you want to start by identifying who at your organization influences pay decisions. This may seem tricky in this case, because the issue affects everyone your organization pays. But typically, there is specific staff with access to company-wide compensation data and oversight on salaries, hiring, and promotions, such as HR and finance leads. To start the process, you should assemble a centralized and streamlined team of people who are capable of assessing old problems from new angles.

As you assess, here are a few questions you can use to determine if you have an equitable approach to your job offers. Also consider who should be owning and supporting each of these:

- Overall, do your people feel fairly compensated and empowered by what you pay?

- Who at your company influences pay equity and are they aware of pay inequity that exists in the workforce?

- Have you assessed the current pay inequity within your organization?

- Do you make your salary ranges transparent internally to your organization's leadership and hiring managers during the hiring process?

- Do you make your salary ranges transparent to candidates early in the hiring process?

- Do you offer holistic compensation and benefits to employees?

- Do you ask your employees what benefits or support they need to thrive at work?

- Do you have ongoing systems in place to assess and maintain pay equity?

For additional resources to assess your diversity hiring efforts visit: http://Mathison.io/Index.

If any of these areas aren't yet part of your efforts to ensure equitable job offers, you have an immediate opportunity. We recommend reevaluating the internal decisions that have a direct effect on your process and determining what you can personally influence.

PERFORMING PAY EQUITY AUDITS

Part of the success of Marc Benioff and the Salesforce team resulted from their willingness to engage in a deep pay equity audit (PEA). PEAs not only shed light on disparities, but also clarify why pay inequities exist in your organization. Some discrepancies can be explained through seniority, education level, or job-experience, for example, all of which are tangible issues to address. Pay equity audits will also illuminate inexplicable differences that are more likely connected to biases. Logistically, PEAs encourage organizations to make adjustments moving forward; trying to provide back pay is generally not considered a best practice.

When considering data analytics, it's important to remember that your results are only as clean and accurate as your data. This means that before your audit even happens, your organization will need a team of people working to ensure all data on employees, job titles, benefits, and so on is fully up to date. It may feel like a lot of work up front, but the process will be more effective with this updated content. Once the team has clean data, auditors will run regression analyses to find outliers in your organization. The outliers will identify individuals and overall trends in pay inequities, so you can consider all of the factors that affect job offers, promotions, and pay scales.

In addition to Salesforce, Adobe and Intel are great examples of organizations that have achieved pay equity as a direct result of their PEAs. After two years of audits, Adobe celebrated pay equity on the basis of gender and race. Intel achieved pay equity based on gender for its entire global workforce.

A pay equity audit is a clear way to demonstrate to your organization that you are actively committed to addressing compensation disparities. According to a 2020 study, only 28 percent of organizations are planning to conduct such audits in the next couple of years, giving you a real opportunity to stay ahead of the curve by taking action now. Regardless of how or why you conduct the process, you will likely see eye-opening results.

Pay equity audits aren't available only to large organizations. Organizations of any size can perform such an analysis. According to Payscale, after briefly analyzing pay history, organizations can get started by looking at these four areas:

- Pay gaps hidden in certain job titles or departments

- Underpaid high performers and overpaid low performers

- Significant differences in promotion rates, raise frequencies, and bonuses

- Men and women who do similar work but are not at the same job level

HOW TO ENSURE EQUITABLE JOB OFFERS

To start, assume that every candidate to whom you extend a job offer is potentially from a community with its own set of cultural norms and its own level of familiarity with the job offer process. Take into account the fact that candidates from underrepresented communities have not always had the benefit of professional mentorship. For many candidates, yours could be the very first job offer they are receiving. And let's not forget that navigating a new job offer can involve a wide range of emotions, complexities, and time sensitivities that can cause candidates to feel pressured.

The high degree of variability and subjectivity that can affect this process reminds us why we need structure and consistency. Equitable job offers and equitable pay depend on a set of clear decisions and processes that are defined well before you extend an offer.

Set Expectations and Build Transparency up Front

Think about the last time you asked a coworker—in the office—how much they get paid. Did you ask in a loud, confident voice? Or did you whisper, gripped by the fear someone would hear you? Or, more likely, would you never dream of asking a colleague that question, especially in the office?

While this instinct is understandable, the truth is that a culture of silence around compensation inadvertently contributes to pay inequity. When we're afraid to talk about compensation, we create a secretive environment in which unequal pay can thrive. Today, equal pay advocates encourage employers and workers to speak up about compensation to help expose and alleviate systemic pay inequity. We have to remember that job seekers already have access to market pay and typical ranges for roles through free job board sites like Glassdoor and

Indeed. Imposing a culture of silence around salaries only pushes the issue underground.

We recommend being upfront about salary ranges with prospective employees. Start by determining a position's salary range ahead of interviewing, and then clearly communicate these ranges both internally with the interviewers and externally with the candidates. Some organizations take the extra step and post salary ranges in the job description. This helps neutralize the discomfort around early salary negotiations. It can also increase efficiency by eliminating candidates seeking a higher salary who might otherwise go through several rounds of interviews before dropping out.

Even if communicating the salary range is not an option for you, do your best to communicate your constraints and set expectations where you can in the process. This will ensure there are fewer surprises and misaligned expectations later on. In 2016, Buffer, a social media company, published a Google document listing all of its employees' salaries and soon saw an increase in job applications. This bold action also helped Buffer pay its employees fairly and without bias, building trust among the team.

Pay transparency is also fast becoming a regulatory norm. As of March 2021, California requires private employers to submit annual pay data reports to the Department of Fair Employment and Housing, which is authorized to investigate and prosecute racial and gender pay disparities. Several other states, including Colorado, have either passed pay transparency bills or have them in the pipeline. Embracing pay transparency now, before it becomes law, can help your organization stay ahead of the curve on pay equity and prepare for a possible transition to mandatory reporting.

Refrain from Questions on Salary History

There is one notable exception to the taboo of discussing money at work: the common practice of asking candidates to disclose their most recent salary. Employers have long felt entitled to ask such questions, and applicants have often felt obligated to answer. This, too, is quickly becoming outdated as people have become aware of how these questions contribute to pay inequity, with more and more organizations instituting salary history bans (SHBs). In the U.S., 29 states have now made it illegal to ask job candidates to disclose their salary history.

Because underrepresented groups are historically underpaid, using their salary history as the proxy for what to pay them perpetuates existing pay inequities. By instituting an SHB, hiring managers are forced to offer positions and compensation packages based solely on a candidate's skills and alignment to the role. Research shows that SHBs have led to increased pay for job changers by about 5 percent, with larger increases for women (8 percent) and African Americans (13 percent).

Even if asking about salary history is legal in your region, we strongly advise against it. Making equitable job offers means leveling the playing field for all applicants, regardless of what they have been paid in the past. Adopting an SHB at your organization will go a long way toward ensuring your job offers are not perpetuating historical pay inequities.

Crafting an Initial Equitable Job Offer

As we discussed above, the inclination to remain flexible when formulating a job offer can often allow bias to creep in. This is why you may want to consider adopting standardized job offers.

Creating standardized job offers means setting a single, non-negotiable salary and benefits package for every role in your organization. Adopting this method will make your job offers more consistent and easier to structure. It will also ensure that the candidate is more equitably slotted into your organization. The approach, however, may be perceived as more rigid or less accommodating for the candidate. Some things to consider for a structured approach:

- Is there a standard salary range for this role in your industry you can reference?

- Is there data on previous job offers your organization has made for this or a similar position or positions that you can reference for consistency?

- What is the salary range for existing people at your organization in this role, function, and level that you can take into account in your process?

- Who in your organization is empowered to ask for an exception to go over the set range for a particular candidate?

Alternately, a customized job offer is one that the hiring manager and other leaders devise based on the individual candidate. It does not have to fit into a set range or structure and gives the company the ability to negotiate with the candidate more freely. But this approach can also lead to inequities. To rely on customized job offers in a fair and consistent manner, you need to carefully identify which specific factors you are basing your decision on and keep an eye open for potential bias. Ask yourself which of these are legitimate factors to consider and which shouldn't even be part of the conversation:

- **Education.** Does a well-known school influence your decision?

- **Salary history.** Does knowing what the candidate made previously influence your offer?

- **Family obligations.** Are you less likely to hire someone who is reluctant to travel or work evenings and weekends?

- **Negotiation.** How much are you willing to let counteroffers determine salary?

- **Age.** Would you prefer someone younger for the role? Why?

- **Referral.** Do you favor candidates recommended by current employees?

- **Comparison to other candidates.** Would your offer be different if the candidate pool had been stronger/weaker?

Remember that job offers are about more than salary. When it comes to benefits, be aware that some may be of greater benefit to some candidates than others. We recommend reviewing your existing benefits package to identify what you could add to better support underrepresented communities, then try to make these a standard part of your package.

For example, visa sponsorship, temporary housing, and relocation expenses could all be helpful to immigrants and refugees. Progressive healthcare subsidies and parental leave for both parents can make a huge difference for the LGBTQ+ community. Subsidizing childcare, professional development opportunities, and additional paid time off can help parents who are trying to return to the workforce after taking time off to raise their children. Floating vacation days can benefit anyone who celebrates nontraditional holidays. Flexible work-from-home policies can make a major difference for older workers as well as the disability community. If we are only considering what we pay in the job offer, we are missing a major opportunity.

Make Your Job Offer and Process Clear and Understandable

Candidates can't make good decisions if they don't fully understand your offer. We recommend being overly communicative to clearly explain the details of your job offer and the timeframe in which you expect them to make a decision. Schedule time to walk candidates through the full package step by step to answer any questions they might have. Make yourself available to answer questions after extending the offer to ensure candidates fully understand the details.

While explanations are helpful, there's nothing like a good visual aid to make sure your offer is clearly laid out and intelligible. Software company Carta has designed an easy-to-read job offer template that is available for download on its website. The template is free of legal jargon and uses engaging graphics to clearly spell out employee compensation packages, including everything from salary to paid time off to an options vesting schedule.

Bonuses and equity packages are common sources of confusion for many candidates. Especially when receiving offers from early stage or start-up companies, candidates often struggle to interpret the value of equity and bonuses compared to a standard base salary. Any detailed estimates you can give to help them gauge the value of these will be clarifying. It's also key to clearly spell out benefits to your candidates and not assume that they fully understand your proposed health coverage and what your 401(k) or retirement packages entail. The more clearly you can walk through all of this, the more candidates will feel confident and informed.

Finally, every touchpoint and interaction in this process should be consistent. As much as possible, all offers should be communicated the same way (phone, in-person, email) and all candidates should have the same amount of time to respond. Even if you have an easy opportunity, don't be tempted to communicate the job offer outside of your usual process. This could create an unfair advantage. Inconsistencies create openings for bias to creep in, so challenge yourself and your team to stick to a consistent process.

How to Handle Job Offer Negotiations

Many employers assume that all candidates are accustomed to negotiating job offers. As a result, many choose to intentionally extend lower initial job offers with the expectation that candidates will negotiate for more. In reality, people from many underrepresented communities and cultures are statistically less likely than white men to negotiate their job offers. A recent study of MBA graduates found that half of men negotiate their job offers compared to only one-eighth of women.

Even as children, boys and girls are often taught to have very different relationships with money and authority, leading to significant differences in how they respond to job offers. And in many cultures, it is simply considered impolite to talk about money or to push back against authority figures. Carta's Mallick says her cultural upbringing is a major reason she has struggled to negotiate her compensation in the past. "As a person of color and someone of South Asian descent, I feel like it is impolite to talk about money or ask for more or question authority," she says. "So, from a cultural lens, it was as if I had been taught to implicitly trust authority and those in decision-making roles. So, if you are going to offer me X, I am going to take it."

Allowing your organization's salaries to be influenced by such widespread and deeply embedded cultural differences is a recipe for long-term pay inequity. It's important that the initial job offer reflects what you believe is fair for the candidate with the full expectation that many will not negotiate.

Be Consistent in Your Approach to Negotiation

As part of its mission to ensure greater pay equity, Industrious, a co-working office space company, decided it would no longer negotiate job offers. Ever. The company designated a single salary for each role and made it transparent to candidates from the onset. Not only did this remove ambiguity and subjectivity from the offer process, but it helped candidates who had previously been the victims of pay inequity get back on track. For example, a candidate who came in making $50,000 less than their fair market rate was automatically brought up to their new predetermined salary, no questions asked. This also saved Industrious many cycles of frustrating back-and-forth negotiations, sometimes to ultimately lose the candidate anyway.

Refusing to negotiate with candidates is a hard policy to adhere to. It requires total pay transparency and a willingness to lose a good candidate who's only asking for a small increase. But given the inconsistency with which different kinds of candidates are likely to negotiate at all, and the major disparities that can arise from even slight differences in starting pay, it is a policy that we believe will become more common in the coming years. If you think it can work for your organization, we recommend making the leap.

If your organization is not yet prepared to take this step, we recommend at least developing a policy on how you will handle negotiations, with an eye toward preventing them from creating disparities that consistently favor one kind of applicant. Having such a policy will make it easier to handle these situations in a consistent and equitable manner rather than improvising responses that are too easily infected by bias.

SUSTAIN AND MONITOR YOUR PAY EQUITY PRACTICES

Even the most equitable job offers depend on having ongoing measures in place to sustain pay equity in the long term. Just as Salesforce learned following its upfront calibration, pay equity gaps can quickly return if systemic bias goes unaddressed. As we turn our attention to pay increases through promotions and steps for recalibration, it's important to lean on any available data to ensure decisions are sound and fair.

HR analytics tools like Syndio can help leaders use real-time insights to measure if their salary decisions fall within an equitable range.

Continued pay equity audits are critical to gauging whether any unexpected gaps have surfaced. Without having an easy and frequent way to make this assessment, your organization could face a very delayed and expensive change.

FIRST STEP TOWARD IMPACT

By enabling more equitable job offers at your organization, you are helping to break the chain of systemic pay inequity that has long kept underrepresented communities at a disadvantage. You are also making your organization more competitive, freeing it from the debilitating effects of undervaluing good workers for bad reasons.

One thing you can immediately do to advance equitable job offers at your organization is share the pay inequity table on page 210 with your other decision makers. This will help increase awareness around pay disparities and hopefully reduce the unconscious bias that leads to formulating inequitable pay packages.

Use these insights to start a conversation around pay inequity that exists in the workforce and what it might mean for your organization. In the conversation, emphasize that this is not only influenced by job offers to new hires but also the ongoing decisions we make around leveling and promotions in our daily work. Just as Marc Benioff learned at Salesforce, without transparency and constant maintenance, it's nearly impossible to ensure long-term pay equity.

To access additional resources and download the tables and charts from this chapter visit: http://Mathison.io/Book.

REFERENCES

Abed, Robbie. "This Company Published All Its Employees Salaries 4 Years Ago. Here's What They Learned." Inc. December 22, 2017. https://www.inc.com/robbie-abed/this-company-published-all-its-employees-salaries-4-years-ago-heres-what-they-learned.html.

Barnard-Bahn, Amii. "How to Identify—and Fix—Pay Inequality at Your Company." *Harvard Business Review*. November 3, 2020. https://hbr.org/2020/11/how-to-identify-and-fix-pay-inequality-at-your-company.

Bernard, Tara Siegel. "Moving Past Gender Barriers to Negotiate a Raise." *New York Times*. March 24, 2014. https://www.nytimes.com/2014/03/25/your-money/moving-past-gender-barriers-to-negotiate-a-raise.html.

Bessen, James E., Chen Meng, and Erich Denk. "Perpetuating Inequality: What Salary History Bans Reveal About Wages." June 1, 2020. https://ssrn.com/abstract=3628729 or http://dx.doi.org/10.2139/ssrn.3628729.

"Black Women and the Wage Gap." National Partnership for Women and Families. March 2021. https://www.nationalpartnership.org/our-work/resources/economic-justice/fair-pay/african-american-women-wage-gap.pdf.

"Carta Offer Letter Template." Carta. Accessed March 24, 2021. https://get.carta.com/rs/214-BTD-103/images/Carta_better_offer_letter.pdf.

Dewar, Jen. "8 Wage Gap Statistics to Know in 2021." *Compa*. Accessed March 24, 2021. https://www.compa.as/blog/wage-gap-statistics.

"Equal Pay Is an LGBT Issue." National LGBTQ Task Force. April 9, 2013. https://www.thetaskforce.org/equal-pay-is-an-lgbt-issue/.

"First Generation Students Earn up to 17% Less than Peers." EAB. July 20, 2019. https://eab.com/insights/daily-briefing/student-affairs/first-generation-students-earn-up-to-17-less-than-peers/.

"Global Gender Gap Report 2020." World Economic Forum. Accessed March 24, 2021. https://www.weforum.org/reports/gender-gap-2020-report-100-years-pay-equality.

Hassan, Adeel, and Audrey Carlsen. "How 'Crazy Rich' Asians Have Led to the Largest Income Gap in the U.S." *New York Times*. August 17, 2018. https://www.nytimes.com/interactive/2018/08/17/us/asian-income-inequality.html?search ResultPosition=24.

Leonhardt, David. "The Black-White Wage Gap Is as Big as It Was in 1950." *New York Times*. June 25, 2020. https://www.nytimes.com/2020/06/25/opinion/sunday/race-wage-gap.html.

Lounsberry, Kaitlin. "A Reminder of Gender Pay Inequity's Toll on Seniors." AARP States. April 13, 2016. https://states.aarp.org/reminder-gender-pay-inequitys-toll-seniors.

McIntosh, Kriston, Emily Moss, Ryan Nunn, and Jay Shambaugh. "Examining the Black-White Wealth Gap." Brookings. February 27, 2020. https://www.brookings.edu/blog/up-front/2020/02/27/examining-the-black-white-wealth-gap/.

Nagele-Piazza, Lisa. "The Importance of Pay Equity." SHRM. February 28, 2020. https://www.shrm.org/hr-today/news/hr-magazine/spring2020/pages/importance-of-pay-equity.aspx.

"New CA Law Requires Employers to Submit Annual Pay Data Reports." *National Law Review*. December 22, 2017. https://www.natlawreview. com/article/new-ca-law-requires-employers-to-submit-annual-pay-data-reports.

"Quantifying America's Gender/Wage Gap by Race/Ethnicity." National Partnership for Women and Families. March 2021. https://www.nationalpartnership.org/our-work/resources/economic-justice/fair-pay/quantiFying-americas-gender-wage-gap.pdf.

"The Racial Wage Gap Persists in 2020." PayScale. Accessed March 24, 2021. https://www.payscale.com/data/racial-wage-gap.

"6 Cutting-Edge HR Metrics to Measure." Payscale. Accessed March 24, 2021. https://cdn2.hubspot.net/hubfs/228948/6%20Cutting%20Edge%20 HR%20Metrics%20PDF.pdf.

Small, D. A., Gelfand, M., Babcock, L., and Gettman, H. (2007). "Who Goes to the Bargaining Table? The Influence of Gender and Framing on the Initiation of Negotiation." *Journal of Personality and Social Psychology* 93(4): 600–613. https://doi.org/10.1037/0022-3514.93.4.600.

Sheth, Sonam, Madison Hoff, Marguerite Ward, and Taylor Tyson. "These 8 Charts Show the Glaring Gap between Men's and Women's Salaries in the US." Business Insider. March 24, 2021. https://www.businessinsider. com/gender-wage-pay-gap-charts-2017-3.

"Trends in US Corrections." Sentencing Project. August 2020. https:// sentencingproject.org/wp-content/uploads/2020/08/Trends-in-US-Corrections.pdf.

"Usual Weekly Earnings of Wage and Salary Workers Fourth Quarter 2020." January 21, 2021. https://www.bls.gov/news.release/pdf/wkyeng.pdf.

"The Wage Gap, by Gender and Race." Infoplease. Accessed March 24, 2021. https://www.infoplease.com/us/society-culture/gender-sexuality/wage-gap-gender-and-race.

Western, Bruce. "The Impact of Incarceration on Wage Mobility and Inequality." Accessed March 24, 2021. https://scholar.harvard.edu/files/brucewestern/files/western_asr.pdf.

"Women Are Paid Less Than Men—and That Hits Harder in an Economic Crisis." Lean In. Accessed March 24, 2021. https://leanin.org/equal-pay-data-about-the-gender-pay-gap.

"Women Had Median Weekly Earnings of $902 in Third Quarter 2020, Compared with $1,104 for Men." U.S. Bureau of Labor Statistics. October 22, 2020. https://www.bls.gov/opub/ted/2020/mobile/women-had-median-weekly-earnings-of-902-in-third-quarter-2020-compared-with-1104-for-men.htm.

CHAPTER 10

Empowering and Advancing Underrepresented Team Members

"Inclusion is the yin to the diversity yang."
—Amy Stern, BI Worldwide

In 2015, Whirlpool took a look at its progress on diversity hiring and discovered an unexpected problem. Despite its success in hiring more diverse employees, the company had a "leaky bucket." Underrepresented employees were leaving at a faster rate than they were being hired.

Whirlpool's leadership team knew that, left unchecked, this trend could have disastrous results for the company and its culture. To fix it, they developed a retention risk assessment toolkit that consisted of three phases:

1. Assess the impact to the organization should a particular employee leave.

2. Assess the likelihood that an employee might leave.

3. Create an action plan to ensure employees would stay and be successful.

Whirlpool decided to test the toolkit on a pilot group of 65 employees identified as top talent from underrepresented communities. To complete the assessment, each of the employee's managers was given a list of 25 questions to answer, such as, "If this employee left Whirlpool, would we lose significant intellectual capital?" and "Would this role be difficult to fill both internally and externally?"

What immediately became apparent was that the managers didn't know their employees well enough to answer the questions. So the company asked the employees to sit for a series of interviews with their managers. Those interviews yielded two major insights. First, the managers thought their relationship with the employees was stronger than the employees did. Second, the managers were unaware of many of the "engagement factors" that employees said were important to them, including feeling valued, being recognized/rewarded, having meaningful work, and working with great people.

One manager even noted that he knew much more about his male employee than his female employee, mostly because he had taken the time to get to know the male employee, with whom he had shared interests outside of work. This may not be surprising given what we know about affinity bias, but it highlights the need to make an effort to get to know employees with whom we don't have much in common.

Building on what they learned, the managers were given a list of concrete actions they could take to make sure employees were getting what they needed from the relationship, such as conducting regular one-on-one meetings, giving recognition for good work, and finding development opportunities that would help the employees reach their career goals.

Ultimately, the attrition rate of employees from underrepresented groups who were in the program was 14 points lower than those not in the program, and the attrition rate for women in the program was 12 points lower.

WHY DIVERSITY DEPENDS ON INCLUSIVE ORGANIZATIONS

Throughout this book, we've explored the full life cycle of strategies for hiring talented people from diverse backgrounds. But hiring for diversity is only the beginning. Maintaining a vibrant, productive community of people from many backgrounds requires us to create cultures that make people feel valued, nurtured, and, above all, included.

Unfortunately, being part of an underrepresented group at work—whether based on race, ethnicity, gender, or any other identifier—often leads to inherent feelings of being excluded and undervalued. A 2020 study from insurance company Cigna found that 39 percent of Hispanic Americans and 30 percent of African Americans felt isolated from their coworkers—a feeling shared by only 25 percent of white Americans.

No organization intentionally sets out to build a hostile or discriminatory culture. But good intentions aren't enough to overcome the human tendency to favor people who look like us, talk like us, or share our interests. Even adopting equitable hiring practices won't build a culture where everyone feels equally empowered or recognized. Creating an inclusive culture requires specific steps that account for everyone's differences and signal acceptance of diverse perspectives.

Some leaders worry about how much of the original culture needs to be changed to foster inclusivity. To that, we can say it's very possible to keep your style and some preferences as long as you do it with the mindset of making sure everyone feels included. Encouraging and fostering inclusion through actionable goals and changed behaviors is what we aim to address in this chapter.

Diversity without inclusion is like being invited to the party but not having a seat at the table. Is it any wonder that new hires from underrepresented communities at such organizations might not stick around long? The result for noninclusive organizations is not just the costs of replacing employees, but the loss of talent and valuable perspectives that help drive innovation, productivity, and profits.

Measuring inclusion is harder and more complex than measuring diversity. Employees who earn top performance ratings and accolades could nonetheless feel limited at a company whose leadership team includes no one who looks like them. Taking the time to develop and implement the tools that reveal such feelings is the first step to addressing them. This chapter will give you the tools to gauge how inclusive your organization is now and to build a culture that makes everyone feel valued, seen, and included.

CULTURAL CHALLENGES WITH INCLUSION

Everyone has an intrinsic need to feel a sense of belonging at work, but studies suggest that too many organizations are failing to meet that need. A 2017 study by the Kapor Center for Social Impact found that the most common reasons for turnover among underrepresented groups in the technology industry are unfairness and mistreatment in the workplace. Underrepresented workers experienced two times the rate of stereotyping compared to Asian and white employees. LGBTQ+ employees were more likely to be bullied at a rate of 20 percent, and nearly one-third of women of color were passed over for promotions—more than any other group. Underrepresented groups were also subject to higher rates of stereotyping and bullying, which helped contribute to high turnover rates. The tech industry is losing an estimated $16 billion a year due to unfairness-based turnover alone, the study said. And research has shown that the tech industry is hardly alone.

A study by Coqual, a DEI research firm, found that only 31 percent of Black full-time employees felt they had access at work to a senior leader who could guide their careers—13 percentage points lower than white men. The lack of equal access to a supervisor and the inability to forge relationships with key decision makers left Black employees frustrated with their career advancement.

The study also found that employees of color encounter workplace prejudice at higher rates than all other professionals. This prejudice is often unintentional, manifesting itself in microinsults, microassaults, and microinvalidations, like constantly being told "you are so articulate," being unfairly characterized as angry, or being mistaken for a coworker of the same race.

Slow career advancement and subtle prejudice are two of the major reasons that 35 percent of Black workers plan to leave their current employer within two years, the study said. Overall, Black employees are 30 percent more likely than their white counterparts to consider leaving their current job.

If you've put the effort into finding and hiring diverse people, it's vital that you make sure they feel welcome and safe at your organization. Otherwise true organization-wide diversity will always remain out of reach.

ASSESSING YOUR DIVERSITY RETENTION STRATEGY

In previous chapters, we've presented a few specific frameworks for assessing your organization's status regarding the topic at hand. But this is different. Yes, you have to assemble various stakeholders to gather the right perspectives so you can decide policy. Yes, any leader can start these discussions, engaging the teams that help create support on an organizational level. But this is a question of how you get started *and* how you maintain momentum. This is a question of cultural transformation.

How does your organization adopt an approach to continual, ongoing assessments of retention and advancement practices?

How do these policies become natural behaviors when conducting your day-to-day business? What are your more frequent checkpoints and metrics to develop an adaptive, incremental approach to needed change?

Here are some areas to consider as you assess how inclusive your organization's practices are and if you are doing everything possible to empower and advance your underrepresented team members. As you go through the following items, consider which team members should own or support each of these areas. Remember, it's not just up to your HR or talent teams to invest in team members from all communities. It is the responsibility of the whole organization to ensure your people feel supported, empowered and set up to advance. Any employee can sign up to be a mentor, recognize their peers, or encourage more work-life balance. Anyone can make a difference.

Area of retention	Questions to ask yourself
Mentorship/ sponsorship	• Does your organization have structured mentorship and sponsorship opportunities for senior leaders to engage with emerging leaders or employee resource groups?
Professional development	• Does your organization provide career development and coaching opportunities?

(*continued*)

Area of retention	Questions to ask yourself
Recognition	• Does your organization have incentives and rewards policies in place to encourage engagement and recognize employees?
Compensation	• Does your organization offer competitive compensation and benefits to your full-time employees?
Work-life balance	• Does your organization have policies in place that encourage flexible work and a healthy work-life balance?
Effective feedback	• Does your organization have systems in place to anonymously collect employee feedback regarding diversity, inclusion, and belonging?
Culture	• Does your organization coordinate formal and informal programming to foster a strong culture and community?
DEI programming	• Does your organization have affinity groups, ERGs, or coordinated diversity events?

For additional resources to assess your diversity hiring efforts visit: http://Mathison.io/Index.

1. *Invest in Formal Mentorship and Sponsorship Relationships*

In a perfect world, each one of your junior team members from an underrepresented community could form a deep connection with someone who would take them under their wing and help them navigate professional challenges. In reality, these relationships are rare, particularly for people from underrepresented groups who may not find many senior staffers who understand their specific challenges. This is why formal mentorship or sponsorship programs are a great way to help those underrepresented workers feel they belong and have a future in your company. (They're also a great way to combat employee turnover and low productivity.)

A 2017 study from executive search firm Heidrick & Struggles found that 30 percent of women and 32 percent of people of color consider mentorship to be very important to their career trajectory. Indeed, people from these groups may find that having a more seasoned professional offering advice or advocating for them can help them overcome systemic bias or avoid common pitfalls that prevent their advancement. A 2019 study from PayScale, a compensation software company, found that employees who have a workplace sponsor earn almost 12 percent more than those who do not.

Though there are countless ways to structure mentorships, the basic idea is simple: a junior employee is paired with a senior employee who can offer advice and guidance on achieving their career goals. Most mentorship programs include regularly scheduled one-on-one meetings, and many come with a termination date, allowing mentees to benefit from the wisdom of multiple mentors during their time with an organization.

Sponsorship programs are similar but focus more on tangible benefits and opportunities for the younger employee. Typically, a sponsor will either bring the junior employee into a project they might not otherwise have access to or simply advocate for them with others in leadership positions. Frederica Peterson is a leadership coach who has helped many organizations mobilize sponsorship and mentorship strategies. "People that are cared for commit," she says. When people are sincerely invested in by their leaders, they are more likely to commit to the leader, to the team and to the organization. This is especially important to team members from underrepresented communities who can often feel isolated and unsupported in organizations. A leader who can build trust through consistency and support will inevitably create an environment that will allow them to thrive and excel."

Such programs are good not just for the employees, but the organization itself. They reduce turnover (and the associated costs), lift employee morale, and help ensure that you're getting the most out of every employee. Plus, incorporating succession planning into mentorship programs can further ensure that the departure of key employees does not significantly affect your organizational flow and structure.

"The reason why growth is so important is that it's not a zero-sum game," PwC partner and chairman Tim Ryan told the *New York Times*. "When you're growing, you're creating more opportunities."

Sponsorship programs needn't be limited to individuals, either. Providing employee resource groups with a liaison who has a direct line of communication to the leadership team can help ensure that their recommendations are heard.

Something you can do today	Something to strive for long term
• Introduce a senior employee to a team member to provide them with guidance and support—this could be the start of a long-term mentorship relationship. • Establish a buddy program for new hires to cultivate relationships and receive guidance from their peers.	• Develop and regularly promote a robust program that incentivizes and commits mid- to senior-level employees to becoming mentors or sponsors for junior employees. • Create a program where executives regularly hold events (e.g., "Lunch and Learns") so employees have a place to ask questions and cultivate relationships with leadership.

2. Commit to Continuous Professional Development

You might have a clear idea of how much it would cost you to train employees. But the real question is, how much will it cost you *not* to train them? Professional development (PD) is one of the most sought-after benefits for applicants and can go a long way toward helping advance underrepresented team members. A 2017 study by the Society for Human Resource Management (SHRM) found that 21 percent of employees cited a lack of PD and career development as the primary reason for leaving a job. For workers from underrepresented communities, the combination of feeling both isolated at work and stuck in their career can be devastating.

Organizations that invest in PD also reap the benefits of having better-educated employees. The American Society for Training and Development found that companies that invest in training have 24 percent higher profit margins. While it's natural to wince at the high cost of conferences, classes, and professional memberships, one doesn't have to look far to see the benefits.

Squarespace is a great example of a company striving to do better in this area. The company, which provides tools for building websites, has invested in learning and development programs to accelerate career progression and to give its employees opportunities to achieve their career goals. Its programs promote continuous learning and include a mix of in-person and virtual classroom development experiences, individual coaching, and self-paced learning resources.

Software company Cornerstone on Demand has geared its professional development to emphasize DEI by hosting development days (Dev Days) internally where team members across the company lead internal training courses. The company has focused a whole series of sessions on DEI, including sessions on Juneteenth, growing your team inclusively, and the benefits of being a working parent at Cornerstone.

Team members who are given the tools to meet their potential will have a higher sense of belonging and, by extension, higher employee satisfaction and retention. PD also creates an environment in which highly engaged and high-performing workers can meet the challenges of your organization. Well-trained workers will be better positioned to take advantage of promotions and career advancement opportunities when they become available and will be less likely to leave an organization that invests in their professional growth.

Something you can do today	Something to strive for long term
• Allot dedicated time for your team to focus on their professional development each quarter. • Create a shared folder or document where your team can populate and share micro-learning (small-scale training sessions, webinars, podcasts, etc.).	• Establish clear internal career paths for all roles to build transparency and common understanding of potential advancement opportunities. • Offer skills trainings for those who want to make lateral moves into other parts of the business.

3. Find Meaningful Ways to Recognize Your Team

Everyone wants to feel that the work they do matters, so the simple act of acknowledging and showing appreciation for an employee's hard work can go a long way in empowering team members from underrepresented communities.

Research from O.C. Tanner, a firm that develops strategic employee recognition and reward solutions, shows that employees are five times more likely to remain in an organization when their achievements are regularly acknowledged. And 37 percent of employees said that the more sincere, specific, and timely the recognition, the more it made them feel encouraged.

Milestones like work anniversaries or big client wins make for great opportunities to show employee recognition, and will certainly help your people feel appreciated. But as with any gift, the more thought you put into the gesture, the more meaningful it will be to the recipient. For example, Taco Bell gave its employee recognition efforts a boost by creating awards and gifts that felt exclusive and authentic to the brand: a golden bell, a solid pewter sombrero, throw pillows shaped like hot sauce packets. "Symbols mean a lot to people," says Frank Tucker, Taco Bell's Chief People Officer. "People love to display them because it communicates to others that this really means something to me and has great value to me."

Like Taco Bell, try using work anniversaries as a simple way to recognize service and celebrate an employee's loyalty to your organization. It doesn't have to be an extravagant celebration—just a simple gathering to toast a worker, or a small but thoughtful token, is enough to lift them up and inspire other employees to look forward to their own milestone. (Do bear in mind that not everyone relishes being the center of attention, so elaborate activities that put individuals on the spot might not yield the results you're hoping for. Take individual preferences and character in mind when planning celebrations.)

Something you can do today	Something to strive for long term
• Prepare a list of employee hire dates and attach it to your organization's calendar so that you can receive reminders to recognize anniversaries. • Recognize your peers through your internal communications channel or intranet. • Build time into each meeting agenda for managers to call out specific employees who are doing a particularly good job.	• Establish a policy depending on your organization's size and budget on how you will celebrate work anniversaries, from private emails or mentions during staff meetings to bigger celebrations for 5- or 10-year anniversaries. • Develop a formal bonus structure based on performance metrics. • Create rewards and incentives systems for employees when they reach new milestones. • Establish formal communication channels dedicated to publicly sharing kudos both vertically and horizontally among colleagues.

4. Design a Fair and Equitable Compensation Program

Offering competitive compensation and benefits packages is a vital part of advancing team members from underrepresented communities. As we discussed in Chapter 9, your benefits package says a lot about what kind of employee you value, so make sure you're offering the kind of benefits that will make it easier for people from diverse backgrounds to stay with you.

For example, you can support your LGBTQ+ community by identifying areas where your benefits favor a heteronormative culture. Do you offer parental leave for all employees, regardless of gender? What about adoption leave and domestic partner benefits? Can your employees take time off to celebrate holidays that aren't historically recognized in the U.S.? Do your contributions to retirement funds support the goals of older workers who may be closer to exiting the workforce? There are many ways we can adjust our existing benefits and adopt low-lift policies to support an inclusive culture.

You may also consider finding ways to link unique benefits, rewards, or bonuses to retention where necessary—for example, bonuses tied to years with the company, or stock options that vest over time. If you want loyalty from your employees, it helps to demonstrate how much you value their commitment.

Something you can do today	Something to strive for long term
• Survey your team members to determine how your current package and offerings match their needs and identify areas of improvement.	• Consider all aspects of holistic well-being (health coverage, car insurance assistance, pension, life insurance, mental health, etc.) while creating your benefits package.

5. Support a Healthy Work-Life Balance for Your Team

High employee burnout has become an all-too-common affliction in the 21st-century workplace, especially for underrepresented communities. Where it once seemed that digital communication tools and portable technology would usher in an age of flexibility and freedom for workers, they have instead blurred the lines between work and personal time, which has left many employees without the luxury of being "unavailable," regardless of their personal obligations.

Not surprisingly, this has disproportionately affected women and people of color. A University of Michigan study found that Black women between the ages of 49 and 55 in the U.S. were 7.5 years biologically "older" than white women of the same age, due largely to work-induced and economic stress. A 2015 Stanford Business School study found that the average Black man with less than a high school degree lost, on average, an estimated 1.7 years of longevity due to workplace stress.

One contributing factor to this disparity is something known as representation burnout, which is the stress and exhaustion brought on by being the only person of a particular identity in an organization. In short, constantly being the exception to the rule is hard, unrewarding work, and it's vital that employers who want to build a diverse workforce do their best to alleviate it.

Some ways to fight representation burnout (beyond trying to hire more diverse workers) include forming affinity groups that help team members feel less alone, mentorship and sponsorship programs, and informal social gatherings that let coworkers get to know one another better. For example, consider starting a book club that focuses on non-white authors or a movie club that focuses on non-white stories. Most important, be aware of who might be suffering from this kind of burnout and don't be afraid to ask what you can do to support them.

Try to be intentional about ensuring that underrepresented team members in your organization are receiving their fair share of recognition and opportunity. As we discussed in the previous section, recognition goes a long way toward alleviating feelings of isolation and frustration at work. You can reduce the incidence of burnout among your people by making sure they feel that their efforts are actually getting them closer to their personal and professional goals.

In general, when advocating for a healthy work-life balance, try to treat employee burnout as a broader organizational issue instead of an individual problem. Consider hosting seminars with a health professional to help your workforce better understand what a good work-life balance looks like and how they can strive to achieve it. Establish policies that enforce work etiquette, such as, "Don't expect your colleagues to respond after 6 p.m.," "Be aware of your colleagues' time zones," "Set your Slack (or communication channel) to *do not disturb* outside of working hours." Discuss these policies during onboarding to let your employees know that these are not simply suggestions but rules.

Your active participation in ensuring mental, social, and emotional health will in turn translate into increased productivity and performance for your organization. Moreover, it will be difficult for an employee to overlook these benefits when contemplating whether to leave or stay. Chevron, for instance, is very deliberate about showing employees that it cares about them. The energy company provides health and fitness centers on site or through health-club memberships and makes other health-oriented programs such as massages and personal training available to its workers.

It also helps to educate your employees on digital overload and how to avoid it. Particularly where remote work has become far more prevalent, it's vital that employees can take regular breaks and set boundaries on how much time they spend in front of a screen each day. As a leader of an organization, you can step in here and set firm boundaries to help protect your workers' mental health. Commit to enforcing work hours so employees don't feel obligated to hop back online at their managers' every request.

It is important to see all your employees first as humans who have achievements outside of work that should be respected as fully as those that benefit the company directly. Strive to make your organization's culture healthy and positive, with clear boundaries separating work time and personal time, and you should lose far fewer people to burnout.

6. Ensure Your Workforce Feels Seen and Heard

In his 2021 report, "Elevating Equity: The Real Story of Diversity and Inclusion," Josh Bersin, founder of talent management consultancy Bersin & Associates, concluded that the most important factor in advancing diversity is the ability to listen—and respond—to your employees.

"Why is listening so important?" he writes. "Because it switches DEI from a compliance program to one focused on performance and growth. When leaders listen and hear what diverse teams need, they understand the small things that make a difference. When we truly feel empathy, listen, hear, and respond—we are naturally inclusive and diverse as a result."

That conclusion is supported by Bersin's research. Organizations that listen to employees, hear what they are saying, and act accordingly are 12 times more likely to engage and retain employees and 8.4 times more likely to inspire a sense of belonging, according to the report.

PREVENTING BURNOUT

One common source of representation burnout is being expected to single-handedly fix a company's DEI issues. Too often, organizations will task their diverse employees with the mission, assuming they are the most qualified, possess the most relevant knowledge, and have the most to gain. This is a serious mistake. You should not ask those who are disadvantaged because of your policies to take on the extra burden of changing those policies. As a leader, it is your responsibility to mend what is broken.

Something you can do today	Something to strive for long term
• Establish hard lines between the workday and time off (e.g., not responding to emails during evenings or weekends), so all employees feel empowered to set their own boundaries.	• Cross-train employees and broaden communications to remove any guilt surrounding time off. • Establish formal policies that promote paid parental leave (regardless of gender, type of birth, etc.).

One way to make employees from vulnerable communities feel heard is to solicit their feedback through anonymous DEI surveys. Questions like "Do you feel that management respects your work?" "Is everyone here treated fairly and equally?" "Are you confident that you will be recognized when you put in extra effort?" can be extremely eye-opening and give you a great starting point for addressing employee concerns. Even just fielding the survey can go a long way toward showing employees you are interested in hearing and responding to their opinions.

Also remember that employees can feel disconnected from senior leadership when there is a lack of transparency around business updates, objectives, and vision. To create a sense of transparency, actively seek feedback to gauge what exactly your employees want to hear about.

Feedback is at the core of every interaction; it does not need to be formal, verbal, or acknowledged. But organizations must do what they can to empower their employees to give intentional feedback that they can trust will be heard and addressed. The way feedback is collected signals how comfortably one can share their observations. It's necessary to keep feedback anonymous and relay a timeline for when employees can expect to hear back. This establishes accountability and will likely lead to more honest, constructive comments.

One of the greatest missteps leaders make is seeking feedback from employees when they don't genuinely want to hear it. In a 2020 Leadership IQ study, researchers found that only 27 percent of the 21,000-plus employees surveyed felt that their managers were always open to feedback and encouraged it. This is an opportunity for your organization to set itself apart.

Something you can do today	Something to strive for long term
• Consider what feedback is most important; seek this out informally to begin integrating feedback loops more organically into your culture. • Find a template for engagement surveys online. You can pilot it within departments before making it more widespread.	• Partner with solutions like Culture Amp for a one-stop solution. They can help you conduct engagement surveys, performance reviews, 360 reviews, etc., and help analyze your results. • Work with managers to communicate to employees how their work contributes to organizational and team goals. This will help all employees develop specific and impactful feedback.

7. Invest in Ways to Build Community and Bring Your People Together

In an age when your team members may be no longer physically sitting next to each other, we can't assume everyone feels connected or has a strong sense of community. Consider your more introverted team members of different backgrounds who aren't typically proactive in reaching out. It's easy for these individuals to feel disconnected or isolated in a remote working world. This is why it's all the more important to act with greater intent to bring everyone on your team together for a broader sense of camaraderie.

This opportunity arises starting on day one with onboarding. Many team members from underrepresented communities may enter the room (physically or virtually) with a subconscious feeling of worry or disconnect. This often stems from an uncertainty as to how they will be perceived or whether they will feel included. Onboarding really sets the tone for what team members can expect as they embark on this new journey, and you have the opportunity to be part of that. We recommend taking the chance to communicate your diversity commitment and your diversity opportunities. Go out of your way to introduce team members. Assign an onboarding buddy to each new hire. Don't let anyone fall between the cracks on their first day.

There are many tools out there that serve this need. For example, the Donut app integration on Slack can be set up so that employees are paired with someone different every one to two weeks for a #virtualdonut. Such opportunities help eliminate the awkwardness of attempted networking. For ERGs or smaller internal gatherings, icebreaker.video is a great online tool that helps you build connections in group settings through guided conversation games on a variety of topics. Sisense has a virtual reality world for their remote workers to take meetings in; for example, you can catch up with your global teams while hanging out in a vineyard overlooking the Mediterranean. In a world that is moving toward more remote teams and hybrid work environments, virtual work is our new reality, and those who embrace it will thrive.

If you recall from Chapter 6, there are many different ways to develop community partnerships as an organization. Doing so not only improves diversity sourcing, but also improves the experience of your employees.

Something you can do today	Something to strive for long term
• Make a big deal out of a new hire joining your team. Coordinate fun exercises where they can get to know the team and the company better. • Send your employees little boxed gifts or snacks to let them know you appreciate them and their hard work.	• Company-wide philanthropic efforts that are steeped into the culture build a more meaningful experience for all employees. • Plan team and company-wide events to enhance employee experience and belonging. • Focus your manager training on being human-centric and responsive.

8. Take an Intentional Approach to Diversity

As we've shared in the previous chapter, a DEI strategy is crucial to your organization's overall progress and development. A 2018 McKinsey report revealed that DEI programming and diverse representation on teams lead to an increase in value creation and financial productivity. It can help explain why diverse organizations are 70 percent more likely to capture new markets.

One way to intentionally communicate your commitment to diversity is to recognize holidays, weeks, and months that are dedicated to celebrating the heritage and history of underrepresented groups. These calendar days offer leaders a more authentic and natural opportunity to develop far-reaching programming for all employees, while building a sense of belonging. For example, June is Pride month for the LGBTQ+ community, which means organizations have an entire month of opportunities to celebrate their colleagues. Many employers now support local Pride parades through sponsorship or simple participation in the event itself.

One way you can bring in stakeholders across the organization is by forming diversity councils or steering committees. These groups can include executives, managers, and individual contributors—anyone who has a passion for driving diversity at work. This can help with gathering various perspectives and having broader reach as each member advocates on behalf of diversity initiatives to their colleagues and teams. ERGs can serve a similar purpose as well. On top of creating a space for underrepresented groups to gather, they can also serve as a great resource for feedback and driving change at the employee level.

In a 2021 study conducted by Mathison, we found that 56 percent of diverse and traditionally underrepresented candidates have questioned whether employers value diversity when viewing a career page or company job posting. Perhaps even more important, we found that 50 percent of participants view being from an underrepresented community as a disadvantage. These statistics drive home the importance of actively working to enhance sustainable and effective DEI programming that goes beyond the hiring process.

Something you can do today	Something to strive for long term
• Begin gauging interest in affinity and ERGs. • Identify leaders within your organization who may establish these ERGs, and share insights gathered from the groups with the entire workforce.	• Diversity audits can help you identify gaps in representation within your organization. • Build stronger connections with the community you serve and use these connections to recruit a more diverse pool.

First Step Toward Impact

Since we know from Bersin that the most important factor in advancing diversity is to listen to your people, that is also the best place to start. As a first step, schedule some time with your team and ask them:

- What are some concrete ideas for how we can improve our culture? How can we make people feel more connected and included?

- Are there individuals who appear more disconnected or not included? How can we bring them into the fold more?

- What role should team members commit to playing in bringing these ideas to life?

If your people know they have a space to share their ideas and know you'll regularly be responsible for sharing information—not just when there's a crisis—diversity will build itself into the culture. It will become a priority.

To access additional resources and download the tables and charts from this chapter visit: http://Mathison.io/Book.

References

"Being Black in Corporate America." Coqual. Accessed March 24, 2021. https://www.kaporcenter.org/wp-content/uploads/2017/08/TechLeavers 2017.pdf.

Bersin, Josh. "Elevating Equity: The Real Story of Diversity and Inclusion." Accessed March 25, 2021. https://ss-usa.s3.amazonaws.com/c/308463326/media/7667603358a67626883312490210463/202102%20-%20DEI%20 Report_Final_V2.pdf.

"Delivering Through Diversity." McKinsey & Company. January 2018. https://www.mckinsey.com/~/media/mckinsey/business%20functions/organization/our%20insights/delivering%20through%20diversity/delivering-through-diversity_full-report.asHx.

Gelles, David. "'There Is a Bigger Role': A C.E.O. Pushes Diversity." *New York Times.* March 5, 2021. https://www.nytimes.com/2021/03/05/business/tim-ryan-pwc-corner-office.html.

Geronimus, Arline T., Margaret T. Hicken, Jay A. Pearson, Sarah J. Seashols, Kelly L. Brown, and Tracey Dawson Cruz. "Do US Black Women Experience Stress-Related Accelerated Biological Aging?: A Novel Theory and First Population-Based Test of Black-White Differences in Telomere Length." *Hum Nat* 21 (2010): 19–38. https://www.ncbi.nlm.nih.gov/pmc/articles/PMC2861506/.

Goh, Joel, Jeffrey Pfeffer, and Stefanos Zenios. "Exposure to Harmful Workplace Practices Could Account for Inequality in Life Spans Across Different Demographic Groups." *Stanford Graduate School of Business.* October 1, 2015. https://www.gsb.stanford.edu/faculty-research/publications/exposure-harmful-workplace-practices-could-account-inequality-life.

Hastwell, Claire. "Creating a Culture of Recognition." Great Place to Work®. Accessed March 26, 2021. https://www.greatplacetowork.com/resources/blog/creating-a-culture-of-recognition#:~:text=Recognition%20helps%20 employees%20see%20that,them%20to%20continue%20great%20work.

Hunter-Gadsden, Leslie. "Why People of Color Feel the Loneliest at Work." *Forbes.* May 19, 2020. https://www.forbes.com/sites/nextavenue/2020/05/19/why-people-of-color-feel-the-loneliest-at-work/?sh=6eb043b61ad8.

Patel, Sujan. "10 Examples of Companies with Fantastic Cultures." *Entrepreneur.* August 6, 2015. https://www.entrepreneur.com/article/249174.

Perez, Teresa. "Sponsors: Valuable Allies Not Everyone Has." PayScale. July 31, 2019. https://www.payscale.com/data/mentorship-sponsorship-benefits.

Rizkalla, Emad. "Not Investing in Employee Training Is Risky Business." HuffPost. August 30, 2014. https://www.huffpost.com/entry/not-investing-in-employee_b_5545222.

"The State of Leadership Development." Leadership IQ. Accessed March 26, 2021. https://www.leadershipiq.com/blogs/leadershipiq/leadership-development-state.

"Taco Bell: Client Case Study." O.C. Tanner—Appreciate Great Work. Accessed March 26, 2021. https://www.octanner.com/case-studies/taco-bell.html.

"Tech Leavers Study." Kapor Center for Social Impact. April 27, 2017. https://www.kaporcenter.org/wp-content/uploads/2017/08/TechLeavers2017.pdf.

"28 Companies Where You'll Never Stop Learning." *Muse.* January 14, 2021. https://www.themuse.com/advice/companies-with-professional-development-opportunities.

"2017 Employee Benefits: Professional Development." SHRM. January 30, 2018. https://www.shrm.org/hr-today/trends-and-forecasting/research-and-surveys/pages/2017-employee-benefits-professional-development.aspx.

"2021 Diversity Hiring Report." Mathison. Accessed March 23, 2021. mathison.io/2021DiversityReport.

Von Rosty, Nicholas, and Phyllis Schneble. "Creating a Culture of Mentorship." Heidrick & Struggles. Accessed March 24, 2021. https://www.heidrick.com/Knowledge-Center/Publication/Creating_a_culture_of_mentorship.

Wheeler, Shertease, and DBP Staff. "Case Study: Whirlpool's Diverse Talent Retention Strategy." Diversity Best Practices. September 8, 2015. https://www.diversitybestpractices.com/news-articles/case-study-whirlpools-diverse-talent-retention-strategy.

Wowk, Amanda. "How to Build the Business Case for Your DEI Strategy." Qualtrics. October 30, 2020. https://www.qualtrics.com/blog/build-a-dei-strategy/.

"Your Essential Guide to Building a Recognition Program." O.C. Tanner. Accessed March 26, 2021. https://www.octanner.com/insights/whitepapers/essential-guide.html.

CHAPTER 11

Mobilizing Your Organization in Diversity Hiring

When 2020 began, Eileen Benwitt, Chief Talent Officer of Horizon Media, the world's largest independent media agency, was already years into leading the company's diversity and inclusion initiatives. Previously, Benwitt and her talent team had been focused mostly on diversity hiring through internship and entry-level recruiting, leading company-wide diversity surveys, and establishing diverse affinity business resource groups. Benwitt had even organized a passionate DEI council in the hopes of engaging the rest of the company in their diversity efforts. Nevertheless, every year, despite enthusiastic praise for the diversity work, there was little to no active engagement from the rest of the organization.

"It felt like we as an HR team were in an echo chamber talking to ourselves about the importance of diversity," says Benwitt. "There wasn't a burning desire to get involved, and motivation was lackluster across the organization."

It's not as though Benwitt and the team lacked a vision or a plan. Much of the foundational work had already been done. The plan, which the team had articulated to the rest of the agency, was *to be an agency of belonging* where DEI would be at the heart of everything Horizon Media did. The team had even created a framework called the "Wheel of Belonging" that laid out 11 functional priorities that could one day be carried out by ten impact teams (community relations, funding and resources, client and vendor management, sourcing talent, training and development, accountability and measurement, communication, compensation and benefits, policies and procedures, and equitable talent practices). Benwitt's team had built all the scaffolding to engage the executive leadership as well as the full Horizon Media team around diversity.

As the events of 2020 unfolded—the killing of George Floyd, the COVID-19 pandemic, the global uprising against racial injustice— Horizon Media felt a newfound sense of urgency. "There was a tremendous amount of pain and anger throughout the company, which created an escalated interest and desire to act," says Benwitt. "Employees expected action, answers, and solutions to what was now a business imperative." Thankfully for Horizon, Benwitt and the team weren't starting from scratch.

During a company town hall led by CEO and founder Bill Koenigsberg, the company reintroduced the vision to become an "agency of belonging," the Wheel of Belonging with its ten impact teams, and a strategic plan. The organization immediately resonated with the vision. Leaders engaged and employees signed up to be a part of the teams. Every team had an action plan, a cross-functional working group, and executive sponsors from across the business. Each team began to meet and contribute in substantive ways.

For the first time, Horizon Media's diversity efforts amounted to more than a handful of people yearning for buy-in. They encompassed every corner of the company, and they started to see progress. "We embraced learning together, making mistakes, and uncovering collective approaches that could really advance access and belonging in everything we do," Benwitt says. "While fear and discomfort still ran high, the level of vulnerability was palpable and an important shift needed to drive change." Looking back now, Benwitt realized the issue was not that her colleagues hadn't cared about diversity. They simply lacked an awareness of the issues and a sense of their importance.

Now that they were on board, the results were compelling. In less than a year, more than 700 employees have joined in and 70 leaders throughout Horizon Media became actively engaged leading impact teams and BRGs. Horizon Media's diversity hiring increased 4 percent in less than a year. But even these numbers did not come close to representing the cultural shift that took place at the company. "For years, there was little dialogue about the importance of DEI, and it was hard to make it a priority," says Benwitt. "It was overwhelming; we were stuck in our own bias. People wanted to engage, but fear was an overwhelming reality. As a result, diversity wasn't part of the daily conversation."

"Today it couldn't be more different," she continues. "Diversity is at the heart of every conversation. It's core to everything we do, and we are running to this instead of running from it. I am inspired on a daily basis by the passion and commitment from our full community. I couldn't be more proud to see we are becoming an agency of belonging."

THE NEW MINDSET OF LEADERS IN ADVANCING DIVERSITY

Too often, it takes a tragedy to create momentum around diversity, equity, and inclusion. A moment of unbearable injustice takes place, and we are compelled to look around us to see who doesn't have a seat at the table and what we can do to change that. We reach out to others. We host listening sessions and town halls. We meet with affinity groups. We have the hard conversations.

If we're lucky, we make some progress before, inevitably, the tragedy fades from memory. As humans tend to do, we move on other things. We return to the status quo.

The pattern constantly repeats. With one significant difference— every time it happens, it gets a little harder to bear. And a little harder to be patient with the pace of progress.

The question is, how do we sustain momentum when the tragedy fades from view? How do we keep the urgency alive even when things for so many of us have seemed to return to "normal"? When it comes to diversifying our workforce, how do we shift from being reactive to proactive?

There is no one answer to this question. But if we've learned anything in doing this work, it's that momentum derives from a culture that fully embraces and aspires to diversity and inclusion. And we build that culture by harnessing the experiences and passions of everyone around us. We bring in different perspectives. We lean on those who can show us who is missing from the conversation. To do this right, everyone needs to be involved. Diversity needs to be an integral and indispensable part of our culture. It can't be something pushed by one department or a handful of leaders. It needs to come from the bottom, the middle, and the top. And it needs to be focused on goals that are at once achievable and aspirational.

More so than any other business objective, growing diversity requires personal involvement, reflection, and commitment—particularly from leaders. People in positions of authority need to understand and acknowledge the systemic inequities that have perpetuated the lack of diversity and how it's affected their own lives. If they're serious about sustaining change, diversity is not a concern that true leaders leave at work at the end of the day.

"You can't begin to advocate for diversity at work if you don't have diversity in your life," says Elliott Masie, the educational technology expert and longtime diversity advocate who coined the phrase "e-learning." "Take a look at who is on your phone, on your social media, and in your birthday pictures. The way to live diversity at work is by authentically embracing it in everything you do." For leaders to be prepared to increase diversity in our organizations, we have to start by authentically living it in our daily lives.

We have to acknowledge that it is no coincidence that diverse representation has been lacking in our workforce for as long as we can recall. Systemic racism and oppression have been baked into most of our institutions and have fueled the continuing marginalization of underrepresented groups. This has led to business systems that reflect the challenges of society in general, with "culture fit" often serving as shorthand for the pursuit of sameness. For leaders, this vividly points to the responsibility we have to mobilize change in our organizations to ensure equity for all groups. Without addressing the inequity of our systems and doing so in a holistic way, we won't break this cycle, and we'll go back to waiting for the next tragedy to motivate us.

The path to making this happen in your workplace isn't easy, but it is necessary. And it's only when you involve everyone in this work that it becomes sustainable. Every step of the way, the more people you enlist as advocates, the easier it becomes. This is what you now have the opportunity to build.

Company-wide empowerment begins by understanding where your organization and people are ready for change. Here are some questions to consider:

- Is there a shared understanding and vision throughout your organization around the need to grow diversity?

- Is everyone aware of your diversity hiring efforts and the progress you have made to date?

- Does everyone know the role they can play in advancing diversity hiring at your organization?

- Are senior leaders actively engaged in your diversity hiring efforts?

- Are hiring managers engaged in this process?

- Do recruiters and the talent team feel supported in diversity hiring efforts?

- Do your broader team members know how they can contribute to growing diversity at your organization?

- Have you considered how an emphasis on diversity influences everything else your organization does, from the product you deliver to the way you operate?

- Is the specific priority for diversity hiring understood across your organization?

- Have you taken steps to make diversity hiring a systemic element of your business?

- How is inclusion incorporated into your hiring approach so that hires are immediately culturally supported before, during, and after hiring?

- How has equity been infused into the full range of your hiring process?

For additional resources to assess your diversity hiring efforts visit: http://Mathison.io/Index.

EMPOWERING YOUR ORGANIZATION TO LEAD IN DIVERSITY HIRING

The leaders who have made the greatest progress in growing diversity in their organizations have recognized that the sustainability and longevity of the work depends on inspiring ownership and involvement across their entire team. Diversity hiring graduates from an initiative to a *movement* at your organization the moment your entire team has a common understanding of your efforts and a shared sense of responsibility for bringing them to life.

The challenges in diversity hiring are intensified when your team isn't aligned around your end goals and the efforts required to achieve them. This happens when your team has a narrow view of diversity itself or doesn't understand all the steps involved to achieve it. You create this alignment for your team by ensuring that everyone shares the same inclusive definition of diversity, and the concrete goals and actions from the underrepresented communities that make it up.

To create momentum across your team, you have to start by understanding each of your organization's stakeholder groups to account for their distinct perspectives, challenges, and drivers. Each of your senior leaders, hiring managers, recruiting and talent team, and broader team members play a critical role in this mission.

While you may recognize common themes in each group, it's important to note that no perspective is universal. Everyone brings their unique viewpoints and degrees of buy-in. You won't convince everyone to be actively engaged immediately, and there will always be some who are resistant to change. But no successful movement has ever had absolute engagement. What you are looking for is a critical mass of employees who are committed to the objective and agree on the basic direction.

Empowering Your Senior Leaders

Ask any senior leader in your organization whether diversity is a priority, and they will almost certainly say yes. But how many of these leaders are actively engaged in the work? How many know where diversity is lacking on specific teams? How many have taken the time to root out their own unconscious biases? How many have asked what they, personally, can do?

Too many senior leaders believe that diversity hiring is someone else's job, which means that too many senior leaders are sitting on the sidelines, cheering on the effort without really engaging. If this is the case in your organization, you have an opportunity to help those leaders feel a sense of ownership—and responsibility—with a clear idea of where they need to act.

When David Hanrahan, the Chief Human Resources Officer of Eventbrite, was mapping his diversity strategy in 2019, he believed that the best way to ensure success was to get enthusiastic buy-in from the company's leaders and inspire them in a way that got them personally tied to the work. So Hanrahan and his team developed a DEI commitment letter for leaders to sign. The letter spelled out each leader's pledge to hire a diverse global team, foster an inclusive culture, and support social impact initiatives.

For Hanrahan and Evenbrite's leaders, this created a philosophical shift. "We all realized as leaders that we had to hold a mirror up to see what we were doing, and we had to say we wanted to be diverse and inclusive if we wanted anything to change," Hanrahan says. To support leaders in their follow-through on the commitment, the HR team offered training and support in measurement and reporting. The results were significant. Within only six months, BIPOC (Black, Indigenous, and People of Color) representation had increased. Employee engagement across the company improved and attrition began to drop, especially among women and ethnically underrepresented team members. Hanrahan and the team attributed this progress to capturing the commitment of leadership.

To reach leaders on diversity, you have to make this personal. Everyone has a connection to diversity, whether as an ally, being from an underrepresented group, or having an experience where they felt they didn't belong. The important thing is to find a way to get your leaders to acknowledge their own connection. If you can also get them to share it with the organization, you will go a long way toward solidifying and amplifying their commitment to the mission.

There are several ways to go about engaging leaders in this work. Nicole Johnson leads DEI at Mathison and has led extensive diversity work with leadership teams. She says, "Mobilizing leaders in this work often requires storytelling around diversity and asking the question 'why now?' One of the most powerful ways you can reach leaders on a personal level is to give them the time to share their personal stories about diversity. Schedule time to meet with your leaders as a group and facilitate a conversation wherein each leader is prompted to share excitements and challenges they may have while approaching this work. Ahead of the session, share an article that resonates with you in your own journey and share why you chose this piece to open the conversation. As you bring the group together, ask leaders to consider what diversity means to them personally, their experience with diversity, where they have experienced privilege or felt disadvantaged, and what they see as their role in advancing diversity. Set the tone and create psychological safety by sharing your personal perspective and diversity story at the forefront. Having this conversation with leaders will help to align your shared vision of growing diversity, prioritizing DEI and the role each leader can play in driving this work forward."

Leaders' diversity stories not only become powerful ways to help them articulate why this work is so personally important. When they share their stories with the broader audience, it inspires the rest of the organization and creates a powerful sense of psychological safety. This exercise also gives you the opportunity to remind leaders of their sphere of influence and to showcase their commitment to diversity as a strong example for the rest of the organization to follow. Here are some specific actions you can challenge leaders to take:

- Share your diversity story and why this work matters personally.

- Commit to growing sustained awareness of biases and under-represented communities.

- Build transparency in diversity goals and efforts throughout the organization.

- Reiterate the strategic priority and commitment to growing diversity.

- Invest resources in and increase attention to diversity hiring efforts.

- Commit to addressing bias and promoting structure throughout the hiring process.

- Mentor and sponsor existing underrepresented employees.

- Ask the broader team how to improve and how they feel: listen to their feedback.

- Invest in the organizational culture to build a place where people feel that they belong.

Many senior leaders feel disconnected from diversity initiatives because they don't know where gaps exist in their own teams. This can be addressed by creating transparency in specific staff needs, then tying leadership goals and incentives to resolving them. It's an approach that worked for Dr. Johné Battle, Vice President of Diversity at Dollar General. "At every business unit of the company, we enabled leaders to have a light bulb moment where we equipped them with information on the diversity of who gets hired on their team, and at what rate, and we tied performance bonuses to these outcomes," he says. "This inspired ownership and accountability."

Leaders also play a unique role in creating transparency in the state of diversity for your broader organization. Leaders are often apprehensive about collecting or reporting diversity data, especially early on, fearing that the results may not show enough progress or could create a backlash if shared. At this juncture, you have a chance to build the case for transparency.

Transparency instills a sense of trust throughout your organization, and this is what inspires shared ownership. The reality is that if your numbers are low, it's likely that your people have already noticed. It's much better to come out in front of the problem, address it head on, and discuss ways you are actively approaching it. And just as transparency regarding need was key to inspiring your leaders to take ownership in diversity hiring, the same goes for your broader organization. Feeling clear on the need and supported in efforts to address it will better inspire everyone to take action.

Empowering Your Talent Team

In most organizations, the talent and recruiting teams typically feel most of the pressure, but little support, to increase diversity among job candidates and, ultimately, the staff. "Historically, recruiting teams have had to shoulder the majority of the weight and responsibility for meeting diversity recruiting goals," says Jill Macri, a partner at recruiting company Growth by Design Talent and former Director of Recruiting at Airbnb. "This uneven approach has made it nearly impossible to scale and sustain diversity recruiting efforts." If we want to empower and support the talent team in diversity hiring, we have to start by better aligning on goals and priorities, role responsibilities, and deadlines.

While it might seem like common sense to put your talent team in charge of diversifying your talent, the reality is that such teams are rarely put "in charge" of anything more than executing the goals and visions laid out by senior leaders. They are commonly given all the responsibility for diversification but little decision-making authority. And if leadership isn't clear or consistent about those goals, the talent team is left struggling to implement incoherent policies with constantly shifting objectives.

For example, if your company's diversity priorities are constantly changing; if diversity goals are unclear or merely symbolic; or if leaders take a "check the box" approach to the entire enterprise, your talent team will inevitably struggle to make progress.

To empower your talent team, we recommend meeting with them to establish clear diversity objectives, define specific underrepresented communities, and set measurable goals. They need to have a clear understanding of the roles that everyone will play in the hiring process, along with shared responsibility and alignment for the process itself. They need a solid, consistent commitment from the top. Such planning will support the talent team by preventing misalignment or drastic process changes later on.

One of the best ways we can support the talent team is to align on a more realistic expectation of how long the work will take. "We often constrain our talent acquisition teams with artificial timelines," says Natasha Kehimkar, CEO of leadership consultancy Malida Advisors and former Chief People Officer of Fandom. "If we are serious about sourcing and recruiting diverse talent, we have to invest the time to cast a wider net. Aligning around timing makes it easier for everyone."

A common complaint we hear from talent teams is that leaders may ask to expand diversity sourcing for a specific role, as if diversity sourcing were a switch that can be turned on and off instead of a complex, time-consuming endeavor. This leads to unnecessary frustration for everyone involved. We recommend empowering your talent team to proactively communicate the amount of time they believe diversity hiring efforts will take and to set proper expectations up front with the broader team. Many talent team members even formalize this process by establishing a service-level agreement (SLA) to define the estimated timing it will take to source and advance through each stage of the hiring process. We recommend encouraging leaders to acknowledge these timing estimates so their expectations accurately reflect what realistically can be delivered.

Empowering Your Hiring Managers

Hiring managers (in this case, the individuals to whom the prospective job seekers will report) sit at a critical intersection when it comes to diversity hiring. They are often the ultimate decision makers regarding who gets hired. But they may not have an inclusive or well-rounded definition of diversity, which often translates to hiring managers not having the full picture about where diversity is lacking on their team. Even with this level of awareness, many hiring managers don't believe diversity recruiting efforts are their responsibility. As such, for many organizations, hiring managers represent the greatest opportunity for making a meaningful difference in their diversity efforts. Bringing hiring managers in as DEI advocates is mission critical, but many organizations struggle immensely with it.

"When goals and efforts are aligned to engage hiring managers in diversity recruiting," says Macri, "you find them opening up the aperture on candidate profiles, building more diverse networks, and investing the time needed to see a representative slate of candidates."

Some of the common pushback you might hear from hiring managers include: *I don't have time for a diverse slate of candidates. This candidate isn't "diverse" enough. I have a gut feeling about the candidate's qualifications.* Or *This candidate was referred, so we can skip the standard hiring process altogether.*

Organizational dynamics can make it hard to engage hiring managers on these issues. Jennifer Brown, author of *Inclusion: Diversity, the New Workplace and the Will to Change* and *How to Be an Inclusive Leader: Your Role in Creating Cultures of Belonging Where Everyone Can Thrive* (and the preface to this book), offers this. It represents a "frozen middle," she says, between leadership (which hands down the orders) and the grassroots (which creates the urgency for change) where diversity initiatives often go to die. "The middle somehow misses the memo from the top and then gets watered down," she adds, "and I think they aren't held accountable in a way. So, there's either a problem of enforceability, or we haven't tapped into or taught these concepts in a way that helps middle managers see that this is actually really helpful for them."

To address these dynamics, we need to find ways to bring in hiring managers as partners on diversity. As with all employees, we can do this by making them a part of the process. Tami Wolownik, Head of Human Resources for global transportation company Siemens Mobility, has found that a collaborative approach makes all the difference. "Rather than mandate a prescriptive approach to diversity hiring, we approach this work together with hiring managers and encourage them to experiment," she says. "When they feel a sense of ownership in the work, they play a much more active role in bringing new candidates to the organization."

Again, we recommend setting timing expectations by establishing SLAs with realistic estimates for how long the process will take. Also, try to reinforce the structures and policies you have in place in the hiring process (many of which we've explored in the book) to avoid bias and the specific role that you'd like hiring managers to play in the process. Here are some specific areas we recommend exploring with hiring managers to better partner in the diversity hiring process:

- Align around an inclusive definition of diversity.

- Commit to growing ongoing awareness of biases and underrepresented communities.

- Articulate specific diversity goals for this role.

- Align around the essential criteria for the role.

- Align around the timing needed to successfully recruit a diverse slate for the role.

- Commit to the specific steps, structures, and systems in the full hiring process.

- Align around the role expectations and final decision-making process.

- Actively focus on ways to ensure existing team members feel included.

Empowering Your Broader Team

One of the most common mistakes organizations make is assuming that employees not directly involved in everyday hiring decisions have no role to play in expanding diversity. "We have to start by recognizing that diversity is owned by every member of the team," says Rocki Howard, Chief Diversity Officer of SmartRecruiter. "Everyone plays an important role and can contribute, but they need to know how." Your team members may have a strong desire to see diversity grow at your organization, but you need to empower them to translate that passion into action. This is best done by involving them early and listening, building transparency for your efforts, and giving them a tangible path for contributing.

Start by asking your team what communities you can do a better job of reaching. Where do they see opportunities to improve accessibility or reduce bias in your process? Ask them where they can commit to being involved in your efforts. You will be navigating a great deal of change together—you will be asking everyone to embrace new systems and play an active role in welcoming new people into your organization. The difference between your team feeling like victims of this change and feeling ownership over it greatly depends on them having a voice.

Of course, your team can't answer these questions if they don't have visibility into your organization's diversity status and challenges. This is where transparency comes in. Does your team know what you're doing to increase diversity, or what you've previously done that didn't work? When people don't have a clear story, they will naturally resort to telling their own. In the case of diversity hiring, without clarity the team may incorrectly assume that nothing is being done, which can have a depressive effect on morale.

Without proper context, employees may resist investing time in your hiring process, or they might resent feeling forced into adopting changes to it. For example, if you're asking your broader team to start playing an active role in referring candidates through a new system you've established, this will require their time above and beyond their existing work. If you're asking team members already involved in your hiring process to start using a new structured interview scorecard, you are likely creating more work for them. If they understand the needs that drove these changes, or the potential benefits of adopting them, they are far less likely to push back. It's vital to give them transparency on the decision-making process and to solicit their feedback on how you can improve your approach. This will create a shared sense of ownership and may even reveal strategies you might have missed.

You can even go a step further than creating transparency and context for your team by inspiring them to take ownership of this work. Invite your team to contribute, and ask for their ideas about improving your process or even reaching new communities. If a team member has a creative idea for a diversity sourcing event to reach an underrepresented community from which you don't normally recruit, encourage them to pursue it. Empower your existing ERGs or diversity councils, if they exist, to get involved.

When getting your team involved in your diversity efforts, resist the urge to single out team members from underrepresented groups. This can feel like the right thing to do, but it's important not to put anyone on the spot. Many team members from underrepresented groups don't want unnecessary attention in this work or to feel called out. Many may not be ready to engage. We should never make them feel like they have the burden of educating or speaking on behalf of all underrepresented people. It's important to be wary of unintentionally tokenizing. For example, say you want to start a DEI employee blog or revamp your careers page. It would be counterproductive to feature the same employees of color over and over again. Instead, invite everyone to engage and make sure there is widespread awareness of how to do so.

Here are some specific ways you can encourage employees who sit outside of hiring functions to contribute:

- Share ideas and feedback on how to improve diversity.
- Commit to growing ongoing awareness of biases and underrepresented communities.

(continued)

- Serve as an ambassador and advocate for the organization to reach new external groups.

- Refer candidates from underrepresented communities for open roles.

- Get involved in the community, volunteering and serving underrepresented groups.

- Use and promote structures and systems to reduce bias in the hiring process.

- Play a role in inclusive interviewing or offer optional informational interviews.

- Take part in onboarding to welcome in new team members.

EMBRACING DIVERSITY IN WHAT YOU DELIVER AS AN ORGANIZATION

Something remarkable happens when you successfully diversify your workforce. By bringing many different perspectives to bear, your organization begins to function differently. You eliminate blind spots and reveal new opportunities. You see not only where your organization has been limiting itself, but new ways to surpass those limits and reach new customers. When everyone in your company can bring their full selves to work every day and provide the full benefit of their experience, you become a better, nimbler, and smarter organization. And it shows in the ways you engage with the world.

In the wake of George Floyd's death, Anne Wojcicki, CEO and cofounder of 23andMe, a genetic testing and research company, published a letter of support for the Black Lives Matter movement in which she stated, "I feel the responsibility to not just talk about Diversity, Equity and Inclusion, but to make meaningful changes and contributions through my own actions and how we operate at 23andMe. Our management team, Board and employee base must have greater diversity." Wojcicki continued to admit, "I am ashamed to say I do not have a single black employee who is at Director level or above. Our product is euro-centric but must expand to be inclusive and equitable. We absolutely have the potential to be better. Despite our efforts, I have to honestly say that we are also part of the problem."

These straightforward declarations encouraged 23andMe employees to come together and organize four pillars of action: Hiring, Employee Experience, Product & Research, and Community Impact. This comprehensive and collaborative approach deepened 23andMe's internal diversity training, increased representation of minority employees, and even shifted the way the company looked at the representation of its customer base and how DEI is reflected in its product. "We focused on improving our process by layering in DEI considerations, helping us to ideate, develop, and deliver products that are better and more inclusive by design," said Shirley Wu, who leads 23andMe's DEI Product & Research efforts.

One year later, Fred Kohler, 23andMe's Vice President of People, said, "By applying a diversity-focused approach to everything we did as a company, it naturally amplified all of our efforts to grow the diversity of our workforce." Diversity will continue to be the lens through which 23andMe looks at everything it does as an organization.

It doesn't matter what industry you're in. Diverse hardware stores are more likely to place items that the disabled community relies on in easier-to-reach spots. Diverse ad agencies are less likely to produce commercials that denigrate women. Cosmetics companies with greater representation are more likely to produce products optimized for non-white skin. Diverse tech companies are less likely to create AI that favors white faces. And on and on and on. The common thread is a culture that values diversity over the status quo, and creating that culture is the opportunity you have now. If you can get your whole team on board, you are closer than you think.

First Step Toward Impact

Throughout this book, we've stressed the importance of setting diversity goals and sticking to them. One reason leaders so often fail to do this is the constantly shifting nature of the problem. There is always a new lens through which we can view diversity. There is always another person to be included in the conversation. Just as we make progress in including one group, we become aware of another we've overlooked. This is the nature of the challenge, and as leaders who have been engaged in this work for years can attest, it's easy to become exhausted or disillusioned.

It's true: Diversifying your workforce takes time, and the work is never truly done. Even if you should reach absolute equity, maintaining it requires hard work and vigilance. But the point does arrive when a diverse workplace becomes self-perpetuating, when we stop reflexively favoring historically advantaged people and start valuing everyone as individuals. That's the ultimate goal we need to keep our eyes on together. And we need to have faith that we will get there sooner than we think.

To be a leader on this topic, it means harnessing the strength and passion of those around you. You need to build a shared aspiration for diversity and belonging. That shared intent will translate to shared impact, and your organization will be stronger as a result.

As you've navigated this book, we hope you've found this to be a journey for yourself personally just as much as it has been for your organization. You may have started this book ready to create change but not quite sure how. We hope you will have discovered here not only what is necessary, but what is possible.

We leave you with an abundance of potential and a reminder that you are not alone. There is an entire community of leaders who share your feelings of frustration and intent to make change and are actively pursuing progress. This is a collective effort, and we are grateful for the opportunity to help you advance the work.

Remember that you have the power to make a difference—not just in your life or at your organization, but in the lives of people who aren't represented and who don't feel like they belong. You have the power to foster a sense of belonging. That's what it truly means to lead.

WORDS OF WISDOM FROM LEADERS ON ADVANCING DIVERSITY

"Weave your DEIB (belonging) strategy into your mission and values so it's integrated into who you are and what you do AND start early, looking at diversifying your team from day one."

—Mark Levy, EX Advisor and Pioneer of the Employee Experience, Airbnb

"Ensure your organization has the level of support that is aligned with your goals and objectives. DEI is owned by all company employees, but anytime you give ownership of something, you must explain to people how it works and their role in maintaining and caring for what you are sharing."

—Rocki Howard, Chief Diversity Officer, SmartRecruiters

"Make it really easy for people to voice their opinions and proactively invite contrary feedback. Even for your diversity initiatives, ask your people questions like 'What are two reasons why this isn't a good idea?' This will empower people to speak up and any effort you lead will become that much stronger for it."

—Angela Lee, Professor at Columbia Business School and Founder of 37 Angels

"Start early, be intentional, and do not compromise. Don't fall into the trap of thinking this will get easier later on. It will not. Ask yourself, what does this team not have? What perspective are we not seeing? What voice are we not hearing?"

—Dave Walsh, CEO, Mathison

"Diversity is not the nice thing to do. It is the essential thing to do. Data show that diverse organizations outperform others. Diversity will boost your bottom line. So act, be intentional, make diversity a core value, practice it from top down, require performance metrics, measure and report on progress, and correct midcourse to meet goals. Action, Intentionality, Measurement (AIM) = Success!"

—Marcela Berland, President and CEO, and
Frank Gómez, Partner, Latin Insights

"Leadership is the foundation of everything DE&I. If you focus on helping leaders see the big picture and empowering them to take the charge, this work will come to life in your organization."

—Sandra Sims-Williams, Chief Diversity Officer, Nielsen

"Sometimes the most visible work to the organization is not the most impactful work to effect change in the long term. If that's the case, take the time to think about how you can communicate the value of the work that needs to be done."

—Emma Ancelle, VP Human Resources

"Focus on the employment journey! Achieving diversity means taking opportunities across the employee lifecycle to foster employee growth and development."

—Dr. Dave Mayers, Chief Scientist, Knockri

"Hiring for diversity isn't just about getting sound bites. It's about taking a stance at the C-level in ensuring great talent isn't falling through the cracks."

—Jahanzaib Ansari, CEO, Knockri

"Always remember to treat people like humans. We often get caught up in increasing revenue, users, sales—forgetting that on the other side of the table we are interfacing with humans. Whether you are hiring or selling, make sure to check your own intentions and lead with empathy and respect."

—Lisa Carmen Wang, Global Head of Brand
and Communications, Republic

"Make exploration a priority. Set aside time for discussions, actively network in the spaces where you currently have the least connection, and listen when you arrive. Exploration is not a luxury; it is the active and exciting search for what's next."

—Graham Nolan, Co-Chair, Storytelling
and Partnerships, Do the WeRQ

"Be bold and be fierce. Do not worry about starting small, and being the only flag bearer! Keep your chin up and take on the D&I agenda!"

—Manjuri Sinha,
Global Head of Talent Acquisition, OLX Group

"Set the stage with diversity as a source of business value and then model the way by sharing your lived diversity experience or showcasing that of the team with courageous vulnerability."

—Suzanne McGovern, Chief Diversity Officer, Splunk

"Ensure you get commitment from the very top and agreement to stay with it through the full journey."

—Margot Slattery, Global Diversity
and Inclusion Officer, Sodexo

"Keep it simple. Focus on your people over process and include everyone in the conversation, not just a select few."

—Tim Cassidy, Head of Global Talent Acquisition,
FMC Corporation

"Ensure diversity is reflected in your recruiting and HR teams—their networks and sources will directly impact your ability to grow your diversity."

—Monique Cadle, Founder, Good Works Consulting

"You will fail if you make this a game of chasing numbers. Do the hard work upfront of readying the organization for meaningful and thoughtful change that impacts people's lives."

—Fran Benjamin, Managing Partner,
Good Works Consulting

"The key to growing diversity is focusing on a strong set of inclusive business practices and hiring for talent, not flashy credentials."

—Joshua Bellis, Global Head of Talent Programs, PTC

"Understand that your main focus in the work of DEI is creating a sense of belonging for those who have been routinely and consistently marginalized—and make peace with the fact that you will not get this correct."

—Jennifer L. Williams, Principal Consultant/CEO,
The J.L. Solution

"Success is not determined by the number of diverse employees you have, but the ways in which you enable them to leverage their diversity as a strength. It's about how you incentivize different perspectives, how you respond to e-mails, how you support your managers, how you greet your team, who you include in meetings, and how you follow up afterwards. The little things matter most."

—Allison Baum Gates, General Partner,
SemperVirens Venture Capital

"Growing diversity within an organization requires a different approach. Leaders must examine their traditional methods and make systemic changes, including modifying internal processes,

expanding the aperture of where they look for and how they define talent, and working with new external partners."

—Tamika Curry Smith, Global HR
and DEI Executive

"Your tireless effort toward diversity will only bear fruit with a concomitant focus on ensuring that diverse employees' feelings of authentic inclusion and belonging are sustained."

—Amit Mohindra, CEO, People Analytics Success

"Improving diversity in the workforce means building a diverse pipeline that starts with sourcing and hiring and ends with facilitating workers' upward mobility within a company. We encourage leaders to collect data that allows them to see who moves up and who stagnates in low-wage jobs, so that they can create training opportunities that align with their organizational goals while making sure no worker is left behind."

—Natalie Geismar, Member of Brookings
Workforce of the Future initiative

"Share your deep passion and conviction on why it is important and then be relentless in executing against your goals."

—Puja Jaspal, VP People & Communities at Cisco

"Remember, diversity is the numbers, inclusion is making the numbers count—a means to an end. The goal is having people feel they belong."

—Robin Dillard, Publisher, Business Equality Network

"Growing diversity in an organization is about blocking and tackling. It is not just recruiting; it is working to create a workplace where every person can thrive. That takes lots of little changes."

—Meg Langan, Chief People Officer, Turbonomic

"Don't forget about diversity of thought. You want different or dissenting viewpoints, opinions, and experiences. They don't just help shape a culture; they can shift or enhance them."

—Alex Seiler, VP, Head of HR, Americas, Control Risks

"Make clear to recruits your long-term company-building commitment to inclusion. Focus on inclusion more than diversity. At parity.org take the parity pledge. At Boardlist.org, find diverse board members."

—Brian Smiga, Alpha Partners

"Increasing DE&I in organizations requires a system of solutions, but starting with two or three things allows the team to stay focused and get the right momentum."

—Elizabeth Spenko, Head of Product, Mathison

"Building inclusive teams, boards, and leadership structures that accurately reflect the reality of your staff, customers, and partners is not just the right thing to do, but also the smarter thing to do for a business. Visible and genuine representation count amongst the best tools to motivate, encourage, and spur teams into action to rise to the challenge and become better employees and leaders."

—Lorenzo Thione, Managing Director, Gaingels

ACKNOWLEDGMENTS

We'd like to thank our amazing team at Mathison (Mathison.io), without whom this book would not be possible: Dave, Nicole, Elizabeth, Ron, Misha, Eden, Giuliana, Isaac, April, Kynzie, Nora, Katty, Jelena, Robert, Kevin, Emanuel, Poti, Andree, Lily, Yori. To our incredible board for their ongoing guidance: Sarah, Ingrid, Chance, Justin, Paul.

To our unstoppable editing and research team who enabled us to bring this to life: Oheneba Nti Osei, Amy Wilson, Graham Nolan, and Doug Quenqua.

To the Wiley team, thank you for everything: Mike, Andrew, Natalia, Amanda, and the team.

Jennifer Brown and Judith Williams, thank you for your inspiration in this work.

To our advisors and contributors for your wisdom and courage: Robby, Allison, Todd, Mark, Sarah, Mita, Rocki, Jill, Adam, Karsten, Mike, Healthline Media Marcela, Frank, Camille, Mark, Eileen, Aaron, Sarah, Nico, Tono, Matt, Lindsay, Barry, Joy, Sam, Alex, Valera, David, Derek, Mary, Francesca, Zeeza, Samir, Knight Foundation, Springbank Collective, ANIMO, Gaingels, Company Ventures, SAP.io Allyn and Fabio.

From Susan: To my family and to my Rutgers squad, thank you for supporting me all these years.

From Arthur: Mom and Jason, I couldn't have done this without you. To my loving family and amazing life-long friends who have always cheered me on—thank you for the love and support.

ABOUT THE AUTHORS

ARTHUR WOODS

Arthur Woods is a social entrepreneur and LGBTQ+ advocate whose work has been at the intersection of equity, inclusion, and technology. He was named to Forbes 30 Under 30 and 40 Under 40 by BEQ. He is the co-founder of Mathison (mathison.io), the leading technology for equitable hiring, giving employers a single system to manage their diversity recruiting, reduce bias from their systems, and mobilize their teams around diversity hiring efforts. Arthur has spearheaded Mathison's research, including the development of its Equal Hiring Index®.

Arthur is a three-time TEDx speaker, has contributed to Fast Company, and has advised leading organizations from the U.S. Navy, Sonos, and MetLife to Disney and the Smithsonian. Arthur came from Google, where he led operations for YouTube's education division and oversaw YouTube for Schools. Arthur previously co-founded Imperative, a social learning platform; Out in Tech, the largest global LGBTQ technology community; and Social Impact 360, a collegiate social enterprise education program. Arthur studied at Georgetown University, Pontificia Universidad Católica de Chile, and HBS online. He is a World Economic Forum Global Shaper, GCT Entrepreneur in Residence, a New York Venture Fellow, and SAP.io Foundries Fellow. He is an active angel investor and advisor to a number of early-stage ventures.

SUSANNA THARAKAN

Susanna Tharakan is a leader and researcher focused on advancing diverse, equitable, and inclusive workplaces. She began her DE&I journey at Snagajob and continued this important work at Mathison by applying her knowledge and understanding of human behavior, coupled with extensive research in DE&I, to develop an Equal Hiring Index®, which provides an in-depth analysis of an organization's hiring process and retention practices. Susanna is currently leading DE&I initiatives at Sisense while working towards becoming a thought leader in the diversity, equity, and inclusion space. She earned her bachelor's in psychology at Rutgers University and a master's in industrial/organizational psychology at Springfield College.

INDEX